Designing Rubrics for Reading and Language Arts

Joan F. Groeber

SkyLight
Professional
Development

Designing Rubrics for Reading and Language Arts

Published by SkyLight Professional Development
2626 S. Clearbrook Dr., Arlington Heights, IL 60005
800-348-4474 or 847-290-6600
Fax 847-290-6609
info@skylightedu.com
http://www.skylightedu.com

LCCN 2002112972
ISBN 1-57517-668-8

V
ZYXWVUTSRQPONMLKJIHGFEDCBA
10 09 08 07 06 05 04 03 02   15 14 13 12 11 10 9 8 7 6 5 4 3 2 1

There are
one-story intellects,
two-story intellects, and
three-story intellects with skylights.

All fact collectors, who have no aim beyond their facts, are

one-story minds.

Two-story minds
compare, reason, generalize,
using the labors of the fact collectors
as well as their own.

Three-story minds
idealize, imagine, predict—their best illumination
comes from above,

through the **skylight**.

—Oliver Wendell Holmes

Dedication

To those individuals in my life who have encouraged me to live, think, and dream outside the world of "what is" and remain steadfast in their loyalty and support as I venture into the universe of "what could be"

CONTENTS

Introduction ix

Chapter 1

Using Rubrics to Assess Literacy

Rubrics to Assess Authentic Learning 2
What Is a Rubric? 2
Why Use Rubrics? 4
When to Use Rubrics 8
Converting Rubric Scores 9
An Assessment Tool and More 9

Chapter 2

Using Rubrics to Assess Reading Comprehension

Examining the Components of Reading Comprehension 14
Poetry 15
How to Use the Poetry Rubrics 16
Fiction 28
How to Use the Fiction Rubrics 29
Nonfiction 43
How to Use the Nonfiction Rubrics 44
Biography 56
How to Use the Biography Rubrics 57
Instructions 69
How to Use the Instructions Rubrics 70

Chapter 3

Literature and the Assessment Rubric

Know the Read Ahead 84
Plot 85
How to Use the Plot Rubrics 86
Character 98
How to Use the Character Rubrics 99
Setting 113
How to Use the Setting Rubrics 114
Theme 130
How to Use the Theme Rubrics 131

Chapter 4

Assessing Student Writing with Rubrics

Rubrics Enhance Instruction 144
How to Use the Five-Step Writing Process Rubric 145
Writing Rubrics 150
How to Use the Poetry Rubrics 153
How to Use the Fiction Rubrics 165
How to Use the Greeting Card Rubrics 177
How to Use the Autobiography Rubrics 185
How to Use the Informational Brochure Rubrics 194
How to Use the Letter Rubrics 204

Chapter 5

Using Rubrics to Assess Listening Skills

The Art and Science of Listening 216
How to Use the Instructions Rubrics 218
How to Use the Stories Rubrics 227
How to Use the Guest Speaker Rubrics 239
How to Use the Informational Speech Rubrics 251

Chapter 6

Assessment Rubrics and Oral Language

Oral Presentations: Beyond Words 264
How to Use the Debate Rubrics 266
How to Use the Oral Report Rubrics 275
How to Use the Storytelling Rubrics 287
How to Use the Dramatic Presentation Rubrics 299
How to Use the Discussion Rubrics 311

Chapter 7

Rubrics and the Research Process

Investigate the Possibilities 320
Research Rubrics 320
How to Use the Reference Materials Rubrics 323
How to Use the First-Hand Experience Rubrics 335
How to Use the Written Report Rubrics 347
How to Use the Collaboration Rubrics 354

Rubrics and Classroom Technology

Preparing for Tomorrow 362
How to Use the Internet Search Rubrics 364
How to Use the E-Mail Message Rubrics 373
How to Use the Web Page Rubrics 375
How to Use the Audio Collage Rubrics 381
How to Use the Video Presentation Rubrics 387

Constructing Rubrics

Teacher-Created Rubrics 392
Constructing a Rubric 392
Student-Created Rubrics 396
The Future of Rubrics 398

Appendix: Internet Sites 399
Online State Content Standards 400
Rubric Related Web Sites 402
General, Useful Web Sites for Teachers 404

Bibliography 405
Index 411

INTRODUCTION

In recent years, many educators have demonstrated genuine interest in exploring authentic learning opportunities for their students. As individual schools and entire districts seek ways to incorporate this approach into the existing curriculum, a major concern is identifying and implementing a form of student assessment tailored to this learning style. The most frequently discussed option: rubrics.

A rubric is a grid or chart that expresses requirements of a task by dividing them into a range of achievement levels. It is an assessment method that identifies specific steps within a multistep process (constructing a Web page), then defines levels of performance for each step from minimal to optimal expectations based on student age and grade level. Rubrics make an excellent assessment tool for authentic learning tasks because they can include all critical steps as well as levels of performance for each step. Authentic learning seeks to replicate real-life experience with tasks that mirror what occurs in the real world. Authentic learning introduces skills that often fall outside the existing curriculum; therefore, assessment of authentic learning tasks requires a new system of measuring student understanding. Rubric assessment is ideal for the multitask nature of authentic learning because it allows for evaluation of several elements at the same time. For example, students participating in a debate can be evaluated on debate content as well as acceptable behaviors related to that type of oral presentation such as no interrupting or respecting time limits.

The use of rubrics to assess authentic learning provides students with a clear understanding of teacher expectations from the onset of the assignment. Rubrics can reduce or eliminate much of the subjectivity of assessment by stating before students even begin an activity which skills, knowledge, and behaviors students must demonstrate to attain a particular grade. When students see the teacher's expectations at the outset, they must assume more responsibility for both learning and assessment. All students can identify the highest performance level and set goals for attaining that level.

While rubrics can assess a wide variety of tasks, one of their more attractive features is an ability to evaluate the performance of students involved in activities specific to an individual classroom or school district. For example, a teacher may develop and implement a simulation activity for students in a middle school government class. The simulation may involve role-playing, math computations, and debates as well as some written reflections about the experience. The teacher can design a rubric to cover each of these individual areas within the simulation, providing teacher and students with a more complete profile of overall performance. Instead of just a letter or number grade, the rubric shows exactly the area of a student's strengths and weaknesses, which helps students and teachers know the direction remediation should take.

A rubric allows teachers or districts to target areas of study specific to their district. For example, a school district may require students to demonstrate understanding of their state's government. A rubric can be designed to accommodate this situation. Students might participate in an authentic learning exercise such as State Governor for a Week. Teachers might evaluate this simulation on a number of levels, ranging from students' knowledge of the function of state government to the duties of the governor. By placing the district requirements on a rubric illustrating lowest to highest performance in each area, the teacher and students can see almost immediately those areas that require instruction and review.

Rubrics can be developed for areas difficult to assess or incorporate into an overall grade by using other types of assessment such as listening skills. In short, rubrics provide a comprehensive profile of student performance in highly readable results that offer teachers, administrators, parents, and students invaluable information for lesson planning and reteaching exercises. Rubrics are more complete because they can cover all the tasks within a multitask procedure, and they identify what is considered mastery in each of these areas.

HOW TO USE THIS BOOK

Designing Rubrics for Reading and Language Arts was written with a dual purpose. One goal is to provide teachers in all settings with rubrics to assess student literacy. To that end, this book contains samples of rubrics for each of the literacy areas tailored to specific grade levels—primary (K–3), intermediate (4–6), middle school (7, 8), and high school (9–12)—so teachers can track student achievement by using a realistic scale. The presence of multiple grade levels allows teachers to see what their students should know in their present grade level as well as what teachers will expect of them as they progress through the school system.

Accompanying each sample rubric are guidelines for using the rubrics. These how-to pages offer sample assignments as well as acceptable responses for these assignments. While teachers should begin their review of rubrics with the grade level they teach, they should not overlook the materials and information available at the other grade levels. They should peruse the other rubrics and how-to pages for alternative activity ideas and assessment options, which may be useful considering that so many students are above and below the stated grade level.

Benchmarks for each level appear as well as suggested activities in many areas. Each sample rubric shows a specific grading scale (93–100 = A; 87–92 = B; 78–86 = C; 70–77 = D; <70 = F). Chapter 1 offers instructions for altering the scales to meet individual needs. Criteria in the rubrics are taken from the Illinois Board of Education Learning Standards for English and Language Arts (available at http://www.isbe.state.il.us/ils/ english/english.html). The appendix contains a list of Internet sites that offers information on standards across the United States, helpful information on rubrics, and other useful teacher-related Web sites.

In addition to providing time-saving preconstructed rubrics, the other goal of this book is to provide teachers with a step-by-step guide to constructing their own rubrics to suit any classroom exercise. Guidelines appear in chapters 1 and 9.

Focusing on understanding and exploring the use of rubrics for assessment, *Designing Rubrics for Reading and Language Arts* consists of nine chapters.

Chapter 1, Using Rubrics to Assess Literacy, examines the anatomy of a rubric as well as the most appropriate time and situation for using this assessment tool.

Chapter 2, Using Rubrics to Assess Reading Comprehension, offers sample reading activities in the areas of poetry, fiction, nonfiction, biography, and instructions.

Chapter 3, Literature and the Assessment Rubric, focuses on the literary elements of plot, characterization, setting, and theme, providing sample activities and rubrics that measure student understanding of these elements.

Chapter 4, Assessing Student Writing with Rubrics, offers a general overview of how to assess the five-step writing process. Other features of this chapter are sample activities and rubrics for assessing student-authored poetry, fiction, greeting cards, autobiographies, informational brochures, and letters.

Chapter 5, Using Rubrics to Assess Listening Skills, uses the sample activities and rubrics format to assess students' listening skills in the areas of instructions, stories, guest speakers, and informational speeches.

Chapter 6, Rubrics and Oral Language, provides sample activities and rubrics for assessing debates, oral reports, storytelling, dramatic presentations, and discussions.

Chapter 7, Rubrics and the Research Process, provides sample activities and rubrics to measure students' ability to conduct research and process information gathered from reference materials and first-hand experiences. The chapter also contains activities and rubrics geared toward individual and collaborative research reports.

Chapter 8, Rubrics and Classroom Technology, offers sample activities and rubrics to assess student ability to conduct an Internet search or send an e-mail message. The chapter also contains guidelines and sample rubrics to measure student ability to construct a Web page, compile an audio collage, and complete a video presentation.

Chapter 9, Constructing Rubrics, offers a comprehensive guide for constructing assessment rubrics to fit individual curriculum needs.

The literature selections used as examples throughout *Designing Rubrics for Reading and Language Arts* represent the types of books teachers can use effectively with the activities. Such lists are available in a number of literature anthologies. Teachers can also use the sample rubrics to assess student-authored poetry and fiction.

Finally, while the primary focus of this book is the language arts of reading, writing, listening, and speaking, teachers of all content area subjects will also find the assessment rubrics useful in their classrooms. Social studies teachers can use debate and oral presentation rubrics to monitor student growth in those areas, and science and math teachers can make effective use of rubrics for instructions or those involving experiments and field trials.

Using Rubrics to Assess Literacy

Suzanne, a first-year teacher, is committed to designing lessons that promote authentic learning for her eighth-grade students. In developing these activities, Suzanne is experiencing difficulty finding a way to assess student understanding of the concepts she presents in class. She is also struggling with assigning letter or number grades that reflect student performance.

RUBRICS TO ASSESS AUTHENTIC LEARNING

Not only beginning educators face Suzanne's problems. As all educators explore new ways of instructing students, they must also identify methods for evaluating students' grasp of concepts and ideas. The growing interest in authentic learning challenges teachers and administrators to examine current evaluation strategies. Many grading practices now in use are unsuitable for recording student performance on authentic learning tasks. Authentic learning uses collaborative effort, problem-solving opportunities, and dialogue with informed sources to create a real-life learning situation. For example, in an authentic learning unit on weather, students would use some of the same tools a meteorologist would, such as a rain gauge and barometer. A simple letter or number grade of traditional assessment practices does not provide enough information for such tasks. The rubric provides an answer to this dilemma as it is "based on the results of stated performance standards . . . composed of scaled descriptive levels of progress toward that result" (Solomon 1998, 120). In other words, the teacher can establish a set of performance guidelines ranging from inadequate to mastery, providing students with a clear understanding of expectations from the onset of an activity.

In addition to offering clear standards to students participating in authentic learning activities, rubrics, with their multitask evaluation, are well suited to a process vs. product approach to learning because teachers can use them to evaluate performance for many phases within a single experience. For example, chapter 4 describes the five-step writing process. Teachers can use a single rubric to assess student performance during each step of the five-step process.

WHAT IS A RUBRIC?

A rubric is a flexible assessment tool. A rubric allows teachers to make more precise and useful measurements because, unlike conventional grading methods in the areas of language arts and reading, the rubric lists criteria necessary to attain graduated levels of mastery. Because language arts is not an exact science like math, where 2 + 2 = 4, the rubric gives teachers the ability to set up criteria for each phase of an activity. For example, when evaluating an oral presentation, the teacher assigns a grade based on a number of factors, including vocal projection, content, nonverbal language, and the ability to capture and maintain audience attention. The teacher can construct the rubric to list each of these criteria with varying levels of performance ranging from "fails to make eye contact" to "uses facial gestures to emphasize remarks" under the nonverbal language area.

The rubric can be tailored to meet individual needs of a teacher or a school district, but all rubrics contain certain elements. Each rubric contains an *objective,* or stated skill, behavior, or attitude, such as comprehension of a passage of expository writing or delivery of an oral report. This objective may contain a number of components. Taking again the example of an oral report, the teacher must look at a number of factors, including vocal projection and clarity, quality of content, nonverbal language, and audience appeal. On a rubric, these areas would appear in a list in a random or specific (alphabetical or order of importance) sequence as in the example in Figure 1.1.

The most common arrangement for a rubric is a grid. The vertical axis lists the skills, behaviors, and attitudes required for successful completion of the task. For example, on the rubric evaluating oral presentations, the list might include the general areas of Quality of Content, Vocal Projection and Clarity, Nonverbal Language, and Audience Appeal (Figure 1.1).

ORAL PRESENTATION RUBRIC

Giving 0 points is an option—no evidence, no credit.

Criteria	1 point	2 points	3 points	4 points	Total Points
Quality of Content					
Vocal Projection and Clarity					
Nonverbal Language					
Audience Appeal					

Figure 1.1

The rubric also includes more detailed features that would enhance or detract from a student's grade. For example, the sample rubric in Figure 1.2 has the beginning of a list of specific elements that fall within these areas of evaluation. For example, under Vocal Projection and Clarity, the ideal includes qualities such as uses suitable volume, enunciates clearly, and exhibits no halting and repetition of words. Students who achieve these criteria receive a grade that reflects mastery in the area of vocal projection and clarity.

Even though all the items appear within one heading in both sample rubrics, the rubrics allow teachers to evaluate for each item. Each rubric contains *a range,* such as 1 to 4 points. The range of achievement on a rubric enables evaluators to gauge student performance against a learning standard rather than simply calling that performance "right" or "wrong." The point values appear at the top of each column so teachers can add them easily to arrive at a final grade. Giving 0 points is always an option: if the student's work demonstrates no evidence of the criterion, the student receives no credit.

Because a simpler rubric is more appropriate at the primary level, the primary-level rubrics in this book have a range of 0 to 2 points.

In the sample rubric in Figure 1.2, the category Vocal Projection and Clarity evaluates three elements. If none of these elements is present in a student's oral presentation, the rubric score would be no credit or 0. If the student makes an attempt to achieve at least two elements under Vocal Projection and Clarity but falls short in his or her efforts, the score would be 1 point to indicate an incomplete attempt. If the student achieves one of the three stated criteria completely, the score would be 2; if the student achieves two of the criteria completely, the score would be 3, and so on. Thinking of the rubric range as it relates to standards may be helpful. A score of 1 is low: the student has not met the standards. Scores of 2 or 3 indicate that the student has met some portion of the overall standard, while a score of 4 indicates the student has met the standards. These rubric scores make up the eventual letter grade (an explanation of this conversion appears later in this chapter in the section Converting Rubric Scores). This feature of the rubric allows educators to pinpoint specific areas of strength or weakness, providing the student with more useful feedback for future presentations than a simple letter grade (A, B, C, etc.) or assigned percentage (96%, 85%, etc.). Teachers can show students how they will convert presence of these criteria to a letter or number grade.

The sample rubric in Figure 1.3 shows another arrangement of criteria as it lists the specific elements in the same row as the main elements.

On many rubrics, certain elements carry more weight than others (spelling is not as critical in a written report as content), and the numbers help teachers and students make that distinction. Some educators refer to rubrics with this feature as weighted rubrics. All the rubrics in this book are weighted; in other words, all assign a larger point value to the most important elements of the lesson.

Weighted rubrics are one way to establish *degrees* of proficiency on the rubric. For example, a rubric assessing research writing will have one criterion that covers the paper's bibliography. Students receive no points, of course, if no bibliography is present, but if their bibliography contains only books, they might receive only 1 point, while a multimedia bibliography that includes journal articles, Web sites, and videos related to their unit topic might receive 4 points. The scope of the bibliography (all book references, all Internet references, a mix of print, Internet, and video references) influences the grade. In short, a solely literature-based bibliography does not represent the highest degree of competency or "correctness" anymore. Because the teacher distributes the rubrics at the start of the research writing unit, students are aware of this expectation before they even begin their research.

As a wide variety of educators in different settings use and modify the rubric, the basic features of objective, range, and degree will remain the principle reasons for using this highly adaptable assessment tool.

WHY USE RUBRICS?

Because using the rubric may require additional planning in an educator's already time-challenged schedule, one might question why this assessment method is worth the extra effort. The most obvious reason is the rubric's unique capacity to quantify student performance in a relatively objective manner. Rubrics enable teachers to establish a set

ORAL PRESENTATION RUBRIC

Giving 0 points is an option—no evidence, no credit.

Criteria	1 point	2 points	3 points	4 points	Total Points
Vocal Projection and Clarity • uses suitable volume • enunciates clearly • exhibits no halting and repetition of words	Evidence of 2+ incomplete elements	1 complete element present	2 complete elements present	3 complete elements	_____ x 4 = _____ points
Quality of Content					
Nonverbal Language					
Audience Appeal					

Figure 1.2

ORAL PRESENTATION RUBRIC

Giving 0 points is an option—no evidence, no credit.

Criteria	1 point	2 points	3 points	4 points	Total Points
Vocal Projection and Clarity	Suitable volume	Suitable volume; clear enunciation	Suitable volume; clear enunciation; no repetition of words	Suitable volume; clear enunciation; no repetition of words, and more	_____ x 4 = _____ points
Quality of Content					
Nonverbal Language					
Audience Appeal					

Figure 1.3

of criteria for completion of specified tasks, and they give students the opportunity to see what skills and behaviors are expected for mastery of each task. For these reasons, teachers must have the rubric ready before they make the assignment, and students need to see the rubric before they undertake the assignment. Seeing the rubric at the beginning of an activity allows students to be fully aware of what the teacher expects of them in the assignment and helps students become actively involved in their learning.

When educators in a particular grade level, school, or district reach a consensus about performance standards for specific tasks, the rubric's benefits become even more apparent. Having a consistent measurement of the standards set by a school district—say, 90 percent on a particular skill to be considered proficient in that skill—benefits teachers and students. For example, when students move from school to school in our mobile society, having some universal form of measurement makes it easier to ease the new student into the classroom.

Rubrics provide students and their parents/guardians with a clear idea of expectations, eliminating confusion and frustration throughout all phases of the learning experience. Knowing what teachers expect reduces students' anxieties as they approach an assigned task. Whether or not they are able to attain mastery of all task-related components, students have an opportunity to examine what level of competency is expected and set goals. With rubrics, students can easily identify their weakest areas and place greater concentration and effort on improving them.

As educators such as the first-year teacher in the scenario at the beginning of this chapter attempt to involve students in more authentic learning, they must identify methods for assessing understanding. They must determine student achievement in a different way because the assignments often fall outside the category of traditional direct instruction (games, simulations, workshops). The flexibility and increased detail of the rubric makes it an obvious choice for assessment purposes.

At the completion of an activity, teachers can use the information the completed rubric provides in a number of ways. The organization of the rubric offers easy identification of patterns that may suggest the need for additional instruction. For example, if all or most students scored low on the Vocal Projection and Clarity component of an oral presentation rubric, educators may find it helpful to work with students in small or large groups in an alternate venue, such as the gym or cafeteria, to strengthen vocal projection. If an individual student consistently scores low on a specific area of the rubric, the teacher may use this information to prepare some sort of remediation exercise for that student. Finally, if all students receive a low score on an element, it may indicate the teacher's inadequate preparation or lack of instruction in that area.

Individual students can also benefit from mining the information on an assessment rubric. At the conclusion of a specific task, teachers should hold a conference with individual students during which they examine together the completed assessment rubric for areas of strength or weakness. Teachers should use the opportunity to encourage students to develop their specific strengths (audience appeal) while offering suggestions on how to target areas of weakness (vocal projection and clarity) with tangible strategies; for example, they might suggest that when students practice their presentation, they stand at the rear of a room and speak to be heard by a classmate at the far end of that room.

RUBRICS VS. CHECKLISTS

Checklists may be regarded as the forerunner of the rubric even though both assessment instruments remain in use. Like the rubric, the checklist lists criteria necessary for mastery of a specific task. (See the sample checklist in Figure 1.4.) Absence of one or more of the stated criteria can detract from a student's overall grade on a particular activity. The checklist and the rubric provide students with a clear idea of educator expectations.

While both assessment tools offer students more information than a letter or number grade, the rubric takes the criteria list one step further by associating stated performance standards with graduated levels of mastery. For example, the sample checklist in Figure 1.4 reminds students that they must edit written reports for punctuation errors. A rubric would state the same objective with graduated levels of mastery: 0–1 errors = 4 points, 2–4 errors = 3 points, and so on. This additional information allows educators to distinguish between minor lapses in punctuation (two or three punctuation errors) and significant lack of understanding of correct punctuation (eight to ten errors). This feature of the rubric makes it a more objective evaluation instrument than the checklist, where educator discrimination determines whether students receive full credit for correcting punctuation errors. In a weighted rubric, of course, teachers would assign a lower value (__ x 1) to punctuation and give more points (__ x 4) to the content and organization of a composition so the number of punctuation errors would not drag down the grades of good but careless writers.

Although the comprehensive nature of the rubric offers students and educators more information regarding performance on specific tasks, the checklist remains a useful assessment instrument, particularly when teachers can evaluate the stated objective with a yes or no response to questions such as Does the written report contain a title?

Punctuation Checklist for Written Report

_____ Does the composition contain appropriate end punctuation (*/?/ /!/ /./*)?

_____ Does the writer use commas to separate a series of items?

_____ Does the writer use colons and semicolons appropriately?

_____ Does the writer use commas appropriately in direct address?

_____ Does the writer use unnecessary punctuation?

_____ Total Points

Figure 1.4

WHEN TO USE RUBRICS

A rubric is appropriate in all learning situations. Teachers can use it to evaluate oral and written assignments and with individual and group presentations. Although regarded largely as an assessment instrument, teachers should make rubrics available to students during early phases of the lesson or unit.

It is essential that educators construct and distribute the assessment rubric for a specific task before designing and executing related activities for three important reasons: (1) to guide lesson planning; (2) to make students aware of lesson objectives and teacher expectations; and (3) to make students assume responsibility for their learning. Having the rubric at the onset of a unit, lesson, or activity assists in lesson planning because it gives teachers the opportunity to reflect on their expectations and make certain that students have ample instruction and opportunities for growth in those areas. For example, if a rubric on debating concentrates on students' ability to stay focused on the topic regardless of the nature of opponents' comments, the teacher must plan instruction time emphasizing this skill. The additional time invested in this area alerts students to its importance in their preparation as debaters.

Second, distributing the rubric at the start of a lesson alerts students to the areas the teacher considers most important for mastery of the unit or task and gives students insight into specific goals the teacher has set for activities. Students can begin to think about these expectations and look for ways to meet the criteria in the most effective manner. Rather than attempting to absorb every piece of information the teacher presents, students are able to rank the information's importance, investing more time and energy on those areas deemed essential to mastery of a specific task. They have time to ask questions and focus their efforts on those areas they are weakest in. For example, if a rubric for oral presentation lists "makes eye contact with audience" or "uses a strong opening statement" as the most essential factors, students can focus their primary attention on those areas of their presentation. Because its purpose is to convey a set of standards for a particular task, presenting the rubric at or near the completion of the task diminishes its function as an organizational tool and guiding force in students' preparation and execution of various tasks.

Finally, when students have an opportunity to view an assessment rubric at the onset of a lesson or unit of study, they gain a feeling of control over their learning; therefore, distributing rubrics at the onset of an assignment helps students become more actively involved in their learning. With the expectations in hand before they even begin an assignment, they must assume responsibility for meeting those expectations. There can be no claims of "I didn't know that's what you wanted" or "You never said we had to do that." Teachers who use rubrics can effectively transfer responsibility for learning to students. This active involvement in their own learning also promotes an increased interest on the part of students.

To help students understand this form of assessment, students should have the opportunity to fill out rubrics, too. They might practice filling them out in workshop settings when reading their peers' essays, they might complete them for their peers giving oral presentations, and so on. They might also create their own rubrics.

Student-Created Rubrics

One of the most effective ways teachers can introduce rubrics to students is by letting them play an active role in constructing the rubrics. The primary reasons for involving students in this capacity are, first, so they can begin to assume responsibility for their own learning by understanding what components of an assignment teachers consider in compiling an overall grade, and, second, to increase student understanding of the evaluation process by making them partners with the teacher in deciding what constitutes an ideal presentation, debate, or report.

CONVERTING RUBRIC SCORES

At present, most school districts continue to use some form of letter or number grading. For the rubric to be an effective assessment tool, a widely accepted method of converting its information to this system must exist. Assigning a particular weight (in numbers) for the inclusion of specific components within a task provides educators with the basis for converting this information into more traditional letter or number grades.

The most direct method of converting rubric scores is by means of a key at the bottom of the rubric that links student performance to a letter grade (Figure 1.5). To arrive at values for a letter grade of A, B, C, and so on, one simply divides the number of points earned by the total number of points available. For example, earning 19 points out of a possible 20 yields a score of 95 percent, which the majority of grading standards would consider an A. A score of 18 out of 20 yields a 90 percent. Depending on the grade scale a school system uses, this grade might be considered an A (in a 90–100 classification) or a B (in a 93–100 classification). When creating the rubric, teachers should calculate the percentages for each possibility, as in the sample in Figure 1.6, and list the results in a key somewhere on the rubric.

Teachers assign a specified number of points for each criterion listed under each objective on a rubric (Figure 1.7). They then combine these individual numbers to report a total score on the task. Since quality of content should be considered more critical than speaker volume on an oral report, criteria under the objective Quality of Content would be worth more points than criteria under the objective Vocal Projection and Clarity. Students who present an oral report of little or no substance would receive a much lower grade than a student whose report contains high quality content but indicates room for improvement in the area of vocal projection. This type of weighted evaluation provides students with clear expectations concerning which aspects of their report preparation and presentation are more important than others.

AN ASSESSMENT TOOL AND MORE

The rubric is much more than an effective assessment tool. It enables teachers to clarify specific components of a task for students at the onset of instruction as well as indicate what parts of the task are most important and what teachers consider an acceptable performance on all components of the task.

Rubric Conversion Key

Total score _____ /20 = _____

19–20 = A
18 = B
16–17 = C
14–15 = D
<14 = F

Figure 1.5

Grade and Percentage Scoring for Rubric Based on a 30-Point Scale

28–30 = A
26–27 = B
23–25 = C
21–22 = D
<20 = F

30 = 100%
29 = 97%
28 = 93%

27 = 90%
26 = 87%

25 = 83%
24 = 80%
23 = 77%

22 = 73%
21 = 70%

<20 = <70%

Figure 1.6

ORAL PRESENTATION RUBRIC

Giving 0 points is an option—no evidence, no credit.

Criteria	1 point	2 points	3 points	4 points	Total Points
Vocal Projection and Clarity • uses suitable volume • enunciates clearly • exhibits no halting and repetition of words	Evidence of 2+ incomplete elements	1 complete element present	2 complete elements present	3 complete elements present	_____ x 2 = _____ points
Quality of Content • presents accurate information • uses most current information • uses only relevant information	Evidence of 2+ incomplete elements	1 complete element present	2 complete elements present	3 complete elements present	_____ x 4 = _____ points
Nonverbal Language • makes eye contact with audience • maintains relaxed and natural posture • uses facial gestures to emphasize remarks	Evidence of 2+ incomplete elements	1 complete element present	2 complete elements present	3 complete elements present	_____ x 3 = _____ points
Audience Appeal • delivers strong opening • involves listeners • fields questions	Evidence of 2+ incomplete elements	1 complete element present	2 complete elements present	3 complete elements present	_____ x 3 = _____ points

Figure 1.7

45–48 = A
42–44 = B
38–41 = C
34–37 = D
<34 = F

Total score _____/48 = _____

The following chapters provide sample rubrics for a wide variety of learning experiences, beginning with the assessment of reading comprehension. Because a clear understanding of the reading process and the selection and use of quality literature are essential components in any curriculum, it is important to invest some time and effort reviewing these areas in detail. For this reason, chapters 2 and 3 include a more in-depth look at the reading process and the elements of story structure, including additional suggestions for class discussion topics and activities. These two chapters lay the foundation for rubric assessment in reading and the language arts, and the remaining chapters on writing, listening, speaking, research, and technology build on this foundation. These chapters contain more self-explanatory rubrics and activities and require only minimal introduction and explanations.

The book's focus is language arts, but the rubrics are not just for use by reading or language arts teachers. Subject area teachers can use the book and benefit from its activities for dealing with areas such as nonfiction, instructions, observation, and experimentation.

Begin by reviewing the rubric and accompanying information at the grade level you teach, but do not overlook the information and rubrics for the other levels. Because so many students are above or below their grade level, the other rubrics might offer alternative activities and assessment options for these students.

The final chapter, chapter 9, contains step-by-step instructions for creating one's own rubrics.

2

Using Rubrics to Assess Reading Comprehension

Robert, a veteran middle school educator, has returned recently from a conference covering a number of assessment tools, including rubrics, and is eager to apply this information in his language arts classes. As Robert begins to construct rubrics for reading assessment, he realizes that because students must use different strategies to deal with different types of printed materials, his rubrics for assessing their performance with each type of material must reflect these differences.

EXAMINING THE COMPONENTS OF
READING COMPREHENSION

Most readers are introduced to printed material in the form of fiction such as bedtime stories and nursery rhymes. Exposure to nonfiction comes later through magazine articles and school textbooks. The fact that most readers are introduced to fiction first is often regarded as one reason most readers prefer stories to nonfiction. But, more likely, readers gravitate to fiction because they share a certain amount of prior knowledge, an essential component for comprehension, with the story characters. In contrast, comprehension of nonfiction texts often requires some knowledge of the specialized vocabulary related to the topic as well as the ability to read and comprehend information contained in graphs and charts. The organization of nonfiction texts generally differs from fiction in its use of such text structures as description, sequence, comparison, cause and effect, or problem and solution. These differences in text structure and organization may account for the difference in reader comprehension of fiction and nonfiction texts. As a result, readers who are able to understand fictional material at a grade or ability level above their own may lack the skills necessary to read and interpret information found on a chart or graph, a deficit that affects their level of comprehension of nonfiction.

Using different rubrics for assessing student comprehension of various reading materials provides educators with a more detailed analysis of students' reading strengths and weaknesses. This information can prove invaluable in designing and executing reinforcement activities that target specific types of printed matter, such as charts and graphs.

POETRY

More than any other genre, poetry challenges readers to use their senses as well as their imaginations to gain a true appreciation of the poet's message. Economical phrasing and an abundance of figurative language combine in a unique form, and in poetry, the rhythm and cadence of a phrase are as important as its meaning. For this reason, poetry is enjoyed most when it is read aloud.

As with other genres, poems contain themes intended to educate and heighten awareness of the poetic form, but unlike fiction or biography, readers and listeners can also simply listen to the sounds of words woven together carefully and create vivid mental images that will last long after the final syllable is uttered. Several varieties of poetry are available for emerging and mature readers. Some examples appear here. (To see examples of formula poems such as these, visit Inky & Taz's Poetry Corner, a middle school Internet site, at http://library.thinkquest.org/11883/.)

- Acrostic: acrostic poetry is created by writing a word vertically on the page and using the letters of that word to begin the first word of each line.
- Ballad: the ballad is a story about a famous person told in short stanzas.
- Clerihew: a clerihew is a four-line poem written in an a-a-b-b pattern about a famous person.
- Concrete: the lines of concrete poetry take the shape or outline of the poem's topic (trees, dogs, flowers, etc.).
- Diamante: a diamante is an eight-line diamond-shaped poem that compares opposites, such as *child* and *adult* or *winter* and *summer*. The first half of the poem describes one word; the second half of the poem describes its opposite.
- Free Verse: free verse poetry does not follow a specific rhyme or rhythm pattern but does have an identifiable cadence that separates it from a work of prose.
- Haiku: a Japanese form of poetry, haiku uses seventeen syllables spread over three lines in a 5, 7, 5 pattern to describe elements in nature.
- Limerick: limericks are a humorous poetic form that follows an a-a-b-b-a pattern and is characterized by stressed and unstressed syllables.

Getting Underway

Conduct some workshop activities before assessing students' understanding of poetry. A few suggestions for workshop activities follow. Because poetry represents a solid connection between printed material and the fine arts, dramatic and artistic responses may be the most effective way to measure student understanding.

- Instruct students to dramatize emotions linked to the theme.
- Ask students to draw sketches that demonstrate their comprehension of figurative language, such as similes and metaphors.

How to Use the

POETRY Rubric

at the Primary Level

Introduce the Rubric

Distribute the rubric and briefly review it with students before reading the poem. Explain that the assessment will focus on their understanding of the language, imagery, and theme of the poem. Review the definitions of these terms, as well as other elements of poetry (rhyme, rhythm), asking students to provide concrete examples of each element. Ask students to keep these terms in mind as they read and listen to the poem.

After reading the poem, discuss the rubric elements thoroughly, making sure students understand what you expect of them and know that they must meet the objective listed to receive full credit.

Make the Assignment

Read the poem aloud to students. Then have students read the poem aloud round-robin style. Repeat the poem as often as necessary so each student has a chance to read aloud.

Assess Student Understanding

Language
- knows difference between prose and poetry
- reads poem with appropriate rhythm

Have students give definitions of *prose* and *poetry;* write them on the board. Then ask students to choose the best definition. Ask them for examples of each term. Give them examples they might not have thought of, such as a newspaper article, a top 40 song, a commercial jingle. Ask them to label the examples as prose or poetry and explain how they determined the correct response.

When students read rhyming poems, listen for appropriate emphasis on rhyming words. (Younger students may benefit from use of a metronome as they read.) With free verse poems, listen for a reader's trouble at line breaks.

POETRY

Task: Student will read and respond to a poem.

Goal/Standard: Demonstrate understanding of poem through verbal or visual response

Criteria	0	1	2	Total Points
Language • knows difference between prose and poetry • reads poem with appropriate rhythm	0 elements present	1 element present	2 elements present	____ x 3 = ____ points
Imagery • describes images in poem • explains images in poem	0 elements present	1 element present	2 elements present	____ x 3 = ____ points
Theme • identifies message poet is expressing • expresses his/her feelings after reading poem	0 elements present	1 element present	2 elements present	____ x 4 = ____ points

19–20 = A
18 = B
16–17 = C
14–15 = D
<14 = F

Total score ____/20 = ____

Chapter 2 • Using Rubrics to Assess Reading Comprehension

Imagery

- describes images in poem
- explains images in poem

Students at this level should be able to recognize and explain all the images their age-appropriate poem contains. They can respond orally or in writing. One appropriate response is a sensory description that identifies the poem's images by their taste, touch, sound, smell, or sight. Or you might ask students to come up with an alternative way to represent the poem's central image such as by drawing or dramatizing the images in the poem. For the dramatization, students might become the tree or wind or other image depicted in the poem.

Theme

- identifies message poet is expressing
- expresses his or her feelings after reading poem

Individually or as a group, students should be able to describe how the poem makes them feel and whether those feelings match the poem's message. For example, if the message conveyed in the poem is a new beginning or starting again, does the student feel eager and hopeful?

How to Use the

POETRY Rubric

at the Intermediate Level

Introduce the Rubric

Distribute and briefly review the rubric with students before reading the poem. Explain that the assessment will focus on their understanding of the language, imagery, and theme of the poem. Review the definitions of these terms, as well as other elements of poetry (rhyme, rhythm), asking students to provide concrete examples of each element. Ask students to keep these terms in mind as they read and listen to the poem.

After reading the poem, discuss the rubric elements thoroughly, making sure students understand what you expect of them and know that they must meet the objectives listed to receive full credit.

Make the Assignment

Have students read the poem aloud in groups of three or four, with each student reading a line in round-robin fashion. Or read the poem aloud as a class, with each student taking a stanza. Repeat the poem as often as necessary so each student has a chance to read aloud.

Assess Student Understanding

Language

- ■ knows difference between prose and poetry
- ■ reads poem with appropriate rhythm
- ■ recognizes figurative language (simile, metaphor)

Have students give definitions of *prose* and *poetry;* write their definitions on the board. Ask students to choose the best definition. Ask them for examples of each term. Give them examples they might not have thought of, such as a newspaper article, a top 40 song, a commercial jingle. Ask them to label the examples as prose or poetry and explain how they determined the correct response.

POETRY

Task: Student will read and respond to a poem.

Goal/Standard: Demonstrate understanding of poem through verbal, visual, or dramatic response

Giving 0 points is an option—no evidence, no credit.

Criteria	1	2	3	4	Total Points
Language • knows difference between prose and poetry • reads poem with appropriate rhythm • recognizes figurative language	Evidence of 2+ incomplete elements	1 complete element present	2 complete elements present	3 complete elements present	____ x 3 = ____ points
Imagery • describes images in poem • understands significance of image to poet's message • discerns what poet does not state directly	Evidence of 2+ incomplete elements	1 complete element present	2 complete elements present	3 complete elements present	____ x 3 = ____ points
Theme • identifies message poet is expressing • relates message to reader's feelings after reading poem • restates poet's message in 2–4 words	Evidence of 2+ incomplete elements	1 complete element present	2 complete elements present	3 complete elements present	____ x 4 = ____ points

37–40 = A
35–36 = B
31–34 = C
28–30 = D
<28 = F

Total score ____/40 = ____

When students read rhyming poems, listen for appropriate emphasis on rhyming words. With free verse poems, listen for a reader's trouble at line breaks. For an activity that demonstrates students' recognition of figurative language, have them write examples of figurative language, such as *quick as a bunny* or *hair like spun silk*. Leave the first or second part of the phrase blank and provide several choices, such as *quick as a ____* with possible answers as *mule* or *turtle*. Have students select an answer and explain, orally or in writing, why they chose that answer. Return to the poem and find examples of figurative language and highlight, or in some way identify, them. Next, have students create their own figurative language, such as *my heart pounded like a bass drum*.

Imagery

- describes images in poem
- understands significance of image to poet's message
- discerns what poet does not state directly

Students at this level should be able to recognize and explain all the images their age-appropriate poem contains in an oral or written description, a drawing, or a dramatization. A description might take the form of a collage of the senses the poem invokes. In a drawing, the more important images might be larger than the other images. For a dramatization, students might become some of the images in the poem, such as the tree or the wind, and interact with each other. Students should also be able to discern what the poet does not state directly. They should see, for example, that a poet describing a dimly lit, empty street is indirectly conveying loneliness.

Theme

- identifies message poet is expressing
- relates message to a reader's feelings after reading poem
- restates poet's message in two to four words

Whether individually or as a group, students should be able to describe the feelings the poet hopes to engender in the poem's readers. Students should refer to phrases in the poem to support their response. Students should also explain how the poem makes them feel and whether those feelings match the poem's message. For example, if the message conveyed in the poem is rebirth or reawakening, does the student feel energized by the poet's words?

For the poem "Trees" by Joyce Kilmer, a student might restate the message as "an appreciation of nature." An unacceptable response is "It's a poem about how trees don't look like poems."

How to Use the

POETRY Rubric

at the Middle School Level

Introduce the Rubric

Distribute and briefly review the rubric with students before reading the poem. Explain that the assessment will focus on their understanding of the language, imagery, and theme of the poem. Review the definitions of these terms as well as other elements of poetry (rhyme, rhythm), asking students to provide concrete examples of each element. Ask students to keep these terms in mind as they read and listen to the poem.

After reading the poem, discuss the rubric elements thoroughly, making sure students understand what you expect of them and know that to receive full credit, they must meet the objectives listed.

Make the Assignment

Have students read the poem aloud in groups of three or four, with each student reading a line in round-robin fashion. Or read the poem aloud as a class, with each student taking a stanza. Repeat the poem as often as necessary so each student has a chance to read.

Assess Student Understanding

Language
- reads poem with appropriate rhythm
- recognizes figurative language
- identifies types of figurative language (simile, metaphor)

When students read rhyming poems, listen for appropriate emphasis on rhyming words. With free verse poems, listen for a reader's trouble at line breaks. Ask students to think about where the poet wants them to take a breath (or not) as they read.

Allow students to draw, dramatize, or describe in writing the poet's use of figurative language. When evaluating an artistic rendering of a metaphor, for example, look for students' attempts to relate the elements of their drawings to the figurative language. In the metaphor "the aging maple was a proud father looming protectively over the tiny garden," a student who magnifies the size of the tree and the expanse of its limbs creates a sense of paternal strength. Some students may even sketch the suggestion of a benevolent fatherly expression on the tree's bole.

POETRY

Task: Student will read and respond to a poem.

Goal/Standard: Demonstrate understanding of poem through verbal, visual, or dramatic response

Giving 0 points is an option—no evidence, no credit.

Criteria	1	2	3	4	Total Points
Language • reads poem with appropriate rhythm • recognizes figurative language • identifies types of figurative language	Evidence of 2+ incomplete elements	1 complete element present	2 complete elements present	3 complete elements present	_____ x 3 = _____ points
Imagery • describes images in poem • links images to poem's theme • offers a reason the poet uses certain images to convey a message	Evidence of 2+ incomplete elements	1 complete element present	2 complete elements present	3 complete elements present	_____ x 3 = _____ points
Theme • restates poet's message in 2–4 words • relates message to a reader's feelings after reading poem • connects theme to real-life experiences	Evidence of 2+ incomplete elements	1 complete element present	2 complete elements present	3 complete elements present	_____ x 4 = _____ points

37–40 = A
35–36 = B
31–34 = C
28–30 = D
<28 = F

Total score _____/40 = _____

Ask students to come up with examples of figurative language not in the poem. If they can generate their own examples, they understand the concept on a higher level than simply memorizing the examples in the poems discussed in class. Once students demonstrate ability to identify images within the poem, the next step in their learning should be extrapolating what they learned in the poem to create their own figurative language. In other words, they should be able to apply what they learned in the poem to write their own poetry.

Imagery

- describes images in poem
- links images to poem's theme
- offers a reason the poet uses certain images to convey a message

Students should be able to recognize and explain all the images in the poem. Ask students to represent the poem's central image in an alternative way through a drawing, dramatization, or description in writing. Have students respond to the last two elements in their journals: have them select one or two images and link them to the poem's theme, then state why they think the author chose those particular images to convey the theme.

Theme

- restates poet's message in two to four words
- relates message to a reader's feelings after reading poem
- connects theme to real-life experiences

Whether individually or as a group, students should be able to describe the feelings the poet hopes to engender in the poem's readers. Students should refer to phrases in the poem to support their response. Students should also explain how the poem makes them feel and whether those feelings match the poem's message. For example, if the message conveyed in the poem is rebirth or reawakening, does the student feel energized by the poet's words?

For the poem "Trees" by Joyce Kilmer, a student might restate the message as "an appreciation of nature." An unacceptable response is "It's a poem about how trees don't look like poems." Ask students to provide a real-life experience, such as walking in the woods or watching a sunset, and explain how that actual experience differs from an artistic rendering of the same experience. A poem, no matter how lovely, pales in comparison to a living tree. An image in a movie, however meaningful, pales in comparison to a sunset. Have students share such examples verbally or in writing.

How to Use the
POETRY Rubric
at the High School Level

Introduce the Rubric

Distribute and briefly review the rubric with students before reading the poem. Explain that the assessment will focus on their understanding of the language, imagery, and theme of the poem. Review the definitions of these terms, as well as other elements of poetry (rhyme, rhythm), asking students to provide concrete examples of each element. Ask students to keep these terms in mind as they read and listen to the poem.

After reading the poem, discuss the rubric elements thoroughly, making sure students understand what you expect of them and know that to receive full credit, they must meet the objectives listed.

Make the Assignment

Have students read the poem aloud in groups of three or four, with each student reading a line in round-robin fashion. Or read the poem aloud as a class, with each student taking a stanza. Repeat the poem as often as necessary so each student has a chance to read aloud.

Assess Student Understanding

Language
- recognizes figurative language
- identifies types of figurative language (simile, metaphor)
- understands significance of poet's choice of word or phrase

Allow students to draw, dramatize, or describe in writing the poet's use of figurative language. When evaluating an artistic rendering of a metaphor, for example, look for students' attempts to relate the elements of their drawings to the figurative language. For example, in the metaphor "the aging maple was a proud father looming protectively over the tiny garden," a student who magnifies the size of the tree and the expanse of its limbs creates a sense of paternal strength. Some students may even sketch the suggestion of a benevolent fatherly expression on the tree's bole.

How to Use the POETRY Rubric at the High School Level

POETRY

Task: Student will read and respond to a poem.

Goal/Standard: Demonstrate understanding of poem through verbal, visual, or dramatic response

Giving 0 points is an option—no evidence, no credit.

Criteria	1	2	3	4	Total Points
Language • recognizes figurative language • identifies types of figurative language • understands significance of poet's choice of word or phrase	Evidence of 2+ incomplete elements	1 complete element present	2 complete elements present	3 complete elements present	_____ x 3 = _____ points
Imagery • links images to poem's theme • offers a reason the poet uses certain images to convey a message • links poem's symbolic images to real life	Evidence of 2+ incomplete elements	1 complete element present	2 complete elements present	3 complete elements present	_____ x 3 = _____ points
Theme • relates theme to a reader's feelings after reading poem • connects theme to real-life experience • recognizes universal emotions readers experience while reading the poem	Evidence of 2+ incomplete elements	1 complete element present	2 complete elements present	3 complete elements present	_____ x 4 = _____ points

37–40 = A
35–36 = B
31–34 = C
28–30 = D
<28 = F

Total score _____/40 = _____

Ask students to come up with examples of figurative language not in the poem. If they can generate their own examples, they understand the concept on a higher level than simply memorizing the examples in the poems discussed in class. In a journal entry, have students explain their understanding of the poet's choice of words or phrases. Correct responses might touch on the poet's use of analogy to convey the theme; for example, using the boundless nature of the ocean to represent freedom.

Imagery

- links images to poem's theme
- offers a reason the poet uses certain images to convey a message
- links poem's symbolic images to real life

Students should be able to recognize and explain all the images in the poem. Ask students to represent the poem's central image in an alternative way through a drawing, dramatization, or description in writing. Rather than simply describing in writing the poem's images, you might have students at this level bring representations of the imagery, such as an object from nature. A twisted branch could express the torment a poem conveys, for example. They should also be able to link the symbolic image (running water, a rainbow) to a real-life emotion. Running water, for example, suggests the notion that life goes on regardless of any obstacles (river rocks) along the way. In a journal entry, have students isolate one or two of the poem's images and analyze why the poet chose those particular images to convey the message.

Theme

- relates theme to a reader's feelings after reading the poem
- connects theme to real-life experience
- recognizes universal emotions readers experience while reading the poem

Students can address all these elements in an informal journal exercise by describing in detail how they felt when they read the poem, how the poem reflects an event in real life, and why they think most people will feel a certain way when they read the poem. For an oral exercise, they can accomplish the same tasks in a small group discussion as you note their responses. Students should provide concrete examples from the poem to support their statements.

FICTION

Fiction, through which most readers are introduced to the world of literature, is often relegated to a secondary position in intermediate, middle, and secondary school. The main reason cited for the shift in emphasis from use of fiction primarily in the early grades of school to nonfiction primarily in the middle and high school grades is the growing amount of factual information students must read within the limited time allotted for readers' formal education.

However, the shift in emphasis does not diminish the value of reading fiction. Contemporary fiction teaches the values, customs, and practices of a culture, while historical fiction offers a glimpse of these areas in another time period. Fantasy and science fiction nurture the imagination. The conflicts (man vs. self; man vs. man; man vs. nature; man vs. society) that fiction explores are the same as those found in the real world. Whether characters live on a remote prairie outpost or aboard a futuristic space station, readers experience their struggles vicariously, gaining insights for tackling problems in their own lives.

Fiction comes in a variety of categories to engage the imagination and suit the personal tastes of almost every reader.

- Contemporary, or realistic, fiction refers to fiction set in the present day. Examples of this genre include Katherine Paterson's *Bridge to Terabithia* and Beverly Cleary's *Dear Mr. Henshaw* for younger readers and S. E. Hinton's *Taming the Star Runner*, J. D. Salinger's *Franny & Zooey*, and Robert Cormier's *After the First Death* for older readers.

- Historical fiction refers to fictional stories set in the past. Examples of this genre include Patricia MacLachlan's *Sarah, Plain and Tall*, Laura Ingalls Wilder's *Little House in the Big Woods*, Mildred Taylor's *Roll of Thunder, Hear My Cry*, Willa Cather's *My Antonia*, and Kay Gibbons' *Charms for the Easy Life*.

- Fantasy or science fiction represents a literary form that extends the suspension of disbelief we accept in literature to include such events as time travel, shape shifting, and talking animals while still pursuing answers to the universal questions of good vs. evil and the meaning of life and death. Examples of fantasy include E. B. White's *Charlotte's Web*, Nancy Bond's *A String in the Harp*, Madeline L'Engle's *A Wrinkle in Time*, and J. K. Rowling's *Harry Potter and the Sorcerer's Stone*. Science fiction examples include Jill Paton Walsh's *The Green Book*, H. M. Hoover's *Orvis*, Jules Verne's *20,000 Leagues Under the Sea*, Frank Herbert's *Dune*, and H. G. Wells' *The Time Machine*.

- Folktales, legends, and myths are tales born of the oral tradition and contain simple, often didactic messages of how humans should conduct themselves. Examples include the tales of the brothers Grimm, Aesop's fables, or epic tales such as Homer's *The Iliad* and *The Odyssey*.

How to Use the

FICTION Rubric

at the Primary Level

Introduce the Rubric

Distribute and briefly discuss the rubric with students before they read the novel or short story. Explain that you will base the assessment on their recognition of story classification, their ability to recount the story with emphasis on significant details, and their understanding of story conflict and theme. Ask students to keep these areas in mind as they read the book or short story.

Once they complete the reading, discuss the rubric elements thoroughly, making sure students understand what you expect of them and know that to receive full credit, they must meet the objectives listed.

Make the Assignment

Introduce the story by examining the cover illustration and discussing the title with students. This activity helps young readers begin thinking about the type of story they will read. Read the story aloud or, in the case of more mature readers, allow students to read the story silently.

Assess Student Understanding

Classification

- identifies story type
- recognizes story mood (happy, sad)

Early readers may not know the terms *fantasy, historical fiction,* or *science fiction,* but they should be able to identify some elements that distinguish the various genres. For example, readers should be able to recognize whether the story is set in the past, present, or future or in an imaginary world. Give each student four different-colored index cards. Then, after they read the story, have students hold up the colored card that designates whether the story is set in the present (blue), past (red), or future (yellow) or in an imaginary world (green). To prevent students from watching the cards of classmates, have students close their eyes or lay their heads on their desks while "voting" for the story type. Conduct a similar activity to determine the mood of the story (happy, sad) with cards printed with happy or sad faces.

READING   **FICTION**   PRIMARY

Task: Student will read and respond to a work of fiction.

Goal/Standard: Demonstrate understanding through oral or written response

Criteria	0	1	2	Total Points
Classification • identifies story type • recognizes story mood	0 elements present	1 element present	2 elements present	____ x 3 = ____ points
Plot • retells story in correct order • distinguishes major events from supporting details	0 elements present	1 element present	2 elements present	____ x 4 = ____ points
Conflict • knows main character's struggle • knows why main character is struggling	0 elements present	1 element present	2 elements present	____ x 4 = ____ points
Theme • knows what author wants to say • restates theme in 1–3 words	0 elements present	1 element present	2 elements present	____ x 4 = ____ points

28–30 = A
26–27 = B
24–25 = C
21–23 = D
<21 = F

Total score ____/30 = ____

Plot

- retells story in correct order
- distinguishes major events from supporting details

Students should be able to recognize the difference between a story-defining event and a detail that supports but does not shape the story and theme. Conduct the following activity with students in small groups or individually. After they read the story, provide students with cards listing several events that took place during the story. Instruct students to arrange the cards in the order the events occurred in the story. Next, have the students separate the ordered pile into major events and supporting details.

Conflict

- knows main character's struggle
- knows why main character is struggling

After students complete the reading, use a small-group discussion to determine the main character's struggle. Before the group members begin their discussion, have each student in the group write down who or what prevents a main character from attaining a certain goal. After the groups have a chance to discuss this topic, have them present a summary of their discussion to the class and discuss the results as a class. Once the class identifies the main character's struggle, have students write why the character is struggling with this situation. Once again, give students a chance to share and elaborate on responses.

Theme

- knows what author wants to say
- restates theme in one to three words

During a post-reading discussion, ask students what they learned about the character while reading the story. Stimulate discussion by asking questions such as How did the character change? How did the character remain the same? By exploring character growth, you can guide students toward a discussion of theme, or the author's underlying message to readers. Offer beginning readers a choice of four themes, and ask them to vote on which theme they think the story wants to convey. Once the class identifies the correct theme, have students write in their journals a one- to three-word restatement of the theme along with an explanation for why they chose those words.

How to Use the

FICTION Rubric

at the Intermediate Level

Introduce the Rubric

Distribute and briefly discuss the rubric with students before they read the novel or short story. Explain that you will base the assessment on their recognition of story classification, their ability to recount the story with emphasis on significant details, and their understanding of story conflict and theme. Ask students to keep these areas in mind as they read the novel or short story.

Once they complete the reading, discuss the rubric elements thoroughly, making sure students understand what you expect of them and know that to receive full credit, they must meet the objectives listed.

Make the Assignment

Preview the book with students, discussing any cover illustrations or graphics and the book's title. This brief group exercise gets students ready to read by helping them focus on their purpose for reading. After the discussion, instruct students to read the book silently or, in the case of less mature or emerging readers, allow students to read with a reading buddy.

Assess Student Understanding

Classification
- identifies story type
- recognizes story mood (happy, sad)
- makes comparisons with similar stories

Students at this level should be able to identify the type of story, such as a historical novel or a science fiction story. If students are unsure, instruct them to reflect on those elements that separate the types of stories. For example, historical fiction is always set in the author's past, while science fiction and fantasy involve unexplained phenomena and frequently take place in a time period or place not governed by the rules of our time period or planet. Folktales are short, simple stories that have a very explicit message, such as he who hesitates is lost or haste makes waste. Have students identify, orally or in writing, three reasons why they say the story is a specific type.

Task: Student will read and respond to a work of fiction.

Goal/Standard: Demonstrate understanding through oral or written response

Giving 0 points is an option—no evidence, no credit.

Criteria	1	2	3	4	Total Points
Classification • identifies story type • recognizes story mood • makes comparisons with similar stories	Evidence of 2+ incomplete elements	1 complete element present	2 complete elements present	3 complete elements present	____ x 3 = ____ points
Plot • retells in correct order • distinguishes major events from supporting details • recognizes subplots	Evidence of 2+ incomplete elements	1 complete element present	2 complete elements present	3 complete elements present	____ x 3 = ____ points
Conflict • identifies main character's struggle • understands why main character is struggling • identifies type of conflict	Evidence of 2+ incomplete elements	1 complete element present	2 complete elements present	3 complete elements present	____ x 4 = ____ points
Theme • knows what author wants to say • restates theme in 1–3 words • identifies passage that conveys story theme	Evidence of 2+ incomplete elements	1 complete element present	2 complete elements present	3 complete elements present	____ x 5 = ____ points

56–60 = A
52–55 = B
47–51 = C
42–46 = D
<42 = F

Total score ____/60 = ____

When students tell why the story is a happy or sad tale, they should be able to provide information from the story as a rationale. For example, a story that contains the tragic death of a major character is sad because of that death. When students offer their choice and reasons for making that choice, instruct them to extend their response by comparing this story with another one that is very similar or very different.

Plot

- retells story in correct order
- distinguishes major events from supporting details
- recognizes subplots

Students should be able to recognize the difference between a story-defining event and a detail that supports but does not shape the story and theme. Instruct students, working in pairs, to use index cards to write several scenes from the story, one scene per card. Next, have students exchange decks and arrange their partner's deck in the proper story sequence. Then have students remove those cards that list minor scenes, that is, scenes that have no direct influence on the story outcome, and respond in writing or orally why they chose to remove certain cards and leave others.

Conflict

- identifies main character's struggle
- understands why main character is struggling
- identifies type of conflict

The first element in this category asks students to name the specific struggle (Harry Potter vs. Lord Voldemort), while the third element asks students to identify the conflict category (man vs. man). After students read the story, instruct them to write a brief entry in their journals identifying the main character's struggle, including why they think the situation is such a struggle for that character. Next, working in a small or large group, discuss the types of conflict that exist in literature. The types are man vs. man, man vs. society, man vs. self, and man vs. nature. Instruct students to reflect on the type of conflict in the story they have just read and write that response along with their reason for choosing it in their journals. Correct responses should cite specific information from the story to support a certain choice.

Theme

- knows what the author wants to say
- restates theme in one to three words
- identifies passage that conveys story theme

After students finish reading the story, have students write what they learned while reading the story. Instruct them to reflect on knowledge they gained beyond concrete facts, such as specific information about the main character's job or place of residence, and what they learned by reading the story that will help them in their own lives. Next, instruct students to rewrite what the author was trying to say in one to three words. The word limit helps students focus on what they are trying to say by reducing a message to its simplest terms. On the third card, instruct students to write down the passage in the story that represents or makes the author's message clear to readers, citing page and paragraph number.

How to Use the
FICTION Rubric
at the Middle School Level

Introduce the Rubric

Distribute and briefly discuss the rubric with students before they read the novel or short story. Explain that you will base the assessment on their recognition of story classification, their ability to recount the story with emphasis on significant details, and their understanding of story conflict and theme. Ask students to keep these areas in mind as they read the novel or short story.

Once they complete the reading, discuss the rubric elements thoroughly, making sure students understand what you expect of them and know that to receive full credit, they must meet the objectives listed.

Make the Assignment

Students at this level should be able to preview the story independently before they begin reading. If you assign a longer work and plan to hold a small- or large-group discussion of the book, it is often best to assign a specified chapter or number of chapters, allowing time for students to reflect on what they have read through discussions and journal entries. They can read short stories in their entirety.

Assess Student Understanding

Classification
- recognizes story mood (happy, sad)
- makes comparisons with similar stories
- makes comparisons with real-life situations

During a post-reading discussion, ask students to identify the story as happy or sad and to offer evidence from plot events to support their choice. Next, have students work independently to create a Venn diagram comparing the story with a similar (happy or sad) story they have read recently. Finally, instruct students to think of a time when they or someone they know had an experience similar to the events in the story. The events need not be identical, but students should be able to draw some similarities between the story and the real-life experience, such as a character facing an unfamiliar situation alone or losing someone or something dear to them.

Task: Student will read and respond to a work of fiction.

Goal/Standard: Demonstrate understanding through oral or written response

Giving 0 points is an option—no evidence, no credit.

Criteria	1	2	3	4	Total Points
Classification • recognizes story mood • makes comparisons with similar stories • makes comparisons with real-life situations	Evidence of 2+ incomplete elements	1 complete element present	2 complete elements present	3 complete elements present	_____ x 3 = _____ points
Plot • distinguishes major events from supporting details • recognizes subplots • recognizes influence of subplots on main plot	Evidence of 2+ incomplete elements	1 complete element present	2 complete elements present	3 complete elements present	_____ x 3 = _____ points
Conflict • knows why main character is struggling • identifies type of conflict • identifies story climax	Evidence of 2+ incomplete elements	1 complete element present	2 complete elements present	3 complete elements present	_____ x 4 = _____ points
Theme • restates theme in 1–3 words • identifies passage that conveys story theme • links theme to reality	Evidence of 2+ incomplete elements	1 complete element present	2 complete elements present	3 complete elements present	_____ x 5 = _____ points

56–60 = A
52–55 = B
47–51 = C
42–46 = D
<42 = F

Total score _____/60 = _____

Plot

- distinguishes major events from supporting details
- recognizes subplots
- recognizes influence of subplots on main plot

Students should be able to recognize the difference between a story-defining event and a detail that supports but does not shape the story and theme. Instruct students to construct a story time line, listing major events in the story along the line. Check the time line for proper sequence before proceeding to the next phase of the activity. Have students use a pen or marker of a different color to list any subplots that took place while the main story line was developing, writing the subplots on branches from the main time line. Finally, instruct students to circle those subplots that had the greatest influence on the main story outcome.

Conflict

- knows why main character is struggling
- identifies type of conflict
- identifies story climax

The first element in this category asks students to name the specific struggle (Harry Potter vs. Lord Voldemort), while the second element asks students to identify the conflict category (man vs. man). Use a post-reading class discussion to clarify what the character is trying to achieve or what obstacle the character is trying to overcome during the course of the plot. Next, place students in smaller groups to discuss the type of conflict present in the story. Finally, have students make journal entries defining the term story climax and what passage they perceive contains the *story climax*.

Theme

- restates theme in one to three words
- identifies passage that conveys story theme
- links theme to reality

After students complete the story, use a group discussion to reflect on what the author is trying to tell readers. Then post three or four theme messages, asking students to identify which message goes with the story they read. On the board, an overhead, or a handout, cite specific passages from the story, instructing students to select the passage that conveys the story's theme and write in their journals why they think this passage conveys the story's theme. Their journal entry should also include how the theme relates to their lives, such as how they will use the theme (love conquers all, honesty is the best policy) to guide their actions.

How to Use the

FICTION Rubric

at the High School Level

Introduce the Rubric

Distribute and briefly discuss the rubric with students before they read the novel or short story. Explain that you will base the assessment on their recognition of story classification, their ability to recount the story with emphasis on significant details, and their understanding of story conflict and theme. Ask students to keep these areas in mind as they read the novel or short story.

Once they complete the reading, discuss the rubric elements thoroughly, making sure students understand what you expect of them and know that to receive full credit, they must meet the objectives listed.

Make the Assignment

Use short stories or full-length novels for high school level fiction reading assignments. Students at this level should be familiar with the elements of story structure as well as an author's use of subplots to add dimension to the story. Instruct students to read the selection, keeping informal journal entries related to elements listed on the rubric as an aid in organizing responses later.

Assess Student Understanding

Classification

- makes comparisons with similar stories
- makes comparisons with real-life situations
- recognizes elements related to each genre of fiction

After students complete the reading assignment, place them in small groups to discuss and compare the story with stories that have similar plots. Instruct students to think about ways the two stories are alike and to think of other stories with similar plots that have similar or different outcomes. Move around the room to monitor their discussions. Next, have groups read newspaper or nonfiction magazines to find examples of similar stories and discuss the similarities they find between the fictional account and reality.

READING — **FICTION** — HIGH SCHOOL

Task: Student will read and respond to a work of fiction.

Goal/Standard: Demonstrate understanding through oral or written response

Giving 0 points is an option—no evidence, no credit.

Criteria	1	2	3	4	Total Points
Classification • makes comparisons with similar stories • makes comparisons with real-life situations • recognizes elements related to each genre of fiction	Evidence of 2+ incomplete elements	1 complete element present	2 complete elements present	3 complete elements present	_____ x 3 = _____ points
Plot • recognizes subplots • recognizes influence of subplots on main plot • identifies pivotal subplot with direct influence on story outcome	Evidence of 2+ incomplete elements	1 complete element present	2 complete elements present	3 complete elements present	_____ x 3 = _____ points
Conflict • identifies type of struggle • identifies story climax • compares stories by identified conflict	Evidence of 2+ incomplete elements	1 complete element present	2 complete elements present	3 complete elements present	_____ x 4 = _____ points
Theme • identifies passage that conveys story theme • links theme to reality • names other stories with similar theme	Evidence of 2+ incomplete elements	1 complete element present	2 complete elements present	3 complete elements present	_____ x 5 = _____ points

56–60 = A
52–55 = B
47–51 = C
42–46 = D
<42 = F

Total score _____/60 = _____

Finally, as a class, construct a chart that lists elements associated with various fiction genres. For example, one correct response might be the common use of allegory in works of science fiction. Transfer the chart to a more permanent material (poster board, transparency) for future reference. As students read various genres throughout the year, the more permanent chart provides a quick reference for students unsure of the elements associated with each genre.

Plot
- recognizes subplots
- recognizes influence of subplots on main plot
- identifies pivotal subplot with direct influence on story outcome

Subplots offer information about story characters in a more active way than descriptive exposition. Readers learn more about a character by how he or she reacts in these minor story events, which authors sometimes include to complicate the character's attainments of a goal. Instruct students to focus on one of the story's subplots and write in their journal about the influence of this subplot on the main plot and the story outcome. Tell them they must offer evidence from the story to support their claims. Correct responses will contain clear references to the story and how the subplot did (or did not) influence the fate of the character and the story outcome.

Conflict
- identifies type of struggle
- identifies story climax
- compares stories by identified conflict

Readers can distinguish stories by the type of conflict the main character faces. Stories that pit the character against another, antagonistic, character have a different tone than those in which the main character faces a personal moral dilemma. Students at this level are capable of identifying the type of conflict the story contains. In a journal writing exercise, instruct students to reflect on story scenes that introduce and develop the story conflict. For a variation of this activity, have pairs or triads of students role-play the scene that introduces the conflict. Then have students write about how the conflict reaches its peak in the story climax. Next, ask students working in small groups to identify other stories they have read that contain the same type of conflict. For example, if students have read *Romeo and Juliet,* where the lovers must deal with the society of their time, instruct students to find examples of other stories containing the man vs. society conflict and offer reasons for their choice.

Theme

- identifies passage that conveys story theme
- links theme to reality
- names other stories with similar theme

All stories contain one or two passages that convey the theme, or author's message, to readers. After students finish reading the selection, have them work in groups of six or eight to prepare a dramatization of that scene for classmates. At the same time, instruct members of another group to prepare and dramatize a present-day scenario that conveys the same theme. Have the actors play the scene from the story passage, then have the actors performing the present-day counterpart to that passage give their performance immediately after it. A third set of actors could follow the second performance with a scene from another story that depicts the same theme message.

NONFICTION

During the early years of formal education, most student reading material is fiction. By the intermediate level, however, students spend approximately half their time exploring nonfiction materials. The use of unfamiliar text structures (description, sequence or process, comparison, cause and effect, and problem and solution, argument, or persuasion) as well as the introduction of charts and graphs and specialized vocabulary present new challenges even for mature readers. Learning to identify text structures is a first solid step in making predictions about the type of information a specific passage may contain. Activities designed to familiarize students with these structures and a review of how to use context cues to new vocabulary are worthwhile exercises that increase reader comprehension of a wide variety of nonfiction materials such as the following:

- magazines
- newspapers
- textbooks
- trade books
- reference materials (encyclopedia, dictionary, atlas)
- World Wide Web pages

For a refresher on text structures, visit Web sites for K–12 teachers such as Teachers.Net (http://www.teachers.net/) and Teachnet.com (http://www.teachnet.com/).

How to Use the
NONFICTION Rubric
at the Primary Level

Introduce the Rubric

Distribute and briefly discuss the rubric with students before they read the nonfiction text. Explain that you will base the assessment on their understanding of the purpose of the text, their ability to recognize nonfiction format elements, their use of text cues to aid their understanding, and their overall comprehension of text content. Ask students to keep these areas in mind as they read the text.

Once they complete the reading, discuss the rubric elements thoroughly, making sure students understand what you expect of them and know that to receive full credit, they must meet the objectives listed.

Make the Assignment

Before beginning a nonfiction reading assignment, it is a good idea to administer an informal assessment of students' prior knowledge. To accomplish this task quickly, use a web. Place the topic in the center of the board or transparency sheet, and ask students to give words or brief phrases that they have heard in association with the topic. Then organize the words and phrases into groups based on their relationship to one another. For example, if the nonfiction article or book deals with the solar system, the students may provide names of planets during the web activity. During the next web step, group the planet names under the heading Names of Planets. Repeat this process until you have organized all the words and phrases in the web under headings. Then instruct students to read the selection silently or, in the case of less mature readers, read the selection aloud to them, instructing them to think about additional words or phrases that they could place under each heading.

NONFICTION

Task: Student will read and respond to a nonfiction book.

Goal/Standard: Demonstrate understanding through verbal, visual, or written response

Criteria	0	1	2	Total Points
Purpose • identifies topic • understands author's purpose	0 elements present	1 element present	2 elements present	_____ x 3 = _____ points
Format • identifies text structure • understands graphic organizers that display data	0 elements present	1 element present	2 elements present	_____ x 3 = _____ points
Content • uses context cues to learn specialized vocabulary • understands link between pictures and text	0 elements present	1 element present	2 elements present	_____ x 4 = _____ points

19–20 = A
18 = B
16–17 = C
14–15 = D
<14 = F

Total score _____/20 = _____

Assess Student Understanding

Purpose

- identifies topic
- understands author's purpose

The initial identification of the topic will, most likely, take place during the prereading phase. After students complete the reading, instruct them to write three sentences about what they learned from the text. Have reluctant writers tell or draw their responses. Discuss the author's purpose for writing about this topic—was it to teach them those things they learned?

Format

- identifies text structure
- understands graphic organizers that display data

Before students begin reading nonfiction material, discuss the various arrangements of nonfiction texts. The most basic types are *description, sequence* (sometimes called *process*), *comparison, cause and effect*, and *problem and solution* (sometimes called *persuasion* or *argument*). To help students deal with nonfiction material, have graphic organizers for each nonfiction text organization on display in the classroom. For the description graphic organizer, use a web with the topic in the center and attributes written on branches extending from the center. For sequence, use a numbered row because order is essential in this type of text. For the comparison organizer, use a Venn diagram to accommodate similarities and differences. For cause and effect, show one line for the effect and several lines extending below it on which to list the causes. For the problem and solution organizer, show two blocks, one listing the problem, the other, a solution. Have examples of the graphic organizers on hand in the classroom and ask students to draw the appropriate organizer for the nonfiction information they have read. Work with students at this level to fill in the organizer with details from the text.

Content

- uses context cues to learn specialized vocabulary
- understands link between pictures and text

After students have completed the reading assignment, distribute a worksheet that contains some sentences from the passage, or post the sentences on a sheet of tag board. Highlight unfamiliar vocabulary words and ask students to supply, in writing, their definition for each word, explaining why they think it is the correct definition. To determine if students understand the link between pictures and text, instruct them to list three things they learned from the text that also appear in the text illustrations.

How to Use the
NONFICTION Rubric
at the Intermediate Level

Introduce the Rubric

Distribute and briefly discuss the rubric with students before they read the nonfiction text. Explain that you will base the assessment on their understanding of the purpose of the text, their ability to recognize nonfiction format elements, their use of text cues to aid their understanding, and their comprehension of text content. Ask students to keep these areas in mind as they read the text.

Once they complete the reading, discuss the rubric elements thoroughly, making sure students understand what you expect of them and know that to receive full credit, they must meet the objectives listed.

Make the Assignment

Before making a nonfiction reading assignment, it is a good idea to assess students' prior knowledge. Accomplish this task with an oral brainstorming activity or an informal inventory that contains terms associated with the topic and asks students to rate their depth of understanding of the terms on a scale of 1 to 3, with 3 the highest level of understanding. This activity is helpful at the beginning of a subject area text chapter, such as a science unit on human anatomy or a social studies chapter on government. The inventory may help determine the level of material students can handle for this particular topic.

After determining degree of prior knowledge, instruct students to read the selection independently and use their reading log to record any questions or observations they have about the material as they read.

Assess Student Understanding

Purpose
- identifies topic
- understands author's purpose
- recognizes significance of topic

How to Use the NONFICTION Rubric at the Intermediate Level

NONFICTION

Task: Student will read and respond to a nonfiction book.

Goal/Standard: Demonstrate understanding through verbal, visual, or written response

Giving 0 points is an option—no evidence, no credit.

Criteria	1	2	3	4	Total Points
Purpose • identifies topic • understands author's purpose • recognizes significance of topic	Evidence of 2+ incomplete elements	1 complete element present	2 complete elements present	3 complete elements present	____ x 3 = ____ points
Format • identifies text structure • understands graphic organizers that display data • can convert information on charts and graphs to paragraph form	Evidence of 2+ incomplete elements	1 complete element present	2 complete elements present	3 complete elements present	____ x 3 = ____ points
Content • uses context cues to learn specialized vocabulary • understands link between pictures and text • can compare text information with prior knowledge of topic	Evidence of 2+ incomplete elements	1 complete element present	2 complete elements present	3 complete elements present	____ x 4 = ____ points

37–40 = A
35–36 = B
31–34 = C
28–30 = D
<28 = F

Total score ____/40 = ____

Students will have had the opportunity to identify the topic during the prereading activity. After students complete the reading assignment, discuss the author's purpose for writing about this topic. Instruct them to use their journals to record five things they learned from the reading and how those things will help them in their daily lives.

Format

- identifies text structure
- understands graphic organizers that display data
- can convert information on charts and graphs to paragraph form

Briefly review the five basic text organization structures with students, instructing them to illustrate the appropriate organizer for their reading assignment. Then tell them to fill in the organizer with information from the reading passage. Finally, select one chart, graph, or other type of organizer from the text, and instruct students to write the numerical information in paragraph form. For a variation of this assignment, have students state (orally) the information in their own words.

Content

- uses context cues to learn specialized vocabulary
- understands link between pictures and text
- can compare text information with prior knowledge of topic

Students at this level are capable of demonstrating their ability to use context cues to learn specialized vocabulary. After students finish the reading assignment, provide them with a list of five to nine unfamiliar vocabulary terms from the text. Instruct them to write the terms and their own definition. Later, working in small groups, students will have an opportunity to compare their definitions with the actual definition. If student responses are incorrect, ask what cues led them to develop their definition. Next, place students in small groups and assign each group an illustration from the passage. Each group is responsible for presenting a comprehensive description of their illustration to the rest of the class by using information from the text to clarify the significance of the picture in relation to the text. For a variation of this activity, have students offer the same explanation in writing in their journals. Finally, instruct students to list five things they knew about the topic before reading the passage. After they have read the assignment, instruct them to write beside each item any new information they received that confirmed or contradicted their prior knowledge. Ask students to clarify orally unclear or incorrect responses.

How to Use the

NONFICTION Rubric

at the Middle School Level

Introduce the Rubric

Distribute and briefly discuss the rubric with students before they read the nonfiction text. Explain that you will base the assessment on their understanding of the purpose of the text, their ability to recognize nonfiction format elements, their use of text cues to aid their understanding, and their comprehension of text content. Ask students to keep these areas in mind as they read the text.

Once they complete the reading, discuss the rubric elements thoroughly, making sure students understand what you expect of them and know that to receive full credit, they must meet the objectives listed.

Make the Assignment

Students at this level are capable of completing previewing exercises (examining title, illustrations, unfamiliar vocabulary) before they begin the reading assignment. Provide time for this exercise before making the reading assignment.

Assess Student Understanding

Purpose
- understands author's purpose
- recognizes significance of topic
- recognizes author bias

After students have completed the reading assignment, instruct them to write in their own words what they believe the author is trying to say. Then, with students in small groups, instruct them to discuss the importance of the topic and develop a list to share with the entire class of three to four reasons the topic is important. Finally, provide students with another source (textbook, encyclopedia, Internet) on the same topic, and instruct them to use a Venn diagram to record similarities and differences between the author's information and the second source. A discussion focusing on author bias should follow, with students offering reasons why an author might want to alter or present a slanted view of the information.

NONFICTION

Task: Student will read and respond to a nonfiction book.

Goal/Standard: Demonstrate understanding through verbal, visual, or written response

Giving 0 points is an option—no evidence, no credit.

Criteria	1	2	3	4	Total Points
Purpose • understands author's purpose • recognizes significance of topic • recognizes author bias	Evidence of 2+ incomplete elements	1 complete element present	2 complete elements present	3 complete elements present	____ x 3 = ____ points
Format • understands graphic organizers that display data • can convert information on charts and graphs to paragraph form • can evaluate effectiveness of format	Evidence of 2+ incomplete elements	1 complete element present	2 complete elements present	3 complete elements present	____ x 3 = ____ points
Content • understands link between pictures and text • can compare text information with prior knowledge of topic • can make text-based generalizations about topic	Evidence of 2+ incomplete elements	1 complete element present	2 complete elements present	3 complete elements present	____ x 4 = ____ points

37–40 = A
35–36 = B
31–34 = C
28–30 = D
<28 = F

Total score ____/40 = ____

Format

- understands graphic organizers that display data
- can convert information on charts and graphs to paragraph form
- can evaluate effectiveness of format

After students have completed the reading assignment, instruct them to choose the most appropriate graphic organizer in the text and explain in their own words why they think this organizer is the most effective way to organize the information in the passage. Next, assign each student (or pair of students) a graph or chart from the passage, instructing them to convert the graphic to paragraph form in their journal.

Content

- understands link between pictures and text
- can compare text information with prior knowledge of topic
- can make text-based generalizations about topic

After students have completed the reading assignment, instruct them to create a Venn diagram comparing the information found in the text and pictures. In what areas do the two information sources overlap? In a second Venn diagram, have students compare what they knew about the topic beforehand with what they have learned. Does the text contain information they did not know, or do they possess information the text does not mention?

How to Use the
NONFICTION Rubric
at the High School Level

Introduce the Rubric

Distribute and briefly discuss the rubric with students before they read the nonfiction text. Explain that you will base the assessment on their understanding of the purpose of the text, their ability to recognize nonfiction format elements, their use of text cues to aid their understanding, and their comprehension of text content. Ask students to keep these areas in mind as they read the text.

Once they complete the reading, discuss the rubric elements thoroughly, making sure students understand what you expect of them and know that to receive full credit, they must meet the objectives listed.

Make the Assignment

Students at this level are capable of previewing their material before reading. Remind students to write notes and questions in their reading logs.

Assess Student Understanding

Purpose
- recognizes significance of topic
- recognizes author bias
- recognizes why author may possess particular point of view

After students have completed the assignment, instruct them to write in their journals why they believe this topic is worthy of an entire article or book. Next, ask them to compare the information in the text with another source on the same topic. Tell them to think about whether the assigned text reveals evidence of author bias. They should be prepared to elaborate on their response, including why they think the author may possess the bias.

READING   **NONFICTION**   HIGH SCHOOL

Task: Student will read and respond to a nonfiction book or article.

Goal/Standard: Demonstrate understanding through verbal, visual, or written response

Giving 0 points is an option—no evidence, no credit.

Criteria	1	2	3	4	Total Points
Purpose • recognizes significance of topic • recognizes author bias • recognizes why author may possess particular point of view	Evidence of 2+ incomplete elements	1 complete element present	2 complete elements present	3 complete elements present	____ x 3 = ____ points
Format • can interpret charts and graphs • can evaluate effectiveness of format • understands author's choice of format	Evidence of 2+ incomplete elements	1 complete element present	2 complete elements present	3 complete elements present	____ x 3 = ____ points
Content • can compare text information with prior knowledge of topic • can make text-based generalizations about topic • can rank information in the text by its significance	Evidence of 2+ incomplete elements	1 complete element present	2 complete elements present	3 complete elements present	____ x 4 = ____ points

37–40 = A
35–36 = B
31–34 = C
28–30 = D
<28 = F

Total score ____/40 = ____

Format

- can interpret charts and graphs
- can evaluate effectiveness of format
- understands author's choice of format

At the conclusion of the reading assignment, instruct each student to rewrite in paragraph form one of the charts or graphs in the passage. Then, in their journals, have students write whether the text organization is effective for the topic. For example, the most effective organization for an article explaining how a bill becomes a law is the sequence format. The students' responses should include their opinion about why the author chose the format.

Content

- can compare text information with prior knowledge of topic
- can make text-based generalizations about topic
- can rank information in the text by its significance

Have students construct a Venn diagram to compare what they know about the topic with what they learned in the passage. Next, have students construct a detailed outline of the text that delineates which areas of the text are more significant than others.

BIOGRAPHY

While fiction is populated by characters who live, play, work, and even die at an author's whim, biographies recount the exploits of real people. Authors of fiction are free to manipulate characters or other literary elements such as conflict and setting to convey their message. Biographers must decide whether a subject's life bears retelling, then extract the theme from actual events that took place in that subject's life.

The benefit of reading biographies lies in the subject's connection to the reader, such as a shared background (single parent household, only child) or interest (sports, music). When readers perceive this connection, they develop an immediate empathy for the subject and gain insight for dealing with similar obstacles that arise in their own lives.

Several varieties of biographies are available to readers. The most popular types appear below.

- Authentic biography is a well-documented and carefully researched account of a person's life. Its construction follows many of the same rules as serious works written for adults. Examples include Jean Fritz's *And Then What Happened, Paul Revere?* and Russell Freedman's *The Wright Brothers: How They Invented the Airplane.*

- Partial biographies chronicle only part of the subject's life (a liberty extended to children's authors), usually focusing on a point of high drama in the subject's life. Examples include Alice Fleming's *George Washington Wasn't Always Old* and David Kherdian's *The Road from Home: A True Story of Courage, Survival, and Hope,* which focuses on the early life of Kherdian's mother, Veron Dumehijan, during a time when the Turkish government was trying to eliminate its Armenian minority.

- Fictionalized biography is grounded in research but lets the author dramatize certain events and personalize the subject rather than present the type of straight reporting found in authentic biography. Examples include F. N. Monjo's *Letters to Horseface: Young Mozart's Travels in Italy* and Jean Fritz's *Homesick: My Own Story,* a fictionalized autobiography about the author's early childhood in China.

- Biographical fiction consists entirely of imagined conversations and constructed events. Examples of this form include Robert Lawson's *Ben and Me,* about a mouse who lived in Ben Franklin's old fur cap, and Robert Lawson's *Mr. Revere and I,* told from the point of view of Paul Revere's horse, Scheherazade.

How to Use the
BIOGRAPHY Rubric
at the Primary Level

Introduce the Rubric

Distribute and briefly discuss the rubric with students before they read the biography. Explain that you will base the assessment on their recognition of the author's purpose for writing the biography, their ability to discern the format of the text, and their understanding of the value and accuracy of the text. Ask students to keep these elements in mind as they read the biography.

Once they complete the reading, discuss the rubric elements thoroughly, making sure students understand what you expect of them and know that to receive full credit, they must meet the objectives listed.

Make the Assignment

Briefly review the definition of *biography* (an account of the life of a real person) with students, discussing why the lives of some people are worth a record for others to read. Then instruct students to read the story silently or, in the case of less mature readers, read the story aloud to the class.

Assess Student Understanding

Purpose
- knows significance of subject
- understands subject's role in shaping history

After students complete the reading, instruct them to write a letter to the biographical subject thanking him or her for the role he or she played in shaping history. Display the letters on a classroom bulletin board. When assessing the letters, look for reference to specific accomplishments in the subject's life that had a dramatic influence on the past, present, and future.

BIOGRAPHY

Task: Student will read and respond to a biography.

Goal/Standard: Demonstrate understanding through verbal, visual, or written response

Criteria	0	1	2	Total Points
Purpose • knows significance of subject • understands subject's role in shaping history	0 elements present	1 element present	2 elements present	_____ x 3 = _____ points
Format • distinguishes between biography and historical fiction • distinguishes between complete and partial biography	0 elements present	1 element present	2 elements present	_____ x 3 = _____ points
Content • identifies subject's accomplishments • can compare account with nonfiction for accuracy	0 elements present	1 element present	2 elements present	_____ x 4 = _____ points

19–20 = A
18 = B
16–17 = C
14–15 = D
<14 = F

Total score _____/20 = _____

Format

■ distinguishes between biography and historical fiction
■ distinguishes between complete and partial biography

After students complete the reading, conduct a discussion about the difference between biography (authentic) and historical fiction (loosely based on historical facts or events). Then ask students to vote secretly (only you will see students' names on the paper ballots) on whether the account was biography or historical fiction. Next, discuss complete and partial biographies and ask students to vote secretly on whether the account was a complete or partial biography. Have students include a reason for their choice.

Content

■ identifies subject's accomplishments
■ can compare account with nonfiction for accuracy

After students complete the reading, instruct them to compile a list of the subject's accomplishments. Then provide encyclopedia and Internet access to verify if other sources credit the subject with the same or different accomplishments.

How to Use the
BIOGRAPHY Rubric
at the Intermediate Level

Introduce the Rubric

Distribute and briefly discuss the rubric with students before they read the biography. Explain that you will base the assessment on their recognition of the author's purpose for writing the biography, their ability to discern the format of the text, and their understanding of the value and accuracy of the text. Ask students to keep these elements in mind as they read the biography.

Once they complete the reading, discuss the rubric elements thoroughly, making sure students understand what you expect of them and know that to receive full credit, they must meet the objectives listed.

Make the Assignment

Discuss the term *biography* with students before the reading, asking them why they believe this individual's life is worthy of retelling. Then instruct students to read the account independently or with a reading buddy.

Assess Student Understanding

Purpose
- knows significance of subject
- understands subject's role in shaping history
- recognizes subject's influence on future

After students complete the reading, instruct them to act as journalists and write an account of at least one of the subject's accomplishments, including in their article how this achievement affected the past, present, and future. Display the completed articles.

Task: Student will read and respond to a biography.

Goal/Standard: Demonstrate understanding through verbal, visual, or written response

Giving 0 points is an option—no evidence, no credit.

Criteria	1	2	3	4	Total Points
Purpose • knows significance of subject • understands subject's role in shaping history • recognizes subject's influence on future	Evidence of 2+ incomplete elements	1 complete element present	2 complete elements present	3 complete elements present	_____ x 3 = _____ points
Format • distinguishes between biography and historical fiction • distinguishes between complete and partial biography • identifies point of view of storyteller	Evidence of 2+ incomplete elements	1 complete element present	2 complete elements present	3 complete elements present	_____ x 3 = _____ points
Content • identifies subject's accomplishments • can compare account with nonfiction for accuracy • links subject's deeds to readers' lives	Evidence of 2+ incomplete elements	1 complete element present	2 complete elements present	3 complete elements present	_____ x 4 = _____ points

37–40 = A
35–36 = B
31–34 = C
28–30 = D
<28 = F

Total score _____ /40 = _____

Format

- distinguishes between biography and historical fiction
- distinguishes between complete and partial biography
- identifies point of view of storyteller

After students complete the reading, instruct them to vote secretly on paper ballots containing their names on whether the work is biography or historical fiction. Tell them to include the reason for their choice. On a second secret ballot, instruct students to identify the work as a complete or partial biography and why they made that choice. Finally, ask students to assume the identity of the author and write in their journals why they wanted to tell the story of the biographical subject.

Content

- identifies subject's accomplishments
- can compare account with nonfiction for accuracy
- links subject's deeds to readers' lives

After students complete the reading, instruct them to compile a list of the subject's accomplishments. Next, have students use a second source (encyclopedia, Internet) to verify the information found in the account. Finally, have students write in their journals the ways the biographical subject's actions have affected their lives or the lives of others in this time period.

How to Use the
BIOGRAPHY Rubric
at the Middle School Level

Introduce the Rubric

Distribute and briefly discuss the rubric with students before they read the biography. Explain that you will base the assessment on their recognition of the author's purpose for writing the biography, their ability to discern the format of the text, and their understanding of the value and accuracy of the text. Ask students to keep these elements in mind as they read the biography.

Once they complete the reading, discuss the rubric elements thoroughly, making sure students understand what you expect of them and know that to receive full credit, they must meet the objectives listed.

Make the Assignment

Students at this level are capable of selecting a biography based on personal interest in the subject. In addition to the more obvious choices of sports and entertainment figures, provide students with biographies of authors (J. K. Rowling is a particular favorite) or individuals from history. Use events such as Black History Month or the anniversary of a subject's birth or death to stimulate student interest in less obvious choices.

Assess Student Understanding

Purpose
- identifies subject's role in shaping history
- relates subject's influence on future
- recognizes author bias

To demonstrate their understanding of the subject's role in shaping history and influencing the future, have students compose a letter to their biographical subjects, thanking them for their contributions to this society and their help in shaping the future of this nation or culture.

Next, have students do some basic research on the book's author and create a Venn diagram comparing similarities and differences between the author and subject. Examining a possible connection between the two individuals may provide some insight on why authors choose a particular viewpoint from which to write the account.

How to Use the BIOGRAPHY Rubric at the Middle School Level

BIOGRAPHY

Task: Student will read and respond to a biography.

Goal/Standard: Demonstrate understanding through verbal, visual, or written response

Giving 0 points is an option—no evidence, no credit.

Criteria	1	2	3	4	Total Points
Purpose • identifies subject's role in shaping history • relates subject's influence on future • recognizes author bias	Evidence of 2+ incomplete elements	1 complete element present	2 complete elements present	3 complete elements present	____ x 3 = ____ points
Format • distinguishes between complete and partial biography • identifies point of view of storyteller • explains effectiveness of format	Evidence of 2+ incomplete elements	1 complete element present	2 complete elements present	3 complete elements present	____ x 3 = ____ points
Content • can compare account with nonfiction for accuracy • links subject's deeds to readers' lives • states unifying theme of subject's life	Evidence of 2+ incomplete elements	1 complete element present	2 complete elements present	3 complete elements present	____ x 4 = ____ points

37–40 = A
35–36 = B
31–34 = C
28–30 = D
<28 = F

Total score ____/40 = ____

Format

- distinguishes between complete and partial biography
- identifies point of view of storyteller
- explains effectiveness of format

Conduct this activity as an informal journal session. In their writing, students should explain why a specific account is a complete or partial biography as well as why this format was more effective than the other. For example, in the case of an individual whose early or later life was somewhat uneventful, a partial biography spotlights that part of the subject's life that had a lasting influence on society. Finally, ask students to assume the identity of the author and write in their journals why they wanted to tell the subject's story.

Content

- can compare account with nonfiction for accuracy
- links subject's deeds to readers' lives
- states unifying theme of subject's life

Instruct students to use Venn diagrams to compare the biographical account with any nonfiction account, such as an encyclopedia entry or Internet site, of the subject's life and accomplishments, commenting on any great disparity between the two accounts. Then, in a journal writing session, instruct students to write about whether the subject's life had some influence on their own life. Note that when students choose the subject they wish to read about, they are more likely to choose someone who has affected their lives in some way. At the end of their journal entry, ask students to sum up the subject's contribution to society in a single sentence. This sentence should contain the underlying message of the biography, such as "hard work and perseverance are rewarded" or "stay close to those who love you."

How to Use the
BIOGRAPHY Rubric
at the High School Level

Introduce the Rubric

Distribute and briefly discuss the rubric with students before they read the biography. Explain that you will base the assessment on their recognition of the author's purpose for writing the biography, their ability to discern the format of the text, and their understanding of the value and accuracy of the text. Ask students to keep these elements in mind as they read the biography.

Once they complete the reading, discuss the rubric elements thoroughly, making sure students understand what you expect of them and know that to receive full credit, they must meet the objectives listed.

Make the Assignment

Students at this level have definite interests and should have the opportunity to choose subjects whom they may see as role models. Initiate a group discussion about heroes and what these individuals have done to earn the respect of others. Next, have students select the biography of someone they consider a hero or heroine.

Assess Student Understanding

Purpose

- relates subject's influence on past and future
- recognizes author bias
- identifies author's possible motive for choosing subject

Instruct students to construct a time line, indicating the life and times of the subject and how segments of the population have felt his or her influence. For example, if students are reading the biography of Martin Luther King, Jr., their time line should include information about racial conditions before, during, and after Dr. King lived and worked in this country. Instruct students to use different-colored markers or printing to show a difference between those events from Dr. King's life that had a direct or indirect effect on the past and future of our culture, one color for direct effect, one color for indirect effect. The notations can be in pencil or ink, such as "Blacks use separate water fountains" or "Blacks ride in back of buses." Then have students circle those items upon

Task: Student will read and respond to a biography.

Goal/Standard: Demonstrate understanding through verbal, visual, or written response

Giving 0 points is an option—no evidence, no credit.

Criteria	1	2	3	4	Total Points
Purpose • relates subject's influence on past and future • recognizes author bias • identifies author's possible motive for choosing subject	Evidence of 2+ incomplete elements	1 complete element present	2 complete elements present	3 complete elements present	_____ x 3 = _____ points
Format • identifies point of view of storyteller • explains effectiveness of format • suggests alternate format for presenting material effectively	Evidence of 2+ incomplete elements	1 complete element present	2 complete elements present	3 complete elements present	_____ x 3 = _____ points
Content • links subject's deeds to readers' lives • states unifying theme of subject's life • identifies specific events that embody theme	Evidence of 2+ incomplete elements	1 complete element present	2 complete elements present	3 complete elements present	_____ x 4 = _____ points

37–40 = A
35–36 = B
31–34 = C
28–30 = D
<28 = F

Total score _____ /40 = _____

which Dr. King and his work had a direct effect with one color marker, and circle those events and situations upon which his effect was indirect with another color.

Next, instruct students to use a marker of a third color to add the author to the time line, noting when the author became interested in writing about Dr. King and what events may have motivated that author to complete the work, reflecting on whether the work represents factual events in Dr. King's life or whether the author has slanted the retelling of events in a positive or negative way.

Format

- identifies point of view of storyteller
- explains effectiveness of format
- suggests alternate format for presenting material effectively

Instruct students to begin a journal entry by identifying the storyteller and giving a brief explanation of why the author chose this particular perspective for sharing the subject's story. Next, instruct students to select another way to tell the story. A different but equally effective point of view may exist and its use might change the story emphasis a great deal. For example, would the story of young Dr. Martin Luther King be more effective if it were told from the viewpoint of one of the protesters who joined him on one of his bus rides through the southern United States? After selecting an alternate viewpoint, instruct students to write three to four paragraphs with that point of view.

Content

- links subject's deeds to readers' lives
- states unifying theme of subject's life
- identifies specific events that embody theme

After students have completed the reading, instruct them to write an open letter to the United States (or the world, depending on the sphere of the subject's influence), stressing the importance of the subject's life and work on the lives of those of the subject's time as well as of future times. The open letter should also contain a unifying statement that sums up the life of the subject—the type of message one might find on the subject's tombstone. For example, "Dr. King had a dream—a dream of people living as one—and he spent his life seeking fulfillment of that dream." Finally, instruct students to cite specific events in the subject's life that testify to the subject's dedication to his or her dream.

INSTRUCTIONS

The ability to follow a set of directions empowers readers to complete a limitless variety of tasks, ranging from filling out a printed form, such as a job application or college entrance questionnaire, to tangible construction, such as building a birdhouse or fixing a leaky faucet. While directions and instructions lack the literary elements of fiction (plot, characterization) or the high interest content of nonfiction, this sequenced reading matter is of critical importance to readers of all ages and ability levels.

The most effective strategy for following directions is to read the entire sequence first, assembling any materials necessary to complete the task. Then readers should read and execute each step before moving on to the next step, reviewing, if necessary, for clarification before proceeding further on the project.

A wide variety of projects or activities are appropriate to complete this assignment. Any sort of how-to project, such as how to build a birdhouse, how to use a camcorder, or how to teach yourself to play an instrument or game, make a craft project, or build a model, is appropriate. Recipes are a natural for this assignment. A preassessment discussion should include emphasis on sequence as well as how and when to incorporate shortcuts (after one has learned how to complete the project without shortcuts). When you design and develop projects, consider, of course, materials your classroom has on hand, or use materials that are inexpensive and easy to access.

How to Use the
INSTRUCTIONS Rubric
at the Primary Level

Introduce the Rubric

Distribute and briefly discuss the rubric with students before they complete this activity. Explain that you will base the assessment on their preparations for completing the instructions, their ability to follow each step accurately and in proper sequence, and their overall attention to the process of completing the task. Ask students to keep these elements in mind as they work.

Once they complete the reading, discuss the rubric elements thoroughly, making sure students understand what you expect of them and know that to receive full credit, they must meet the objectives listed.

Make the Assignment

Choose an art project that requires students to follow a specific sequence to complete the project. Read the directions aloud to them or, in the case of more mature readers, allow students to read the directions silently. Observation is the most influential form of assessment for this type of assignment. Work with students in small groups so observation is practical. You also have the option of grading students as a group to assess their cooperative learning skills.

Assess Student Understanding

Preparation
- assembles all materials beforehand
- reads every direction before attempting task

After presenting the art project to students, note whether they assemble materials and read the directions before beginning the project.

Task: Student will read and follow written instructions.

Goal/Standard: Demonstrate understanding by producing desired outcome of directions

Criteria	0	1	2	Total Points
Preparation • assembles all materials beforehand • reads every direction before attempting task	0 elements present	1 element present	2 elements present	_____ x 3 = _____ points
Sequence • completes steps in proper order • exhibits no omissions or reversals	0 elements present	1 element present	2 elements present	_____ x 3 = _____ points
Implementation • completes each step before attempting another step • keeps written directions at hand throughout entire process	0 elements present	1 element present	2 elements present	_____ x 4 = _____ points

19–20 = A
18 = B
16–17 = C
14–15 = D
<14 = F

Total score _____/20 = _____

Sequence

- completes steps in proper order
- exhibits no omissions or reversals

Note whether any student omits or reverses the order of steps. The finished product should reflect inclusion of all steps in proper sequence.

Implementation

- completes each step before attempting another step
- keeps written directions at hand throughout entire process

Note whether students complete each step before they move on to the next step and whether they keep written directions close at hand for consultation during the construction of the project. In the case of oral directions, permit students to ask for repetition of the sequence, but do not offer assistance unless students request it.

How to Use the
INSTRUCTIONS Rubric
at the Intermediate Level

Introduce the Rubric

Distribute and briefly discuss the rubric with students before they begin the activity. Explain that you will base the assessment on their preparations for completing the instructions, their ability to follow each step accurately and in proper sequence, and their overall attention to the process of completing the task. Ask students to keep these elements in mind as they work.

Once they complete the reading, discuss the rubric elements thoroughly, making sure students understand what you expect of them and know that to receive full credit, they must meet the objectives listed.

Make the Assignment

Students at this level enjoy constructing three-dimensional objects. Provide a choice of projects, such as birdhouses or feeders, wind chimes, or other projects you find in how-to informational books. Give students the text and instruct them to complete the project. Observation is the most effective form of assessment for this type of assignment. Work with students in small groups so observation is practical. You also have the option of grading students as a group to assess their cooperative learning skills.

Assess Student Understanding

Preparation
- assembles all materials beforehand
- reads every direction before attempting task
- uses context cues for unfamiliar vocabulary

Note whether students assemble all materials beforehand and whether they read all directions before attempting the task. Next, ask students about the definition of less familiar vocabulary, allowing them to explain how they determined what the word means.

READING   **INSTRUCTIONS**   INTERMEDIATE

Task: Student will read and follow written instructions.

Goal/Standard: Demonstrate understanding by producing desired outcome of directions

Giving 0 points is an option—no evidence, no credit.

Criteria	1	2	3	4	Total Points
Preparation • assembles all materials beforehand • reads every direction before attempting task • uses context cues for unfamiliar vocabulary	Evidence of 2+ incomplete elements	1 complete element present	2 complete elements present	3 complete elements present	____ x 3 = ____ points
Sequence • completes steps in proper order • exhibits no omissions or reversals • understands importance of proper order	Evidence of 2+ incomplete elements	1 complete element present	2 complete elements present	3 complete elements present	____ x 3 = ____ points
Implementation • completes each step before attempting another step • keeps written directions on hand during entire process • reviews steps if error occurs	Evidence of 2+ incomplete elements	1 complete element present	2 complete elements present	3 complete elements present	____ x 4 = ____ points

37–40 = A
35–36 = B
31–34 = C   Total score ____/40 = ____
28–30 = D
<28 = F

Sequence

- completes steps in proper order
- exhibits no omissions or reversals
- understands importance of proper order

After observing students in their groups during the completion of the task, noting any omissions or reversals, instruct them to rewrite the steps in their own words on index cards, one instruction per card. Next, shuffle the cards and ask students in the group to complete the task with the cards in that order, allowing them to explain why this sequence is or is not possible.

Implementation

- completes each step before attempting another step
- keeps written directions at hand during entire process
- reviews steps if error occurs

Note whether students complete steps in proper sequence and keep written directions nearby for easy reference. Ask students what they would do if they found an error at some point in their project. The correct response should be that the student would review the steps of the project to determine where the error occurred.

How to Use the
INSTRUCTIONS Rubric
at the Middle School Level

Introduce the Rubric

Distribute and briefly discuss the rubric with students before they begin this activity. Explain that you will base the assessment on their preparations for completing the instructions, their ability to follow each step accurately and in proper sequence, and their overall attention to the process of completing the task. Ask students to keep these elements in mind as they work.

Once they complete the reading, discuss the rubric elements thoroughly, making sure students understand what you expect of them and know that to receive full credit, they must meet the objectives listed.

Make the Assignment

Students at this level are capable of working with minimal guidance in a kitchen setting. Instruct students to bring their favorite no-bake recipes to class. Compare the ingredient lists to find the most cost-effective recipe before printing up copies of the recipe for each student or group of students. Observation is the most effective form of assessment for this type of assignment. Work with students in pairs or triads so observation is practical. You also have the option of grading students as a group to assess their cooperative learning skills.

Assess Student Understanding

Preparation

- assembles necessary materials and reads every direction before attempting task
- uses context cues for unfamiliar vocabulary
- reflects on desired outcome before beginning task

Provide students with the recipe and the opportunity to assemble materials beforehand. Point out some unfamiliar vocabulary and ask students to provide the word's meaning, probing for what cues they used to arrive at the definition.

INSTRUCTIONS

Task: Student will read and follow written instructions.

Goal/Standard: Demonstrate understanding by producing desired outcome of directions

Giving 0 points is an option—no evidence, no credit.

Criteria	1	2	3	4	Total Points
Preparation • assembles necessary materials and reads every direction before attempting task • uses context cues for unfamiliar vocabulary • reflects on desired outcome before beginning task	Evidence of 2+ incomplete elements	1 complete element present	2 complete elements present	3 complete elements present	_____ x 3 = _____ points
Sequence • exhibits no omissions or reversals • understands importance of proper order • can make predictions about next step in process	Evidence of 2+ incomplete elements	1 complete element present	2 complete elements present	3 complete elements present	_____ x 3 = _____ points
Implementation • keeps written directions on hand during entire process • reviews steps if error occurs • replicates desired outcome	Evidence of 2+ incomplete elements	1 complete element present	2 complete elements present	3 complete elements present	_____ x 4 = _____ points

37 – 40 = A
35 – 36 = B
31 – 34 = C
28 – 30 = D
<28 = F

Total score _____ /40 = _____

Next, discuss the recipe they are preparing to make, asking them to explain why certain steps are necessary. For example, if the recipe is a cake, ask students if they can omit or replace the step involving the oven.

Sequence

- exhibits no omissions or reversals
- understands importance of proper order
- can make predictions about next step in process

After noting whether students made any omissions or reversals, ask each group to write the directions on cards, one direction per card. Shuffle the deck and ask group members if they can still make the recipe in the deck's new order. Correct responses should address the fact that sequence is often essential in preparing a recipe. Next, choose a new recipe (one the students have not yet prepared) and write instructions, one per card. Show students the ingredients and the first card and ask them to predict what they think the next step is in the recipe. Repeat this process, calling on students randomly within the small group.

Implementation

- keeps written directions at hand during entire process
- reviews steps if error occurs
- replicates desired outcome

Students at this level are capable of completing a cooking recipe with no omissions or reversals. During the completion of the recipe, ask students how they would determine if the recipe was correct (taste? appearance?). If they determined there was an error, how would they correct this error? Correct responses should refer to a check of the sequence to determine where the error occurred.

How to Use the
INSTRUCTIONS Rubric
at the High School Level

Introduce the Rubric

Distribute and briefly discuss the rubric with students before they begin this activity. Explain that you will base the assessment on their preparations for completing the instructions, their ability to follow each step accurately and in proper sequence, and their overall attention to the process of completing the task. Ask students to keep these elements in mind as they work.

Once they complete the reading, discuss the rubric elements thoroughly, making sure students understand what you expect of them and know that to receive full credit, they must meet the objectives listed.

Make the Assignment

Students at this level are capable of producing culinary dishes, woodworking projects, or needlework items. Let students choose a project but require that they bring the written instructions and materials to class to complete the project. Observation is the most effective form of assessment for this type of assignment. Work with students in small groups so observation is practical. You also have the option of grading students as a group to assess their cooperative learning skills. The other alternative is to use the small-group setting to stimulate student thinking before moving on to independent completion of the project.

Assess Student Understanding

Preparation

- assembles necessary materials and reads every direction before attempting task
- uses context cues for unfamiliar vocabulary
- reflects on desired outcome before beginning task

Students at this level should be able to explain verbally beforehand what they intend to produce and how each of the materials factors into the production. They should also be able to decode any unfamiliar vocabulary by using context cues. Instruct students working in their small groups to rephrase the instructions in their own words to determine if they understand the steps well enough to paraphrase them.

How to Use the INSTRUCTIONS Rubric at the High School Level

INSTRUCTIONS

Task: Student will read and follow written instructions.

Goal/Standard: Demonstrate understanding by producing desired outcome of directions

Giving 0 points is an option—no evidence, no credit.

Criteria	1	2	3	4	Total Points
Preparation • assembles necessary materials and reads every direction before attempting task • uses context cues for unfamiliar vocabulary • reflects on desired outcome before beginning task	Evidence of 2+ incomplete elements	1 complete element present	2 complete elements present	3 complete elements present	____ x 3 = ____ points
Sequence • understands importance of proper order • can make predictions about next step in process • suggests shortcuts that will not sacrifice integrity of outcome or can show no shortcuts exist	Evidence of 2+ incomplete elements	1 complete element present	2 complete elements present	3 complete elements present	____ x 3 = ____ points
Implementation • reviews steps if error occurs • replicates desired outcome • improves on desired outcome through use of shortcuts or enhanced strategies	Evidence of 2+ incomplete elements	1 complete element present	2 complete elements present	3 complete elements present	____ x 4 = ____ points

37–40 = A
35–36 = B
31–34 = C
28–30 = D
<28 = F

Total score ____/40 = ____

Sequence

- understands importance of proper order
- can make predictions about next step in process
- suggests shortcuts that will not sacrifice integrity of outcome or can show no shortcuts exist

Provide printed instructions for writing a formula poem or a math tessellation. Students must follow the sequence as they "construct" the poem or tessellation. Observe to see whether students follow the prescribed sequence through the implementation phase. Ask students to consider whether a workable shortcut exists.

Implementation

- reviews steps if error occurs
- replicates desired outcome
- improves on desired outcome through use of shortcuts or enhanced strategies

Science experiments, particularly in chemistry, are a natural for this type of assessment. Math exercises involving the creation of tessellations or polygons are also a good choice. However, if you want to confine the entire exercise to paper and pencil, you can simply have students create formula poems, such as acrostics, cinquains, or sonnets because it is necessary to follow a particular sequence on those creations as well. When assessing the activity, compare the formula to make sure student work matches the sequence.

3

Literature and the Assessment Rubric

Peggy, the school librarian, is working with teachers on a project to help students make more informed literature choices. By determining students' understanding of literary elements, Peggy hopes to find clues to their method of selecting books. Mature readers rely on certain factors such as genre, specific character types, or story settings to choose new books to read, while inexperienced readers rely on more superficial elements such as book length or cover illustration. Peggy decides to design rubrics that measure student understanding of literary elements.

KNOW THE READ AHEAD

Rather than selecting the same book over and over again, mature readers are able to identify those elements they enjoyed in that book to initiate a search for similar material. For example, if readers know that they like to read stories set in another time period, past or future, they can use that preference to make other selections in historical or science fiction. Readers who gravitate to plots containing suspense or mystery can turn to books of that genre for a guaranteed satisfying read. Less experienced readers, however, may become frustrated in their search for new reading materials because they are unable to identify those elements that they find enjoyable in previous books and must depend on less reliable elements such as cover illustrations for choosing new books.

Readers who possess a clear understanding of literary elements become lifelong readers since they know how to select materials they are likely to enjoy. Executing and assessing activities that focus on understanding plot, characterization, setting, point of view, and theme help students develop literature selection skills that will serve them beyond classroom walls.

Some of these elements, such as plot, also appear in chapter 2; however, that chapter focuses on overall comprehension of a text, while this chapter, with its focus on individual literary elements, gives teachers a chance to test the depth of student understanding of story structure. In addition, chapter 2 covers all types of reading material, while this chapter focuses on fictional literature.

PLOT

Use one or two of the following activities to help students think about the plot, or sequence of events, in a story. Some are discussion options, others require a written or artistic response, but all encourage students to start thinking in terms of sequence, conflict, summary, and prediction and prepare them for the assessment activity. The activities focus on student ability to recount sequence, recognize major events (vs. supporting details), and demonstrate understanding of the conflict in the story. Students can complete most of the activities individually, in pairs, or in small groups, while some, such as the directed reading thinking activity, are effective with an entire classroom of students. Appropriate grade levels follow the activity description: P = primary, I = intermediate, MS = middle school, and HS = high school. Base the assessment on student participation in these preliminary workshops, the discussions stemming from them, and the suggested assessment activities that correspond with the rubrics.

- Construct a time line of major events that take place during the story, and use different-colored markers to denote their level of importance in the story's outcome. I/MS/HS
- Write a newspaper article (include who, what, where, when, how, and why) about what happens in the story. Newspaper space is limited so make certain to include only the most important information. I/MS/HS
- Participate in a directed reading thinking activity (Stauffer 1969) in a large or small group, making predictions about what will happen next in the story. (I/MS/HS; with primary students, teachers read the story aloud in a directed listening thinking activity)
- Construct a class or small group mural depicting the major and minor events of a story and arranging the pictures in sequential order. P/I/MS/HS
- Select a favorite story and tell it to classmates, focusing on the order in which events occur. P/I/MS
- Draw a series of pictures that depict the sequence of a story. P/I

How to Use the

PLOT Rubric

at the Primary Level

Introduce the Rubric

Distribute and briefly discuss the rubric with students before they read the story. Explain that you will base the assessment on their understanding of sequence and their ability to recognize story conflict, predict upcoming events in the story, and summarize the story. Ask students to keep these elements in mind as they read.

After reading the story, discuss the rubric elements thoroughly, making sure students understand what you expect of them and know that to receive full credit, they must meet the objectives listed.

Make the Assignment

Discuss the story title and cover illustration (if available) before you begin reading so students can think about the type of story they will read. Read the story aloud to students or, in the case of more mature readers, allow them to follow along with their own copies of the book or short story or to read silently.

Assess Student Understanding

Prediction

- predicts next event in sequence
- uses prior knowledge to make predictions

Conduct this activity before you finish reading the story aloud or before students finish the story if they are reading independently. Instruct students to work individually (through writing) or in groups (orally) to make educated guesses about what they think will happen next in the story. Move among students and, when necessary, prompt them with open-ended questions (What do you think will happen?), and ask them to explain their prediction (Why do you feel that way?). Note which students are consistently able (or unable) to make accurate predictions. In the students' reasons for their predictions, consider how they use information from the earlier part of the story. For example, if students hear or read that two of the three Billy Goats Gruff go over the bridge, they should be able to predict the third crossing. An inappropriate answer and its accompanying reason would contain no information from the earlier part of the story.

PLOT

Task: Student will participate in activities that focus on story plot.

Goal/Standard: Demonstrate understanding of plot through verbal or written response

Criteria	0	1	2	Total Points
Prediction • predicts next event in sequence • uses prior knowledge to make predictions	0 elements present	1 element present	2 elements present	_____ x 4 = _____ points
Sequence • has no substitutions or omissions in oral retelling • has no reversal of events in oral retelling	0 elements present	1 element present	2 elements present	_____ x 3 = _____ points
Conflict • identifies characters in conflict • describes type of conflict	0 elements present	1 element present	2 elements present	_____ x 4 = _____ points
Summary • summarizes major events • excludes minor details	0 elements present	1 element present	2 elements present	_____ x 4 = _____ points

28–30 = A
26–27 = B
24–25 = C
21–23 = D
<21 = F

Total score _____/30 = _____

Chapter 3 • Literature and the Assessment Rubric

Sequence

- has no substitutions or omissions in oral retelling
- has no reversal of events in oral retelling

Place students in small groups, instructing them to discuss the events in the story with one another. If you haven't already, introduce the term *brainstorming,* and demonstrate how to brainstorm about events in the story. Provide students with two different-colored index cards, and have them write major events—ones that had a direct and dramatic effect on the main character and/or story outcome—on one color card (one event per card) and supporting details (one detail per card) on the other-colored cards. Challenge students to place the event cards in proper sequence of the story—first with their own cards, then with a classmate's deck of event cards.

Conflict

- identifies characters in conflict
- describes type of conflict

Discuss the meaning of conflict, sharing the four main types of story conflict—man vs. man, man vs. self, man vs. nature, man vs. society—and provide literary examples of each type of conflict. Ask students to identify which type of conflict exists in the story and explain their choice.

Summary

- summarizes major events
- excludes minor details

Assign a word count of no more than 50 to 75 words, and have students write a summary of the story. Or for an oral version of this assignment, assign a time limit (no more than five minutes) in which the student must recount the entire story. To prevent students from simply repeating what their classmates have said, it is a good idea to complete the oral option during reading conferences when you meet individually with students to discuss what they are reading. You might also conduct the oral option with a group of students or even the whole class, with each student providing one event in the plot sequence. Another alternative is to assign a time limit and allow two or more students to dramatize the entire story. With a limit on the amount of time or number of words students can use, they must make decisions about eliminating less significant events and details from their retelling.

PLOT Rubric

Introduce the Rubric

Distribute and briefly discuss the rubric with students before they read the story. Explain that you will base the assessment on their understanding of sequence, ability to recognize story conflict, ability to predict upcoming events in the story, and, after completing their reading, ability to summarize the story. Ask students to keep these elements in mind as they read the story.

Once they complete the reading, discuss the rubric elements thoroughly, making sure students understand what you expect of them and know that to receive full credit, they must meet the objectives listed.

Make the Assignment

Initiate a brief discussion based on the story title about the type of story the students will read. This exercise helps students focus on their purpose for reading. After the discussion, instruct students to read the story silently.

Assess Student Understanding

Prediction

- predicts next event in sequence
- uses prior knowledge to make predictions
- predicts story climax

Conduct this activity while students are still reading the story. Assign a section or chapter. Then instruct students to work individually (through writing) or in groups (orally) to make educated guesses about what they think will happen next in the story. Move among students and, when necessary, prompt them with open-ended questions (What do you think will happen?), and ask them to explain their prediction (Why do you feel that way?). Note which students are consistently able (or unable) to make accurate predictions. An appropriate response has evidence that the student reflected on the story to make his or her predictions. For example, a student might respond, "I feel this way because the last time something like this happened to the main character, she reacted this way, so I figured she would react that way again."

How to Use the PLOT Rubric at the Intermediate Level

PLOT

Task: Student will participate in activities that focus on plot.

Goal/Standard: Demonstrate understanding through verbal or written response

Giving 0 points is an option—no evidence, no credit.

Criteria	1	2	3	4	Total Points
Prediction • predicts next event in sequence • uses prior knowledge to make predictions • predicts story climax	Evidence of 2+ incomplete elements	1 complete element present	2 complete elements present	3 complete elements present	____ x 5 = ____ points
Sequence • has no substitutions or omissions in oral retelling • has no reversal of events in oral retelling • emphasizes major events in oral retelling	Evidence of 2+ incomplete elements	1 complete element present	2 complete elements present	3 complete elements present	____ x 3 = ____ points
Conflict • identifies characters in conflict • describes type of conflict • can compare with conflict in other stories	Evidence of 2+ incomplete elements	1 complete element present	2 complete elements present	3 complete elements present	____ x 3 = ____ points
Summary • summarizes major events • excludes minor details • understands why certain details are not vital to story outcome	Evidence of 2+ incomplete elements	1 complete element present	2 complete elements present	3 complete elements present	____ x 4 = ____ points

56–60 = A
52–55 = B
47–51 = C
42–46 = D
<42 = F

Total score ____/60 = ____

Sequence

■ has no substitutions or omissions in oral retelling

■ has no reversal of events in oral retelling

■ emphasizes major events in oral retelling

Have students brainstorm individually or in small groups about events in the story. Distribute two different-colored index cards, and have students write major events—ones that had a direct and dramatic effect on the main character and/or story outcome—on one color card (one event per card) and supporting details (one detail per card) on the other-colored cards. Challenge students to place the event cards in proper sequence of the story—first, with their own cards, then with a classmate's deck of event cards. Collect the cards to see whether students have listed major events and supporting details correctly on the colored cards.

Conflict

■ identifies characters in conflict

■ describes type of conflict

■ can compare with conflict in other stories

Discuss the meaning of conflict, sharing the four main types of story conflict—man vs. man, man vs. self, man vs. nature, man vs. society—and providing literary examples of each type of conflict. Have students offer literary examples of the different types of conflict as well. Ask them to identify which type of conflict exists in the story they read and to explain their choice. Have students compare the conflicts in the literary examples they give to determine which story conflicts are similar and which are not.

Summary

■ summarizes major events

■ excludes minor details

■ understands why some details are not vital to story outcome

Students might fulfill this objective through one of three methods. Assign a word count (no more than 100 to 125 words), and have students write a summary of the story. For an oral version of this assignment, assign a time limit (no more than five minutes) in which the student must recount the entire story. (Use student conference time for oral responses, working with individual students while others are involved in exercises that do not require direct instruction.) A third alternative is to assign a time limit and allow two or more students to dramatize the entire story. With a limit on the amount of time or words students can use, they must make decisions about eliminating less significant events and details from their retelling.

How to Use the

PLOT Rubric

at the Middle School Level

Introduce the Rubric

Distribute and briefly discuss the rubric with students before they read the novel or short story. Explain that you will base the assessment on their understanding of sequence, ability to recognize story conflict, ability to predict upcoming events in the story, and, after completing their reading, ability to summarize the story. Ask students to keep these elements in mind as they read the novel or short story.

Once they complete the reading, discuss the rubric elements thoroughly, making sure students understand what you expect of them and know that to receive full credit, they must meet the objectives listed.

Make the Assignment

Initiate a brief discussion based on the book or short story title about the type of story the students will read. This exercise helps students focus on their purpose for reading. After the discussion, instruct students to read the book or short story.

Assess Student Understanding

Prediction
- uses prior knowledge to make predictions
- predicts story climax
- predicts story outcome

Conduct this activity while students are still reading the story. Assign a section or chapter. Then instruct students to work individually (through writing) or in groups (orally) to make educated guesses about what they think will happen next in the story. Move among students and, when necessary, prompt them with open-ended questions (What do you think will happen?), and ask them to explain their prediction (Why do you feel that way?). Note which students are consistently able (or unable) to make accurate predictions. Appropriate responses should contain information from earlier in the story to justify why students feel a certain event will occur. An inappropriate response has no reason or a vague reason that does not relate to earlier parts of the story.

PLOT

Task: Student will participate in activities that focus on plot.

Goal/Standard: Demonstrate understanding through verbal or written response

Giving 0 points is an option—no evidence, no credit.

Criteria	1	2	3	4	Total Points
Prediction • uses prior knowledge to make predictions • predicts story climax • predicts story outcome	Evidence of 2+ incomplete elements	1 complete element present	2 complete elements present	3 complete elements present	_____ x 5 = _____ points
Sequence • has no reversal of events in oral retelling • emphasizes major events in oral retelling • identifies story climax	Evidence of 2+ incomplete elements	1 complete element present	2 complete elements present	3 complete elements present	_____ x 3 = _____ points
Conflict • describes type of conflict • can compare with conflict in other stories • can compare with conflict in real-life situations	Evidence of 2+ incomplete elements	1 complete element present	2 complete elements present	3 complete elements present	_____ x 3 = _____ points
Summary • excludes minor details • understands why some details are not necessary • emphasizes story climax	Evidence of 2+ incomplete elements	1 complete element present	2 complete elements present	3 complete elements present	_____ x 4 = _____ points

56–60 = A
52–55 = B
47–51 = C
42–46 = D
<42 = F

Total score _____/60 = _____

Sequence

- has no reversal of events in oral retelling
- emphasizes major events in oral retelling
- identifies story climax

Conduct an oral exercise in which you either call on students randomly or start at one end of the room and have students respond in the order of their seating arrangement. Ask the first student to name the first important event in the story, the second student the next important event, and so on. Tell the other students to interject if a student skips a major event or names an event out of order. This exercise gives you an idea of who has read the text and who can recount story events accurately.

Conflict

- describes type of conflict
- can compare with conflict in other stories
- can compare with conflict in real-life situations

Discuss the meaning of conflict, sharing the four main types of story conflict—man vs. man, man vs. self, man vs. nature, man vs. society—and brainstorm as a class for literary examples of each type of conflict. Ask students to identify which type of conflict exists in the story they just read and to explain their choice. Once able to give literary examples of the types of conflicts, students at this level should be able to compare these conflicts, noting similarities and differences, as well as compare one of the types with a real-life conflict; for example, violent crime is often a case of man vs. man.

Summary

- excludes minor details
- understands why some details are not necessary
- emphasizes story climax

Students can fulfill this objective through one of three methods. Assign a word count (no more than 150 to 200 words), and have students write a summary of the story. For an oral version of this assignment, assign a time limit (no more than five minutes) in which the student must recount the entire story. (Use student conference time for oral responses, working with individual students while others are involved in exercises that do not require direct instruction.) A third alternative is to assign a time limit and allow two or more students to dramatize the entire story. With a limit on the amount of time or words students can use, they must make decisions about eliminating less significant events and details from their retelling.

How to Use the
PLOT Rubric
at the High School Level

Introduce the Rubric

Distribute and briefly discuss the rubric with students before they read the novel or short story. Explain that you will base the assessment on their understanding of sequence, ability to recognize story conflict, ability to predict upcoming events in the story, and, after completing their reading, ability to summarize the story. Ask students to keep these elements in mind as they read the novel or short story.

Once they complete the reading, discuss the rubric elements thoroughly, making sure students understand what you expect of them and know that to receive full credit, they must meet the objectives listed.

Make the Assignment

Initiate a brief discussion based on the book or short story title about the type of story the students will read. This exercise helps students focus on their purpose for reading. After the discussion, instruct students to read the book or short story.

Assess Student Understanding

Prediction
- predicts story climax
- predicts story outcome
- identifies plot twists

Conduct this oral activity while students are still reading the story. Assign a section or chapter. Then ask students to make educated guesses about what they think will happen next in the story. Students at this level should be able to provide specific passages from the story that convinced them a certain event or action is inevitable. Likewise, they should be able to predict the story outcome. If necessary, prompt them with open-ended questions, such as asking them to specify what events or dialogue in the story make them think their prediction is accurate. Take note of which students are consistently able (or unable) to make accurate predictions. Inappropriate responses are vague with no connection to earlier parts of the story. As an alternative, have students work individually and in writing.

How to Use the PLOT Rubric at the High School Level

PLOT

Task: Student will participate in activities that focus on plot.

Goal/Standard: Demonstrate understanding through verbal, visual, or written response

Giving 0 points is an option—no evidence, no credit.

Criteria	1	2	3	4	Total Points
Prediction • predicts story climax • predicts story outcome • identifies plot twists	Evidence of 2+ incomplete elements	1 complete element present	2 complete elements present	3 complete elements present	____ x 5 = ____ points
Sequence • emphasizes major events in oral retelling • identifies story climax • identifies influence of specific events on story outcome	Evidence of 2+ incomplete elements	1 complete element present	2 complete elements present	3 complete elements present	____ x 3 = ____ points
Conflict • compares with conflict in other stories • compares with conflict in real-life situations • identifies events that introduce conflict	Evidence of 2+ incomplete elements	1 complete element present	2 complete elements present	3 complete elements present	____ x 3 = ____ points
Summary • understands why some details are not necessary • emphasizes story climax • understands effect of plot twist on outcome	Evidence of 2+ incomplete elements	1 complete element present	2 complete elements present	3 complete elements present	____ x 4 = ____ points

56–60 = A
52–55 = B
47–51 = C
42–46 = D
<42 = F

Total score ____/60 = ____

Sequence

- emphasizes major events in oral retelling
- identifies story climax
- identifies influence of specific events on story outcome

Hold a discussion with students about events in the story, and ask them to define what elements constitute a major event (ones that have a direct and dramatic effect on the main character or story outcome) and what elements constitute a supporting detail. Next, with students working individually, in small groups, or as a class, ask them to list major events on a story map graphic organizer with supporting details surrounding each event.

Conflict

- compares with conflict in other stories
- compares with conflict in real-life situations
- identifies events that introduce conflict

Discuss the meaning of conflict, sharing the four main types of story conflict—man vs. man, man vs. self, man vs. nature, man vs. society. As a class, name literary examples of each type of conflict. Ask students to identify which type of conflict exists in the story they just read and to explain their choice. Once able to give examples of literary conflicts, students at this level should be able to compare these conflicts, noting similarities and differences, as well as compare one of the types with a real-life conflict; for example, violent crime is often a case of man vs. man.

Summary

- understands why some details are not necessary
- emphasizes story climax
- understands effect of plot twist on outcome

Students can fulfill this objective in a number of ways. Assign a word count (no more than 150 words), and have students write a summary of the story. Another alternative is to assign a time limit and allow two or more students to dramatize the entire story. With a limit on the amount of time or words students can use, they must make decisions about eliminating less significant events and details from their retelling.

CHARACTER

Readers tend to be drawn to or repelled from a story based on the connection they have with the characters, so it is a good idea for readers to spend time getting to know these individuals during and after the reading of the story. Authors use characters to convey a story's theme, or underlying message, and if readers do not connect with the characters, they miss the author's message.

The activities in this section require students to focus on the main character(s) in the story. Some activities ask students to provide information from the story, such as creating a Venn diagram to compare characters with each other or the reader, while other activities ask students to extrapolate new information based on what they have read. For example, drawing a character's bedroom requires the student to reflect on what is important to that character (sports, music, friends) and include it in the drawing. Also, the character's personality (shy, outgoing, creative) would influence the décor (paint color, technique, theme of wallpaper border) and the overall appearance (neat, cluttered, cozy) of the room.

Getting Underway

Conduct some workshop activities to get students thinking about characterization in fiction. Some suggestions for activities appear below. Appropriate grade levels follow the activity description: P = primary, I = intermediate, MS = middle school, and HS = high school. Base the assessment on student participation in these preliminary workshops and the discussions stemming from these and the suggested assessment activities that correspond with the rubric. The first few times students complete this type of assignment, allow them to work in pairs or triads, thus fostering discussion about characters. As students become more comfortable with the assignment, they can work independently.

- Draw or describe a character's bedroom. Include the belongings there that bring the character happiness as well as the color and style of the furnishings. P/I/MS/HS
- Create a character "zoo," drawing and describing what type of animal each of the characters might be and how they would behave with one another. P/I/MS
- Write letters to one of the story characters, offering advice or encouragement regarding the character's planned course of action. I/MS/HS
- Plan and celebrate a birthday party for the story's main character. Use the color scheme, decorations, food, and games that character would enjoy most. Draw or construct a gift for the character. P/I/MS
- Use videotape, still camera, or drawing supplies to create "a day in the life" of the story's main character, recounting with pictures what that character does during the course of a normal day. I/MS/HS

How to Use the
CHARACTER Rubric
at the Primary Level

Introduce the Rubric

Distribute the rubric to students, discussing it briefly before they read the story. Explain that the assessment will focus on their ability to describe the character and compare that character with other characters as well as with themselves. They are also expected to draw inferences about the character based on that character's words and actions and to evaluate that character's behavior. Remind students to keep these tasks in mind as they read the story.

After reading the story, discuss the rubric elements thoroughly, making sure students understand what you expect of them and know that to receive full credit, they must meet the objectives listed.

Make the Assignment

Read the story aloud to students, or in the case of more mature readers, instruct students to follow along with their own copies of the story or to read silently.

Assess Student Understanding

Description

- describes character appearance
- describes character personality

For this objective, devise activities that require students to describe physical, mental, and emotional aspects of the story character(s). Make sure students can give reasons for their responses based on the text. For example, you might give the following instructions:

Physical—pretend you are the main character. Look in the mirror. Describe what you see.

Mental—pretend you are the main character. Write a letter to a friend telling him or her how school is going this year. What are your favorite subjects? Which ones give you the most trouble? Use information the author provides about the character to determine which subjects would be easy or difficult for the character. Does the author describe the character as organized? poetic? artistic?

How to Use the CHARACTER Rubric at the Primary Level

CHARACTER

Task: Student will participate in activities that focus on characterization.

Goal/Standard: Demonstrate understanding through verbal, visual, or written response

Criteria	0	1	2	Total Points
Description • describes character appearance • describes character personality	0 elements present	1 element present	2 elements present	____ x 3 = ____ points
Comparison • compares characters based on physical description • compares characters based on actions	0 elements present	1 element present	2 elements present	____ x 3 = ____ points
Inference • links behavior to personality traits • predicts behavior based on personality traits	0 elements present	1 element present	2 elements present	____ x 4 = ____ points
Evaluation • identifies behaviors in specific situations as wise or foolish • identifies character as good or evil	0 elements present	1 element present	2 elements present	____ x 5 = ____ points

28 –30 =A
26 –27 =B
24 –25 =C
21 –23 =D
<21 =F

Total score ____ /30 = ____

Emotional—pretend you are the main character and write one or two entries in your diary explaining how you feel before, during, or after an event [teacher supplies event]. Use what you have learned from the story about the character and how he or she behaves and reacts to imagine what that character might feel.

Comparison

- compares characters based on physical description
- compares characters based on actions

Comparison activities have two related components. First, students must demonstrate ability to identify a character's attributes (physical, mental, emotional) and then compare these attributes with those of another character or with their own attributes. Students should give accurate descriptions of character traits and specific locations in the text where characters exhibit these attributes.

Inference

- links behavior to personality traits
- predicts behavior based on personality traits

The ability to determine what a story character might think or say requires readers to use information in the book to form their response. A written or dramatized response to the question What career would the story character choose and why? requires readers to make inferences based on information the story provides and what they already know— their prior knowledge—about human nature. For example, if readers think a lively, outgoing boy would be happy as a monk, they may have ignored or misread the story cues that indicate the boy would be happier and more fulfilled in a job that involves more interaction with people. Be sure students offer some explanation for why they think the character would be a good doctor, teacher, or dictator.

Evaluation

- identifies behaviors in specific situations as wise or foolish
- identifies character as good or evil

Once readers are able to infer, or predict, character responses to a certain situation, they can use this information to evaluate that character's behavior. If, for example, a character's stubbornness, illustrated by the character's refusal to make even the smallest compromise, causes the character to lose a friend, readers might judge this behavior as negative. Instruct students to write letters to characters, sharing their opinion of the character's behavior along with advice about how to alter a negative situation, for example, "Try listening to other people's ideas," or "Be willing to make some compromises." If a student fails to see the role a character's stubbornness plays in the breakup of a friendship, ask how he or she would feel if he or she were the character's friend.

How to Use the

CHARACTER Rubric

at the Intermediate Level

Introduce the Rubric

Distribute the rubric to students, discussing it briefly before they read the story. Explain that the assessment will focus on their ability to describe the character and compare that character with other characters as well as with themselves. They are also expected to draw inferences about the character based on that character's words and actions and to evaluate that character's behavior. Remind students to keep these tasks in mind as they read the story.

Once they complete the reading, discuss the rubric elements thoroughly, making sure students understand what you expect of them and know that to receive full credit, they must meet the objectives listed.

Make the Assignment

Instruct students to read the story silently.

Assess Student Understanding

Description

- describes character appearance
- describes character personality
- links character actions to personal tastes

Devise activities that require students to describe physical, mental, or emotional aspects of the story character(s). Make sure students can give reasons for their responses based on the text.

For example, you might give the following instructions:

Physical—pretend you are the main character. Look in the mirror. Describe what you see.

Mental—pretend you are the main character. Write a letter to a friend telling him or her about how school is going this year. What are your favorite subjects? Which ones give you the most trouble? Use information the author provides about the character to determine which subjects would be easy or difficult for the character. Does the author describe the character as organized? poetic? artistic?

CHARACTER

Task: Student will participate in activities that focus on characterization.

Goal/Standard: Demonstrate understanding through verbal, visual, or written response

Giving 0 points is an option—no evidence, no credit.

Criteria	1	2	3	4	Total Points
Description • describes character appearance • describes character personality • links character actions to personal tastes	Evidence of 2+ incomplete elements	1 complete element present	2 complete elements present	3 complete elements present	____ x 3 = ____ points
Comparison • compares characters based on physical description • compares characters based on actions • compares characters' behavior with that of real people	Evidence of 2+ incomplete elements	1 complete element present	2 complete elements present	3 complete elements present	____ x 3 = ____ points
Inference • links behavior to personality traits • predicts behavior based on personality traits • predicts how character behavior will affect story outcome	Evidence of 2+ incomplete elements	1 complete element present	2 complete elements present	3 complete elements present	____ x 4 = ____ points
Evaluation • identifies behavior in specific situations as wise or foolish • identifies character as good or evil • understands character actions	Evidence of 2+ incomplete elements	1 complete element present	2 complete elements present	3 complete elements present	____ x 5 = ____ points

56–60 = A
52–55 = B
47–51 = C
42–46 = D
<42 = F

Total score ____/60 = ____

Emotional—pretend you are the main character and write one or two entries in your diary explaining how you feel before, during, or after an event [teacher supplies the event]. Use what you have learned from the story about the character to imagine what that character might feel.

Comparison

■ compares characters based on physical description
■ compares characters based on actions
■ compares characters' behavior with that of real people

Comparison activities have two related components. Students must be able, first, to identify the character's characteristics and, second, to contrast these attributes with the attributes of another character or with their own attributes. Readers should pay attention to the physical, mental, and emotional attributes an author ascribes to a character, including those such as courage, honesty, and humor. For physical characteristics, students should look beyond height, weight, and color of hair to such details as neat or scruffy. Also under physical characteristics are characters' actions. Mentally, a slow-witted or naïve person might not make the same kinds of judgments as a very bright person. Emotionally, characters' thoughts tell a lot about how they will react to situations. Activities that ask the student to respond to such questions as Why would (or wouldn't) you want to have the story character as a best friend? require students to make this type of comparison. They might, for example, want to have Harry Potter as a friend because they admire and aspire to emulate some of his attributes such as bravery and honesty. Their response may be verbal or written. Look for students' ability to describe character traits accurately and locate places in the text where characters exhibit these attributes.

Inference

■ links behavior to personality traits
■ predicts behavior based on personality traits
■ predicts how character behavior will affect story outcome

The ability to determine what a story character might think or say requires readers to use information in the book to form their response. A written or dramatized response to the question What career would the story character choose and why? requires readers to make inferences based on information the story provides and what they know—their prior knowledge—about human nature. For example, if readers think a lively, outgoing boy would be happy as a monk, they may have ignored or misread the story cues that indicate the boy would be happier and more fulfilled in a job that involves more interaction with people. Be sure students offer some explanation for why they think the character would be a good doctor, teacher, or dictator.

Evaluation

- identifies behaviors in specific situations as wise or foolish
- identifies character as good or evil
- understands character actions

Once readers are able to infer, or predict, character responses to a certain situation, they can use this information to evaluate that character's behavior. If, for example, a character's stubborn attitude, illustrated in the story by the character's refusal to make even the smallest compromise, causes the story character to lose a friend, readers might judge this behavior as negative. Instruct students to write letters to story characters, sharing their opinion of the character's behavior along with advice about how to alter a negative situation, for example, "Try listening to other people's ideas," or "Be willing to make some compromises." If a student fails to see the role a character's stubborn attitude plays in the breakup of a friendship, ask that student how he or she would feel if he or she were the character's friend.

How to Use the
CHARACTER Rubric
at the Middle School Level

Introduce the Rubric

Distribute the rubric to students, discussing it briefly before they read the story. Explain that the assessment will focus on their ability to describe the character and compare that character with other characters as well as with themselves. They are also expected to draw inferences about the character based on that character's words and actions and to evaluate that character's behavior. Remind students to keep these tasks in mind as they read the story.

Once they complete the reading, discuss the rubric elements thoroughly, making sure students understand what you expect of them and know that to receive full credit, they must meet the objectives listed.

Make the Assignment

Instruct students to read the story silently.

Assess Student Understanding

Description

- describes character personality
- links character actions to personality traits
- explains how character personality influences actions/choices

Devise activities that require students to describe the physical, mental, or emotional aspects of the story character(s). Some information will come directly from the book (hair color, height, origin), while students must extrapolate other attributes (intelligent, confident, lazy) from the character's behavior and interactions with other characters. For the extrapolations, require students to give reasons for their statements regarding the character. For example, you might give the following instructions:

Physical—pretend you are the main character. Look in the mirror. Describe what you see.

CHARACTER

Task: Student will participate in activities that focus on characterization.

Goal/Standard: Demonstrate understanding through verbal, visual, or written response

Giving 0 points is an option—no evidence, no credit.

Criteria	1	2	3	4	Total Points
Description • describes character personality • links character actions to personality traits • explains how character personality influences actions/choices	Evidence of 2+ incomplete elements	1 complete element present	2 complete elements present	3 complete elements present	____ x 3 = ____ points
Comparison • compares characters based on actions • compares characters with real-life counterparts • compares character with self	Evidence of 2+ incomplete elements	1 complete element present	2 complete elements present	3 complete elements present	____ x 3 = ____ points
Inference • predicts behavior based on personality traits • predicts personal tastes • constructs profile of character	Evidence of 2+ incomplete elements	1 complete element present	2 complete elements present	3 complete elements present	____ x 4 = ____ points
Evaluation • identifies character as good or evil • understands character actions • offers alternative actions for character to attain goal	Evidence of 2+ incomplete elements	1 complete element present	2 complete elements present	3 complete elements present	____ x 5 = ____ points

56–60 = A
52–55 = B
47–51 = C
42–46 = D
< 42 = F

Total score ____/60 = ____

Chapter 3 • Literature and the Assessment Rubric

Mental—pretend you are the main character. Write a letter to a friend telling him or her about how school is going this year. What are your favorite subjects? Which ones give you the most trouble? Use information the author provides about the character to determine which subjects would be easy or difficult for the character. Does the author describe the character as organized? poetic? artistic?

Emotional—pretend you are the main character and write a letter to a friend explaining how you feel about a current dilemma (i.e., the story conflict). Use what you have learned from the story about the character to imagine what that character might feel.

Comparison

- compares characters based on actions
- compares characters with real-life counterparts
- compares character with self

Comparison activities have two related components. Students must be able to identify the character's attributes (physical, mental, emotional) and contrast these attributes with the attributes of another character or with their own attributes. Ask students to respond to such questions as Why would (or wouldn't) the story character be a good presidential candidate (or other elected official such as mayor of his or her town)? This activity requires students to determine, first, what makes a suitable elected official and, second, whether the character fits the criteria. Their response may be verbal or written.

Inference

- predicts behavior based on personality traits
- predicts character personal tastes
- constructs profile of character

A written or dramatized response to the question What career would the story character choose and why? requires readers to make inferences based on information the story provides and what they know—their prior knowledge—about human nature. In the case of older characters, have students reflect on the type of career that might have given the character a more fulfilling life. Be sure students offer some explanation for why they think the character would be a good doctor, teacher, or dictator.

Evaluation

- identifies character as good or evil
- understands character actions
- offers alternative actions for character to attain goal

Once readers are able to infer, or predict, character responses to a certain situation, they can use this information to evaluate that character's behavior. Instruct students to write letters to one of the story characters, telling the character how much they respected a decision the character made or saying why the character might have made a different choice. This activity requires students to evaluate character actions as good or poor. If the student feels the character made a poor choice, he or she must offer the character advice on what the character might have done differently and why that path would have been more beneficial to the character. Ask students to justify their responses with information from the story.

How to Use the

CHARACTER Rubric

at the High School Level

Introduce the Rubric

Distribute the rubric to students before they read the story. Explain that the assessment will focus on their ability to describe the character and compare that character with other characters as well as with themselves. They are also expected to draw inferences about the character based on that character's words and actions and to evaluate that character's behavior. Remind students to keep these tasks in mind as they read the story.

Once they complete the reading, discuss the rubric elements thoroughly, making sure students understand what you expect of them and know that to receive full credit, they must meet the objectives listed.

Make the Assignment

Instruct students to read the story.

Assess Student Understanding

Description

- links character actions to personality traits
- explains how character personality influences actions/choices
- presents examples of how character behavior alters story outcome

Tell students to pretend they are the main character and write a journal entry describing themselves, including their physical, mental, and emotional attributes and the reasons they take certain actions in the story. Some information will come directly from the book (hair color, height, origin), while students must extrapolate other attributes (intelligent, confident, lazy) from the character's behavior and interactions with other characters. Encourage them to use the freedom of a journal entry to let the character reflect in a way that promotes candid remarks. Romeo exploring his feelings about Juliet in a journal, for example, is less likely to worry about posturing for the "boyz" and be more interested in saying how she has touched and, ultimately, changed his life with her challenge to "deny thy father and refuse thy name."

Ask them to consider how the character's behavior influenced the story outcome and to support their response by giving examples of different behavior that would have changed the outcome.

CHARACTER

Task: Student will participate in activities that focus on characterization.

Goal/Standard: Demonstrate understanding through verbal, visual, or written response

Giving 0 points is an option—no evidence, no credit.

Criteria	1	2	3	4	Total Points
Description • links character actions to personality traits • explains how character personality influences actions/choices • presents examples of how character behavior alters story outcome	Evidence of 2+ incomplete elements	1 complete element present	2 complete elements present	3 complete elements present	____ x 3 = ____ points
Comparison • compares characters with one another • compares character with self • compares character with other literary characters	Evidence of 2+ incomplete elements	1 complete element present	2 complete elements present	3 complete elements present	____ x 3 = ____ points
Inference • predicts character personal tastes • constructs profile of character • predicts character choice of idol, friend, foe, etc.	Evidence of 2+ incomplete elements	1 complete element present	2 complete elements present	3 complete elements present	____ x 4 = ____ points
Evaluation • understands character actions • offers alternate actions for character goal attainment • cites which character actions had an effect on character reaching goal	Evidence of 2+ incomplete elements	1 complete element present	2 complete elements present	3 complete elements present	____ x 5 = ____ points

56–60 = A
52–55 = B
47–51 = C
42–46 = D
<42 = F

Total score ____/60 = ____

Comparison

- compares characters with one another
- compares character with self
- compares character with other literary characters

Students must be able to identify the character's attributes (physical, mental, emotional), then contrast these attributes with the attributes of another character or with their own attributes. Effective activities ask students to examine characters' attributes and note whether those characters made the most of themselves in their chosen path in life. This comparison encourages students to compare characters with other literary characters who possess similar attributes but made different choices and with themselves. Their response may be verbal or written.

Inference

- predicts character personal tastes
- constructs profile of character
- predicts character choice of idol, friend, foe, etc.

The ability to determine what a story character might think or say in any situation requires readers to use information in the book and what they know—their prior knowledge—about human nature to form their response. Ask students to use the story information to reach a conclusion about whether characters made the most of their lives. Another option is to ask students to respond to a question such as Would the story character make a good [insert occupation]? Make sure students defend their response. If a student feels that strong-willed and determined Juliet would do well in a job that requires a great degree of compromise (politics), that reader is ignoring story cues about that character.

Evaluation

- understands character actions
- offers alternate actions for character goal attainment
- cites which character actions had an effect on character reaching goal

Once readers are able to infer, or predict, character responses to a certain situation, they can use this information to evaluate that character's behavior. Have students role-play, taking the parts of two story characters, with one character defending his or her actions to the other character. For a different twist on this activity, have characters from different books interact with one another in the same "here's why I did what I did" situation.

LITERATURE

SETTING

Before evaluating students on their understanding of the role setting plays in fiction, try some of these workshop activities to get students thinking about describing, comparing, and contrasting various story settings before proceeding to the rubric activities. Activities that focus on story setting help students gain an increased awareness of the influence time and place have on the story outcome. Activities that require students to describe, compare, and contrast various story settings provide the basis for later, more in-depth study of why certain times and places are more critical to the plot and outcome.

Appropriate grade levels follow the activity description: P = primary, I = intermediate, MS = middle school, and HS = high school. Base the assessment on student participation in these preliminary workshops and the discussions stemming from these and the suggested assessment activities that correspond with the rubric. The first few times students complete this type of assignment, allow them to work in pairs or triads, thus fostering discussion about setting. As students become more comfortable with the assignment, they can work independently.

- Draw a series of various settings in the story, arranging them in the order of their importance to the story outcome. P/I/MS/HS
- Construct a Venn diagram comparing two or more of the story settings. I/MS/HS
- Create a diorama of one of the story's main settings, making sure to include items that are significant to the plot or character. P/I/MS
- Pretend to be a tour guide and conduct a guided tour of the story's main settings, pointing out important features to "tourists." P/I/MS
- Write a poem about the story settings. Include verses for each important setting and a refrain to unite the composition. P/I/MS/HS
- Construct a Venn diagram comparing the story setting with your own environment. I/MS/HS

How to Use the
SETTING Rubric
at the Primary Level

Introduce the Rubric

Distribute and briefly review the rubric before reading the book or story. Explain to students that the assessment will focus on their understanding of the importance of setting on character behavior and story outcome and that they will examine various settings to determine which are most and least important to these areas.

After students read the book or story, discuss the rubric elements thoroughly, making certain students understand what you expect of them and know that to receive full credit, they must meet the objectives listed.

Make the Assignment

Read the story aloud or, in the case of more mature readers, instruct students to follow along with their own copies of the story or to read silently.

Assess Student Understanding

Description

- provides sensory account of setting
- understands attributes of primary setting (time period, time of day, climate)

The more information readers gather and internalize regarding story setting, the easier it is for them to decide the influence setting has on a character's response, behavior, and choices. For example, if a story character is afraid of thunderstorms and is stranded alone during a particularly violent outburst, that character may do or say things that are somewhat out of character. If students fail to see any connection between the story character and this setting, initiate a discussion about how those students feel when it is dark, sunny, bitterly cold, windy, and so on to point out the influence weather can have on an individual. You might have students respond orally to the following questions: How do you think the story character will behave during a thunderstorm? Why? Think about something that frightens you. How do you behave during this situation? Are you more or less likely to help another person? to behave calmly? to feel the way you usually feel?

SETTING

Task: Student will participate in activities that focus on setting.

Goal/Standard: Demonstrate understanding through verbal, visual, or written response

Criteria	0	1	2	Total Points
Description • provides sensory account of setting • understands attributes of primary setting	0 elements present	1 element present	2 elements present	____ x 3 = ____ points
Comparison • sees differences between settings • compares setting with real life	0 elements present	1 element present	2 elements present	____ x 3 = ____ points
Inference • understands importance of setting • explains influence of setting on story	0 elements present	1 element present	2 elements present	____ x 4 = ____ points
Evaluation • identifies setting as safe or unstable location • explains character's response to setting	0 elements present	1 element present	2 elements present	____ x 5 = ____ points

28 – 30 = A
26 – 27 = B
24 – 25 = C
21 – 23 = D
<21 = F

Total score ____/30 = ____

Chapter 3 • Literature and the Assessment Rubric

For the assessed activity, have students use all five senses to create a "picture" of the primary story setting. Acceptable responses should identify the story's main setting correctly and give a complete (five senses) sensory re-creation of that setting. Students can complete this activity in writing or orally during student reading conference time.

Comparison

■ sees differences between settings
■ compares setting with real life

The ability to compare settings within a single story or between those in the story and those in real life helps students see the influence story setting can have on character behavior and, ultimately, story outcome. Finding scenes where characters face similar problems in different settings is one way of determining the extent of the role setting plays in the characters' actions. Have students use a Venn diagram to illustrate the similarities and differences between different settings within the story and between the story setting and real life. Members of a reading group could share their completed Venn diagrams orally. For another activity, have students choose a scene where two characters face the same problem, then, in writing or in a dramatization in pairs, describe how each of the characters behaves. Or use two stories, and have students choose a similar scene and tell, in writing or in a dramatization in pairs, how the characters in each story handle the situation. To ensure no two dramatizations are the same for these last two options, write scenes on strips of paper and have pairs of students draw the slips of paper. Discuss the reasons students believe the characters respond the way they do.

Inference

■ understands importance of setting
■ explains influence of setting on story

The ability to infer, or make predictions about, how a character will respond in a particular setting is another way of examining the role story setting plays in story outcome. A painfully shy character, for example, thrust into a very public situation might behave differently than he or she would in a situation that allowed him or her to remain anonymous. The highly visible setting might cause the shy character to come out of his or her shell and reach out to others, thus altering the story outcome.

Compile a list of several settings and probable character responses (fear, calmness, happiness). Before students complete the reading, provide them with the settings and character responses and ask them to match the setting with the character's probable response. After matching the setting and response, have students write a brief statement (two to four sentences) about why they think the character would react in that way.

Evaluation

- identifies setting as safe or unstable location
- explains character's response to setting

Have students give an artistic response for this activity. Instruct them to draw the story character in a setting where the character would be most at home, such as a cowboy on a ranch, teacher in a classroom, child on a playground. Ask them to draw a second picture depicting the character in the most uncomfortable setting, such as a small child wandering through a dense and dark forest. A brief oral discussion with each student could clarify any doubts about the quality of the response.

SETTING Rubric

at the Intermediate Level

Introduce the Rubric

Distribute and briefly review the rubric before reading the novel or short story. Explain to students that the assessment will focus on their understanding of the importance of setting on character behavior and story outcome and that they will examine various settings to determine which are most and least important to these areas.

After students read the book or story, discuss the rubric elements thoroughly, making certain students understand what you expect of them and know that to receive full credit, they must meet the objectives listed.

Make the Assignment

Instruct students to read the story with their reading buddies or alone silently.

Assess Student Understanding

Description

- provides sensory account of setting
- understands attributes of primary setting (time period, time of day, climate)
- sketches primary setting

The more information readers gather and internalize regarding story setting, the easier it is for them to decide the influence setting has on a character's response, behavior, and choices. For example, if a story character is afraid of thunderstorms and is stranded alone during a particularly violent outburst, that character may do or say things that are somewhat out of character. If students fail to see any connection between the story character and this setting, initiate a discussion about how those students feel when it is dark, sunny, bitterly cold, windy, and so on to point out the effect weather can have on an individual. Have students write a journal entry and respond to these questions: How do you think the story character will behave during the thunderstorm? Why? Think about something that frightens you. How do you behave during this situation? Are you more or less likely to help another person? to behave calmly? to feel the way you usually feel? Then have students sketch the setting and use color to signify those areas that have

Task: Student will participate in activities that focus on setting.

Goal/Standard: Demonstrate understanding through verbal, visual, or written response

Giving 0 points is an option—no evidence, no credit.

Criteria	1	2	3	4	Total Points
Description • provides sensory account of setting • understands attributes of primary setting • sketches primary setting	Evidence of 2+ incomplete elements	1 complete element present	2 complete elements present	3 complete elements present	____ x 3 = ____ points
Comparison • sees differences between settings • compares setting with real life • lists similarities and differences between two settings	Evidence of 2+ incomplete elements	1 complete element present	2 complete elements present	3 complete elements present	____ x 3 = ____ points
Inference • understands importance of setting • explains influence of setting on story • identifies setting elements that influence outcome	Evidence of 2+ incomplete elements	1 complete element present	2 complete elements present	3 complete elements present	____ x 4 = ____ points
Evaluation • identifies setting as safe or unstable location • explains character's response to setting • identifies importance of setting on story outcome	Evidence of 2+ incomplete elements	1 complete element present	2 complete elements present	3 complete elements present	____ x 5 = ____ points

56–60 = A
52–55 = B
47–51 = C
42–46 = D
<42 = F

Total score ____/60 = ____

greater influence on the story. Have students create a word "picture" of the primary story setting to accompany the sketch. Acceptable responses should identify the story's main setting correctly and give a complete (five senses) sensory re-creation of that setting.

Comparison

- sees differences between settings
- compares setting with real life
- lists similarities and differences between two settings

The ability to compare settings within a single story or between the story and real life helps students see the influence story setting can have on character behavior and, ultimately, story outcome. Finding scenes where characters face similar problems in different settings is one way of determining the extent of the role setting plays in the characters' actions. Have students use a Venn diagram to illustrate the similarities and differences between different settings within the story and between the story setting and real life. Members of a reading group could share their completed Venn diagrams orally. For another activity, have students choose a scene where two characters face the same problem, then, in writing or in a dramatization in pairs, tell how each of the characters behaves. Or use two stories, and have students choose a similar scene and tell, in writing or in a dramatization in pairs, how the characters in each story handle the situation. To ensure no two dramatizations are the same, write scenes on strips of paper and have pairs of students draw the slips of paper. Discuss the reasons students believe the characters respond the way they do.

Inference

- understands importance of setting
- explains influence of setting on story
- identifies setting elements that influence outcome

The ability to infer, or make predictions about, how a character will respond in a particular setting is another way of examining the role story setting plays in story outcome. A painfully shy character, for example, thrust into a very public situation might behave differently than he or she would in a situation that allowed him or her to remain anonymous. The highly visible setting might cause the shy character to come out of his or her shell and reach out to others, thus altering the story outcome.

Before students complete the reading, provide them with several settings and several character responses and ask them to match up the setting with the character's probable response.

Evaluation

- identifies setting as safe or unstable location
- explains character's response to setting
- identifies importance of setting on story outcome

Readers can evaluate story settings from a number of perspectives. They might examine setting from the viewpoint of the main character and examine that character's behavior, stating whether that behavior is wise or foolish in different settings. Readers might also identify the various story settings as safe and secure or unstable for the story characters. Another method of evaluating story setting is to make judgments on whether the author chose a good backdrop to tell the story. In a story set in Victorian England, for example, it would be difficult to portray a female character as completely free to do as she wishes given the constraints of society during that period. For the assessment activity, have students write a journal entry analyzing the influence of the setting on the story outcome. To support their opinions about setting influence, tell them to describe a different setting for the story and explain how placing the story in that setting would change the story outcome.

How to Use the
SETTING Rubric
at the Middle School Level

Introduce the Rubric

Distribute and briefly review the rubric before reading the novel or short story. Explain to students that the assessment will focus on their understanding of the importance of setting on character behavior and story outcome and that they will examine various settings to determine which are most and least important to these areas.

After students read the book or story, discuss the rubric elements thoroughly, making certain students understand what you expect of them and know that to receive full credit, they must meet the objectives listed.

Make the Assignment

Instruct students to read the story silently.

Assess Student Understanding

Description

- understands attributes of primary setting (time period, time of day, climate)
- uses adjectives to create visual image of setting
- relates characters' response to setting

The more information readers gather and internalize regarding story setting, the easier it is for them to decide the influence setting has on a character's response, behavior, and choices. For example, if a story character is afraid of thunderstorms and is stranded alone during a particularly violent outburst, that character may do or say things that are somewhat out of character. If students fail to see any connection between the story character and this setting, initiate a discussion about how those students feel when it is dark, sunny, bitterly cold, windy, and so on to point out the effect weather can have on an individual. Instruct students to reflect on how a particular setting, such as a loud party, would affect the actions, feelings, responses of a painfully shy character. The goal here is to identify how characters behave differently when they are outside their comfort zone. To stimulate thinking along those lines, ask students to think of a time when they have felt particularly uncomfortable and discuss the source of their discomfort. Do they feel more uncomfortable when the cause of the anxiety is something physical, such as a

SETTING

Task: Student will participate in activities that focus on setting.

Goal/Standard: Demonstrate understanding through verbal, visual, or written response

Giving 0 points is an option—no evidence, no credit.

Criteria	1	2	3	4	Total Points
Description • understands attributes of primary setting • uses adjectives to create visual image of setting • relates characters' response to setting	Evidence of 2+ incomplete elements	1 complete element present	2 complete elements present	3 complete elements present	____ x 3 = ____ points
Comparison • compares setting with real life • lists similarities and differences between two settings • sees importance of setting on story outcome	Evidence of 2+ incomplete elements	1 complete element present	2 complete elements present	3 complete elements present	____ x 3 = ____ points
Inference • explains influence of setting on story • identifies setting elements that influence outcome • explains why author chose specific setting	Evidence of 2+ incomplete elements	1 complete element present	2 complete elements present	3 complete elements present	____ x 4 = ____ points
Evaluation • explains character's response to setting • evaluates importance of setting on story outcome • evaluates author's choice of specific setting	Evidence of 2+ incomplete elements	1 complete element present	2 complete elements present	3 complete elements present	____ x 5 = ____ points

56 – 60 = A
52 – 55 = B
47 – 51 = C
42 – 46 = D
<42 = F

Total score ____/60 = ____

Chapter 3 • Literature and the Assessment Rubric

dentist's office, or by something emotional, such as being the only person without a date at a dance? Finally, have students describe the primary story setting by using as many appropriate adjectives as they can to draw the setting in words.

Comparison

- compares setting with real life
- lists similarities and differences between two settings
- sees importance of setting on story outcome

The ability to compare settings within a single story or between the story and real life helps students see the influence story setting can have on character behavior and, ultimately, story outcome. Finding scenes where characters face similar problems in different settings is one way of determining the extent of the role setting plays in the characters' actions. Have students use a Venn diagram to illustrate the similarities and differences between different settings within the story and between the story setting and real life. For example, in Shakespeare's *Romeo and Juliet*, one aspect of setting is the home of each main character. Both Romeo and Juliet come from affluent backgrounds, so while the two characters have this setting in common, the setting probably differs greatly from the homes in which most of us were raised. The street scenes might be an area of similarity since it consists of local haunts where Romeo and his friends hang out.

For another activity, have students choose a scene where two characters face the same problem and, in writing, compare how each of the characters behaves. Or use two stories, and have students choose a similar scene and, in writing, tell how the characters in each story handle the situation. After students complete their descriptions, discuss the reasons they believe the characters respond the way they do.

Inference

- explains influence of setting on story
- identifies setting elements that influence outcome
- explains why author chose specific setting

The ability to infer how a character will respond in a particular setting is another way of examining the role story setting plays in story outcome. For example, it is clear by the way Romeo finds some solace in spending time shut away from others that a setting crowded with people and excitement might have a negative effect on his behavior.

Assign students a chapter and ask them to make predictions about the setting based on what they have read thus far. Have them record their predictions in a reading journal at school, and after they complete the reading assignment, they can confirm or refute their original predictions. The purpose of this activity is to get students thinking about what comes next in a story. By practicing this technique in class, readers will, one hopes, use the same strategies of making use of story information when they read outside the classroom. For the last element, have students write in their journals why they think the author chose a particular setting, for example, the author places the story in a large city to give characters access to more cultural and government activities.

Evaluation

- explains character's response to setting
- evaluates importance of setting on story outcome
- evaluates author's choice of specific setting

Readers can evaluate story settings from a number of perspectives. They might examine setting from the viewpoint of the main character and analyze the character's behavior, stating whether that behavior is wise or foolish in different settings. Readers might also identify the various story settings as safe and secure or unstable for the story characters. Another method of evaluating story setting is to make judgments on whether the author chose a good backdrop to tell the story. Take the example, again, of *Romeo and Juliet*. In modern times where young people enjoy more freedom concerning their choice of mate as well as the means to travel somewhere to wed that mate without parental interference, the present time would have afforded Romeo and Juliet a few more options. In choosing a setting, Shakespeare placed characters in a setting where parental control was the order of the day.

For the assessment activity, have students move the character in both directions along a time line. Then during a discussion or journal writing session, have students answer the following question: When would the story character enjoy the most/least freedom to pursue a goal?

How to Use the

SETTING Rubric

at the High School Level

Introduce the Rubric

Distribute and briefly review the rubric before reading the novel or short story. Explain to students that the assessment will focus on their understanding of the importance of setting on character behavior and story outcome and that they will examine various settings to determine which are most and least important to these areas.

After students read the book or story, discuss the rubric elements thoroughly, making certain students understand what you expect of them and know that to receive full credit, they must meet the objectives listed.

Make the Assignment

Instruct students to read the novel or story.

Assess Student Understanding

Description

- uses adjectives to create visual image of setting
- relates character response to setting
- recognizes setting as silent story character

Initiate a discussion about the influence setting has on a character's response, behavior, and choices. For example, story characters placed outside their comfort zone may act and speak in an unpredictable manner. The gentle soul Romeo, placed in a street fight with Tybalt, behaves in a more violent manner than he exhibits in the rest of the tale. Have students write a journal entry and respond to the following: Think about something that frightens you. How do you behave during this situation? Are you more or less likely to help another person? to behave calmly? to feel the way you usually feel? How might setting push you to behave a certain way, just as another person might? Finally, have students describe the primary story setting by using as many appropriate adjectives as they can to draw the setting in words.

SETTING

Task: Student will participate in activities that focus on setting.

Goal/Standard: Demonstrate understanding through verbal, visual, or written response

Giving 0 points is an option—no evidence, no credit.

Criteria	1	2	3	4	Total Points
Description • uses adjectives to create visual image of setting • relates character response to setting • recognizes setting as silent story character	Evidence of 2+ incomplete elements	1 complete element present	2 complete elements present	3 complete elements present	____ x 3 = ____ points
Comparison • lists similarities and differences between two settings • sees importance of setting on story outcome • identifies setting elements with greatest/least influence on story events and outcome	Evidence of 2+ incomplete elements	1 complete element present	2 complete elements present	3 complete elements present	____ x 3 = ____ points
Inference • explains influence of setting on character • explains why author chose specific setting • extrapolates alternate outcome in new setting	Evidence of 2+ incomplete elements	1 complete element present	2 complete elements present	3 complete elements present	____ x 4 = ____ points
Evaluation • evaluates importance of setting on story outcome • evaluates author's choice of specific setting • offers personal response to setting	Evidence of 2+ incomplete elements	1 complete element present	2 complete elements present	3 complete elements present	____ x 5 = ____ points

56–60 = A
52–55 = B
47–51 = C
42–46 = D
< 42 = F

Total score ____/60 = ____

Comparison

- lists similarities and differences between two settings
- sees importance of setting on story outcome
- identifies setting elements with greatest/least influence on story events and outcome

The ability to compare settings within a single story or between the story and real life helps students see the influence story setting can have on character behavior and, ultimately, story outcome. Analyzing scenes where characters face similar problems in different settings is one way of determining the extent of the role setting plays in the characters' actions. In a journal writing session, have students describe the similarities and differences between different settings within the story and between the story setting and real life. To assess students' understanding of the importance particular settings have on story events and outcome, have them list the settings along the horizontal axis of a bar or line graph. Instruct students to assign the settings a value based on their influence; for example, they would assign a low value to a setting that has minimal influence on story events or outcome. If students create a bar graph, have them use one color to shade the events that had the greatest influence on story outcome and another color to shade the settings that had an influence on a specific story event.

Inference

- explains influence of setting on character
- explains why author chose specific setting
- extrapolates alternate outcome in new setting

The ability to infer how a character will respond in a particular setting is another way of examining the role story setting plays in story outcome. A painfully shy character, for example, thrust into a very public situation might behave differently than he or she would in a situation that allowed him or her to remain anonymous. The highly visible setting might cause the shy character to come out of his or her shell and reach out to others, thus altering the story outcome.

Have students create scenarios and exchange them with their classmates. Tell them to write in their journals how the character might react in that particular setting and how the story might have ended differently in that alternate setting. Tell students to include, as part of this journal entry, the reasons they think the author chose the setting he or she did.

Evaluation

- evaluates importance of setting on story outcome
- evaluates author's choice of specific setting
- offers personal response to setting

Readers might examine setting from the viewpoint of the character and examine the character's behavior in a number of settings, stating whether that behavior is wise or foolish. Readers might also identify the various story settings as safe and secure or unstable for the story characters. Another method of evaluating story setting is to make judgments on whether the author chose a good backdrop to tell the story. In a story set in Victorian England, for example, it would be difficult to portray a female character as completely free to do as she wishes given the constraints of society during that period. If readers are unable to see how one setting might be more effective than another to tell a particular story, use examples such as an African-American character holding public office in a pre-Civil War story and how setting would dictate some of that character's behaviors and responses. For the assessment activity, have students move the character in both directions along a time line. Then during a discussion or journal writing session, have students answer the following questions: When would the story character enjoy the most/least freedom to pursue a goal? Why did the author choose the settings he or she did?

Finally, in a journal writing exercise, have students describe how they would feel about the setting if they were in the same circumstances as the story character.

THEME

When students read fiction, they tend to think more in terms of plot and characterization than story theme. The theme, or author's underlying message, is the thread that runs through the entire story, binding plot, characters, and setting to one another. To prepare students for a more formal evaluation of their understanding of story theme, conduct some of the suggested workshop activities that follow while they read the assigned text. These activities help students think about how the author uses character interaction in various situations to convey a specific message. The activities encourage students to focus on identifying the author's underlying message and the author's effectiveness in conveying that message to readers.

Appropriate grade levels follow the activity description: P = primary, I = intermediate, MS = middle school, and HS = high school. Base the assessment on student participation in these preliminary workshops and the suggested assessment activities that correspond with the rubric. The first few times students complete this type of assignment, allow them to work in pairs or triads, thus fostering discussion about theme. As students become more comfortable with the assignment, they can work independently.

- Write a letter to remind yourself of ways to apply the story's theme to your own daily life. P/I/MS/HS
- Find real-life examples of the story's theme in the daily newspaper such as a real-life example of "love one another" or "good triumphs over evil," common literature themes. I/MS/HS
- Select scenes from the story that illustrate the theme, and work in small groups to act out those scenes for classmates. P/I/MS/HS
- Find and share a natural object (leaf, stone) or a picture of an element of nature (storm, tree) that embodies the story theme and explain why the element of nature reminds you of the theme. I/MS/HS
- Design and draw a symbol that represents the story's theme and explain why you chose certain elements to create the symbol, such as clasped hands if the theme is "reaching out to others," or a symbol that incorporates a sunrise if the theme is "each day brings new promise." I/MS/HS
- Reflect on the story's theme, and brainstorm alone or in a small group about sensory images (sight, sound, taste, touch, smell) that remind you of the theme as in the examples that follow: sight, a sunrise for the theme of "new beginnings"; sound, triumphant brass section to symbolize "good over evil"; taste and smell, homemade bread with a theme of "there's no place like home"; and touch, the feel of a warm hand wrapped around your own hand for a theme of "I'll always be there for you." P/I/MS/HS

How to Use the

THEME Rubric

at the Primary Level

Introduce the Rubric

Distribute and briefly review the rubric before reading the story. Explain to students that the assessment will focus on their understanding of the author's underlying message and how the author uses plot, characters, and setting to convey that idea. Ask students to keep these ideas in mind as they read.

After students read the book or story, discuss the rubric elements thoroughly, making certain students understand what you expect of them and know that to receive full credit, they must meet the objectives listed.

Make the Assignment

Read the story aloud or, in the case of more mature readers, have the students follow along in their own copies of the story or read it silently.

Assess Student Understanding

Identification
- knows author's message
- knows story event that contains author's message

Use oral, written, or artistic activities to determine students' ability to identify the author's message. For example, have students give the story a new title that conveys the theme. Then have them create a book poster, placing the new title across the top of the poster. Below the title, have them draw the scene that conveys the main theme. At the bottom of the poster, instruct students to write a sentence or two paraphrasing the author's message. Students' inability to complete any or all of these types of tasks may indicate that they have only a literal understanding of plot.

LITERATURE   **THEME**   PRIMARY

Task: Student will participate in activities that focus on theme.

Goal/Standard: Demonstrate understanding through verbal, visual, or written response

Criteria	0	1	2	Total Points
Identification • knows author's message • knows story event that contains author's message	0 elements present	1 element present	2 elements present	_____ x 3 = _____ points
Comparison • identifies stories with similar themes • links appropriate character with theme	0 elements present	1 element present	2 elements present	_____ x 3 = _____ points
Application • finds real-life examples of theme • draws or locates pictures emphasizing theme	0 elements present	1 element present	2 elements present	_____ x 4 = _____ points
Evaluation • expresses feelings regarding the story theme • determines whether other stories with the same theme convey theme more or less effectively	0 elements present	1 element present	2 elements present	_____ x 5 = _____ points

28 – 30 = A
26 – 27 = B
24 – 25 = C
21 – 23 = D
<21 = F

Total score _____/30 = _____

Comparison

- identifies stories with similar themes
- links appropriate character with theme

Comparing stories with similar themes but different plots requires students to examine the stories for common elements that convey the underlying message. As a class, create a list of stories with similar themes but different plots, then have students select one and explain in one or two sentences how the story is similar to the assigned story. Next, ask students to compare story characters in the assigned story to determine which character—not always the main character—most effectively conveys the author's message. Have students create a three-way Venn diagram, with two circles representing two characters and a third circle representing ideas (honesty, bravery) related to the theme. Ask students to identify which character conveys the theme more accurately by demonstrating the elements more often.

Application

- finds real-life examples of theme
- draws or locates pictures emphasizing theme

An author's primary purpose for incorporating a theme in a story is to give readers something to think about that will, perhaps, change their lives in a positive way. Once students are able to identify the story's theme, instruct them to connect that message in some way with their own lives. For example, if the story's theme is to treat others as you would like to be treated, initiate a discussion that helps students reflect on their behavior and how closely that behavior measures up to the story theme. Have students create a collage of pictures that emphasize the theme and share the reasons for their choices in a small-group sharing exercise.

Evaluation

- expresses feelings regarding the story theme (agrees/disagrees with underlying message)
- determines whether other stories with the same theme convey theme more or less effectively

Even young readers should be able to identify the story theme and offer their opinion about it. After identifying the story theme, have students write their feelings regarding that theme. In their response, have students identify other stories with the same theme that they consider more/less effective in conveying the theme. As an alternative assignment, have students tape record their responses for you to listen to.

How to Use the
THEME Rubric
at the Intermediate Level

Introduce the Rubric

Distribute and briefly review the rubric before reading the novel or short story. Explain to students that the assessment will focus on their understanding of the author's underlying message and how the author uses plot, characters, and setting to convey that idea. Ask students to keep these ideas in mind as they read the novel or short story.

After students read the book or story, discuss the rubric elements thoroughly, making certain students understand what you expect of them and know that to receive full credit, they must meet the objectives listed.

Make the Assignment

Instruct students to read the story with their reading buddies or alone silently.

Assess Student Understanding

Identification

- knows author's message
- knows story event that contains author's message
- restates author's message in a single statement

To determine students' ability to identify the author's message, ask them to give the story a new title that conveys the theme. Then have them describe the scene or event that conveys the theme, and write the author's message in one sentence. Students' inability to complete these tasks may indicate that they have only a literal understanding of plot.

Comparison

- identifies stories with same themes
- links appropriate character with theme
- compares stories with similar theme for similarities and differences in plot development

Task: Student will participate in activities that focus on theme.

Goal/Standard: Demonstrate understanding through verbal, visual, or written response

Giving 0 points is an option—no evidence, no credit.

Criteria	1	2	3	4	Total Points
Identification • knows author's message • knows story event that contains author's message • restates author's message in a single statement	Evidence of 2+ incomplete elements	1 complete element present	2 complete elements present	3 complete elements present	____ x 3 = ____ points
Comparison • identifies stories with similar themes • links appropriate character with theme • compares stories with same theme for similarities and differences in plot development	Evidence of 2+ incomplete elements	1 complete element present	2 complete elements present	3 complete elements present	____ x 3 = ____ points
Application • finds real-life examples of theme • draws or locates pictures emphasizing theme • explains how theme applies to reader's life	Evidence of 2+ incomplete elements	1 complete element present	2 complete elements present	3 complete elements present	____ x 4 = ____ points
Evaluation • rates theme by personal opinion • determines whether other stories with same theme convey theme more or less effectively • judges author's success in conveying theme	Evidence of 2+ incomplete elements	1 complete element present	2 complete elements present	3 complete elements present	____ x 5 = ____ points

56–60 = A
52–55 = B
47–51 = C
42–46 = D
<42 = F

Total score ____/60 = ____

Comparing stories with similar themes but different plots requires students to examine the stories for common elements that convey the underlying message. Ask students to name two stories with similar themes. Have them create a Venn diagram that illustrates the way the two stories are alike and different in plot development. By comparing such facets as how the story introduces conflict and the use of subplots to support the theme, students can discern a pattern in the development of similar-themed stories. For example, stories whose theme is "love conquers all" typically contain an event that takes the lovers apart, but their desire to be together drives them toward reunion, as in *Romeo and Juliet*. Next, have students compare story characters in the assigned story to determine which character most effectively conveys the author's message. Have students create a three-way Venn diagram with two circles representing two characters and a third circle representing ideas (honesty, bravery) related to the theme. Ask students to identify which character conveys the theme best by demonstrating the elements more often.

Application

- finds real-life examples of theme
- draws or locates pictures emphasizing theme
- explains how theme applies to reader's life

An author's primary purpose for incorporating a theme in a story is to give readers something to think about that will, perhaps, change their lives in a positive way. Once readers are able to identify the story's theme, instruct them to connect that message in some way with their own lives. For example, if the story's theme is "treat others as you would like to be treated," initiate a discussion that helps students reflect on their behavior and how closely that behavior measures up to the story theme.

Evaluation

- rates theme by personal opinion
- determines whether other stories with the same theme convey theme more or less effectively
- judges author's success in conveying theme

In addition to identifying the story theme, more mature readers should be able to find its meaning in their own lives and determine whether the author did an effective job of conveying the theme. Discuss with students whether they find the theme carefully woven into story events and characters' responses to a variety of situations, or if the theme is didactic and explicit, deliberately drawing the readers' attention with phrases like "and the moral of this story is . . ." or "what this story has taught us is. . . ." Ask students to choose a scene that best conveys the theme and write, in their own words, a journal entry that explains why they believe that scene conveys the theme. Tell them also to state whether they agree with the story's theme.

How to Use the
THEME Rubric
at the Middle School Level

Introduce the Rubric

Distribute and briefly review the rubric before reading the novel or short story. Explain to students that the assessment will focus on their understanding of the author's underlying message and how the author uses plot, characters, and setting to convey that idea. Ask students to keep these ideas in mind as they read the novel or short story.

After students read the book or story, discuss the rubric elements thoroughly, making certain students understand what you expect of them and know that to receive full credit, they must meet the objectives listed.

Make the Assignment

Instruct students to read the story silently.

Assess Student Understanding

Identification

- knows story event that contains author's message
- restates author's message in a single statement
- explains how character's actions express theme

To determine students' understanding of the author's message, ask them to identify the event in the story that conveys the author's message and write the author's message in one sentence. As the stimulus for a class discussion of how the author uses character actions to emphasize theme, you might have students select and dramatize the scene in the story that conveys theme.

THEME

Task: Student will participate in activities that focus on theme.

Goal/Standard: Demonstrate understanding through verbal, visual, or written response

Giving 0 points is an option—no evidence, no credit.

Criteria	1	2	3	4	Total Points
Identification • knows story event that contains author's message • restates author's message in a single statement • explains how character's actions express theme	Evidence of 2+ incomplete elements	1 complete element present	2 complete elements present	3 complete elements present	____ x 3 = ____ points
Comparison • links appropriate character with theme • compares stories with same theme for similarities and differences in plot • contrasts stories containing another theme	Evidence of 2+ incomplete elements	1 complete element present	2 complete elements present	3 complete elements present	____ x 3 = ____ points
Application • draws or locates pictures emphasizing theme • explains how theme applies to reader's life • sees theme as a model of how to solve real-life conflict	Evidence of 2+ incomplete elements	1 complete element present	2 complete elements present	3 complete elements present	____ x 4 = ____ points
Evaluation • determines whether other stories with same theme convey theme more or less effectively • judges author's success in conveying theme • identifies effect of story theme on his or her life	Evidence of 2+ incomplete elements	1 complete element present	2 complete elements present	3 complete elements present	____ x 5 = ____ points

56 – 60 = A
52 – 55 = B
47 – 51 = C
42 – 46 = D
<42 = F

Total score ____/60 = ____

SkyLight Professional Development

Comparison

- links appropriate character with theme
- compares stories with same theme for similarities and differences in plot
- contrasts with stories containing other themes

Instruct students to write a journal entry identifying the story character who most effectively conveys the author's message. Tell them to support their response with specific examples from the story. Comparing stories with similar themes but different plots requires students to examine the stories for common elements that convey the underlying message. Have students choose two additional stories, one that has a similar theme and one with a different theme. Have students compare the three stories, reflecting on similarities and differences that exist among the stories.

Application

- draws or locates pictures emphasizing theme
- explains how theme applies to reader's life
- sees theme as a model of how to solve real-life conflict

An author's primary purpose for incorporating a theme in a story is to give readers something to think about that will, perhaps, change their lives in a positive way. Once readers are able to identify the story's theme, instruct them to connect that message in some way with their own lives. For example, if the story's theme is "treat others as you would like to be treated," initiate a discussion that helps students reflect on their behavior and how closely that behavior measures up to the story theme. Have students write a journal entry that states how the story theme could serve as a guideline in real-life situations such as divorce, lying, assault, and so on. Finally, have students create a collage of drawn or collected pictures that embody the theme.

Evaluation

- determines whether other stories with same theme convey theme more or less effectively
- judges author's success in conveying theme
- identifies effect of story theme on his or her life

Initiate a group discussion about whether the author did an effective job of conveying the theme. Did students find the theme carefully woven into story events and characters' responses to a variety of situations? Next, discuss the idea that many stories use a similar theme. Have students name some common themes; then ask them to name stories they know that are most effective in conveying some of those themes. Have students write a journal entry in which they select one of the themes and describe an experience when the theme was true in their own lives.

How to Use the

THEME Rubric

at the High School Level

Introduce the Rubric

Distribute and briefly review the rubric before reading the novel or short story. Explain to students that the assessment will focus on their understanding of the author's underlying message and how the author uses plot, characters, and setting to convey that idea. Ask students to keep these ideas in mind as they read the novel or short story.

After students read the book or story, discuss the rubric elements thoroughly, making certain students understand what you expect of them and know that to receive full credit, they must meet the objectives listed.

Make the Assignment

Instruct students to read the story silently.

Assess Student Understanding

Identification

- restates author's message in a single statement
- explains how character's actions express theme
- explains how character's beliefs express theme

Have students write a journal entry in which they identify the author's message and state how characters' actions and beliefs brought that theme to life.

Comparison

- uses plot to compare stories with similar theme
- contrasts with stories containing other themes
- compares characters in stories with similar themes

Task: Student will participate in activities that focus on theme.

Goal/Standard: Demonstrate understanding through verbal, visual, or written response

Giving 0 points is an option—no evidence, no credit.

Criteria	1	2	3	4	Total Points
Identification • restates author's message in a single statement • explains how character's actions express theme • explains how character's beliefs express theme	Evidence of 2+ incomplete elements	1 complete element present	2 complete elements present	3 complete elements present	____ x 3 = ____ points
Comparison • uses plot to compare stories with similar theme • contrasts with stories containing other themes • compares characters in stories with similar themes	Evidence of 2+ incomplete elements	1 complete element present	2 complete elements present	3 complete elements present	____ x 3 = ____ points
Application • explains how theme mirrors real life • sees theme as a model of how to solve real-life conflict • identifies story theme in daily media	Evidence of 2+ incomplete elements	1 complete element present	2 complete elements present	3 complete elements present	____ x 4 = ____ points
Evaluation • judges author's success in conveying theme • compares author's ability to convey theme with other authors in same genre • identifies theme as implicit or explicit	Evidence of 2+ incomplete elements	1 complete element present	2 complete elements present	3 complete elements present	____ x 5 = ____ points

56 – 60 = A
52 – 55 = B
47 – 51 = C
42 – 46 = D
< 42 = F

Total score ____/60 = ____

Ask students to select three stories—two stories with similar themes and a third story with a different theme. Instruct students to use a Venn diagram to compare the stories with similar themes, noting similarities and differences in plot events. Have them create a second Venn diagram to compare the third story with a different theme with one of the stories in the first exercise, noting any similarities and differences in plot events. Finally, have them focus on the assigned story and create a third three-way Venn diagram, with two circles representing two characters and a third circle representing ideas (honesty, bravery) related to the theme. Ask students to identify which character conveys the theme more accurately by demonstrating the elements more often.

Application

- explains how theme mirrors real life
- sees theme as a model of how to solve real-life conflict
- identifies story theme in daily media (news, Web)

An author's primary purpose for incorporating a theme in a story is to give readers something to think about that will, perhaps, change their lives in a positive way. Once readers are able to identify the story's theme, instruct them to connect that message to their own lives in some way. For example, if a story's theme is "treat others as you would like to be treated," initiate a discussion that helps students reflect on their behavior and how closely that behavior measures up to the story theme. Have students write a journal entry that states how the story theme could serve as a guideline in real-life situations such as divorce, lying, assault, and so on; then, ask students to find concrete examples of the theme being played out in real life in the daily media (news, Web).

Evaluation

- judges author's success in conveying theme
- compares author's ability to convey theme with other authors in same genre
- identifies theme as implicit or explicit

Ask students to locate in the text concrete examples of the theme and state whether the author did an effective job of conveying the theme. Discuss what makes a theme implicit or explicit and how to recognize each type. Did they find the theme carefully woven into story events and characters' responses to a variety of situations, or is the theme didactic and explicit, deliberately drawing the readers' attention with phrases like "and the moral of this story is . . ." or "what this story has taught us is . . . "? As an extension, they might also come up with an implicit way to convey an explicit theme or a way to state an explicit theme implicitly. Have students select another text with the same theme. Instruct students to write a journal entry in which they refer to the second story and explain why they think that author is more or less effective than the first author in conveying the common theme.

4

Assessing Student Writing with Rubrics

Concerns over student writing scores on state proficiency tests have prompted school leaders in the Midland district to examine their current instructional methods. At a meeting to discuss solutions, Janet, an intermediate grade teacher and member of the district's literacy committee, suggests adopting a rubric assessment method. In addition to providing students with guidelines for completing written assignments, rubrics pinpoint individual weaknesses, streamlining remedial sessions. Chuck, a middle school teacher, adds that teachers can modify rubrics for specific writing assignments. The meeting chair asks Janet and Chuck to present the rubrics assessment approach to the entire faculty.

RUBRICS ENHANCE INSTRUCTION

Janet and Chuck are not alone in their belief that assessment with rubrics can actually enhance the instructional phase of writing. Rubrics contain standards of performance, so students and teachers have access to "indicators of what constitutes a quality performance to attain the standards or earn an 'A' or 'B'" (Burke 1999, 84). The rubric acts as a blueprint for instruction, highlighting what criteria teachers should introduce and reinforce with students; therefore, for the rubric to be most effective, teachers must construct and share it with students before students begin the writing assignment.

The Five-Step Writing Process

Rubric assessment allows teachers and students to focus on a writing assignment as a *process* rather than an isolated *product*. And rather than assessing just the product (a specific type of writing such as a research paper, description, letter, etc.), teachers assess each step in the widely accepted five-step writing process—prewriting, drafting, revising, editing, and publishing. Teachers can gain valuable insight concerning student writing performance with a rubric assessment of the five-step process because the process requires certain behaviors and skills at each step. In addition, teachers at all levels can use a single rubric for the five-step writing process because the process does not change. It is consistent whether the final product is a one-page story or a thirty-page research paper. For this reason, only one rubric appears in this chapter for all levels.

Getting Underway

A prewriting activity should precede the actual drafting process in all writing exercises. During the prewriting stage, students discuss with their peers and their teacher their topic and their audience—what they want to write and whom they want to read it. This activity provides student authors with an opportunity to focus on a topic and make decisions about how to organize the material for the audience. Making these decisions early in the writing process makes subsequent steps less difficult. Examples of activities to use as a stimulus for writing for all grade and ability levels appear below.

- Field trip or guest speaker
- Film or video
- Work of literature
- Group discussion of a specific topic (rainforests, friendship, conflict)
- Participation in a simulation (mayor for a day, city government simulation)

The prewriting stage should follow as soon as possible after students have completed one of these activities, or any activity that stimulates thinking and imagination. The more time that passes between the experience and the prewriting activity, the less likely students will be to recall valuable information that will enhance their compositions. Student authors can complete prewriting activities as a class, in small groups, or individually.

How to Use the

FIVE-STEP WRITING PROCESS Rubric
at All Levels

Introduce the Rubric

Young authors need to understand that composing is just one part of the writing process. Equally important to the creation of a written product are prewriting, revising, editing, and publishing. The sequence and procedure of this five-step writing process remain consistent no matter what the writing assignment.

Before the writing assignment, share the rubric with students, reviewing the steps of the writing process. The format of the assignment directs the decisions young authors must make during the prewriting stage such as the why (purpose), how (format), and who (audience) of their proposed composition and how they plan to share the writing (publishing), but it is critical that young authors understand the need for the steps that will help them convey their ideas to an audience.

Make the Assignment

The writing assignment can be any type, structure, and length that is appropriate to the grade level.

Assess Student Understanding

Whether writing instruction takes place in a workshop or lecture format, the criteria students must meet during the steps of the writing process do not change, and students must participate in each step to demonstrate understanding of the writing process.

Prewriting
- identifies topic and purpose
- identifies form
- identifies audience
- uses graphic organizers to relate ideas

Students must identify topic, purpose, form, and the intended audience for their composition before they begin writing. Meet briefly with each student early in the writing process to determine the topic he or she has chosen. After students select a topic, individual or small-group discussion can guide them toward the most effective way to organize their composition.

How to Use the FIVE-STEP WRITING PROCESS Rubric at All Levels

FIVE-STEP WRITING PROCESS

Task: Student will produce a written composition by using the five-step writing process.
Goal/Standard: Demonstrate understanding of the writing process through written sample

Giving 0 points is an option—no evidence, no credit.

Criteria	1	2	3	4	Total Points
Prewriting • identifies topic and purpose • identifies form • identifies audience • uses graphic organizers to relate ideas	1 complete element present	2 complete elements present	3 complete elements present	4 complete elements present	_____ x 4 = _____ points
Drafting • generates and organizes ideas • composes lead statement • develops appropriate topic sentence • writes rough draft	1 complete element present	2 complete elements present	3 complete elements present	4 complete elements present	_____ x 4 = _____ points
Revising • rereads rough draft • shares with partner(s) • makes changes based on feedback • creates unifying title	1 complete element present	2 complete elements present	3 complete elements present	4 complete elements present	_____ x 4 = _____ points
Editing • proofreads for errors • creates edit checklist • makes corrections • shares edited draft with partner(s)	1 complete element present	2 complete elements present	3 complete elements present	4 complete elements present	_____ x 4 = _____ points
Publishing • adds illustrations or graphics • identifies appropriate method for sharing work • incorporates media when appropriate • shares with intended audience	1 complete element present	2 complete elements present	3 complete elements present	4 complete elements present	_____ x 4 = _____ points

74–80 = A   62–69 = C
70–73 = B   56–61 = D
          < 56 = F

Total score _____/80 = _____

By answering two questions—Why am I writing about this topic? and What do I want to tell readers about this topic?—students should be able, with minimal guidance, to select a suitable format for the ideas. For example, students who wish to share their thoughts about current conditions in the regional or global environment with an elected official will decide quickly that the most effective form for such communication is a formal letter. Primary students may find a paragraph is the best format for telling the rest of the class about their favorite summer vacation.

Decisions about form also stem from the intended audience for the composition. In the case of the letter on the environmental topic, the intended audience might be one or more elected officials. Because of these individuals' knowledge of the situation, students can assume some prior knowledge and use more advanced environment-related terminology in their letter. Students writing about their favorite vacation destination should include a description for those classmates who may not be familiar with the location. To assess student understanding at the prewriting step, have students share in a written or oral format what they are writing about, why they chose the topic, what they hope to convey, and whom they would like to read their ideas. Provide students with concrete examples and keep samples available for examination in the classroom. You can also work with students in small or large groups to discuss what formats work best with various purposes.

Drafting

- generates and organizes ideas
- composes lead statement
- develops appropriate topic sentence
- writes rough draft

Students may first wish to organize their ideas by using an outline or graphic organizer such as a web to ensure that they include important points and details. After composing the critical lead statement designed to arouse audience interest, students can complete an initial draft of the composition, getting their thoughts on paper. They can give attention to spelling and grammatical errors in later steps. To help students work on good lead statements, have them read their opening statements aloud to one another to see if the statement gets readers interested in reading more. Like a good newspaper lead statement, the student author's lead statement should draw readers in and make them want more information. Allow students a significant number of drafting sessions during class time so you can monitor student work habits. Keep the time frame for writing fairly brief to ensure that students are not trying to correct and rewrite at this phase. For teachers, this is the most hands-off part of the writing process since writing is a solitary exercise.

Revising

- rereads rough draft
- shares with partner(s)
- makes changes based on feedback
- creates unifying title

Assign students to work in pairs or triads to read one another's compositions so student authors can receive feedback not only from the teacher but from classmates. Make sure students read the work aloud to one another; the oral recitation helps them hear poor or awkward phrasing. Before working in revision groups, provide students with guidelines for feedback exercises. For example, you might tell students they must offer one positive comment for each criticism. Also, student critics must give specific examples of what they like and dislike about the work rather than a generic statement such as "I like what you wrote." The more specific information helps student authors make corrections. You might also share a piece of student writing that could use some work with the entire class, and have students revise it as a group, offering ideas for ways to improve the content, organization, style, and so on. You gain information about student understanding when you hear their ideas, and the student author gets many options for revising the piece.

Editing

- proofreads for errors
- creates edit checklist
- makes corrections
- shares edited draft with partner(s)

You and your students can conduct the more objective exercise of editing by using a checklist of criteria to check for and correct before submission of the final draft. The checklist should list such areas as spelling, punctuation, capitalization, and grammar and include places for classmates, the student author, and the teacher to initial that they have checked the composition before students return to their revision groups for a final read of the material. You might create a checklist with two columns. One column is for peer editors to check off, indicating that they have checked spelling, grammar, and so on. The other column is for you. Check the work after the peer editors and return it to the student author to make any corrections. Base the grade for the editing element on how well students correct the mistakes, not on the number of initial mistakes.

Publishing

- adds illustrations or graphics
- identifies appropriate method for sharing work
- incorporates media when appropriate
- shares with intended audience

During this final step of the writing process, students can work individually or in small groups or participate in a more general class discussion as they reflect on the inclusion of any illustrations, photos, graphics, or media that might enhance their work. Give students time to gather feedback from classmates. For media, students might use music in the background of a poetry reading or use a slide show to accompany a nonfiction article. Primary students can use a CD or cassette player, while high school students might use a slide show or PowerPoint presentation. Next, work with each student to reach a consensus about how to share the work. In the example of the letter about the environment to the elected official, the final step would involve addressing an envelope and mailing the letter to its intended audience. Students might share other writing in a different way; for example, a student poet might read his poem from the author's chair. Newsletters, author's chair, and anthologies are only a few ways to accomplish the publishing element. Assessment at this step is a last look at the polished product, which should be error-free and accomplish whatever purpose (entertainment, information) was set forth in the prewriting phase.

WRITING RUBRICS

The remaining rubrics cover student-authored poetry, fiction, greeting cards, autobiographies, informational brochures, and letters. All the rubrics and suggested activities are based on use of the five-step writing process.

The writing rubrics offer teachers a clear example of what is age- and grade-level appropriate for student authors rather than simply noting the presence or absence of specific skills (the format of the rubrics in chapters 2 and 3). The rubrics arrange the required elements in columns rather than under a main heading in the first column. This format of listing full-credit responses provides teachers with more concrete examples of what they may see in student work. Because writing is a generative process (as opposed to the more receptive nature of reading), it is a good idea for teachers to have these concrete guidelines for what a certain student response is worth and when a particular response receives full credit. The more specific nature of these rubrics helps teachers easily identify student submissions as above or below normal expectations for that age and grade level. A brief overview of each section follows.

Poetry: The Poet's Corner

These rubrics assess students' use of the five-step writing process to compose a poem that demonstrates their understanding of figurative language and imagery. The goal, or highest degree of accomplishment on the rubric, for each grade level follows:

Primary—student composes a poem that has an appropriate title, some complete sensory images, correct use of figurative language, and adequate rhythm.

Intermediate—student composes a poem that has a title that sets its mood, several complete sensory images, correct use of figurative language, and appropriate rhythm.

Middle School—student composes a poem that has a title that is appropriate on literal and inferential levels, images that stimulate the senses, vivid figurative language, and a rhythm appropriate to the poem's mood.

High School—student composes a poem that has a title that uses literary devices, imaginative sensory images, figurative language that paints word pictures, and a rhythm appropriate to the poem's mood and topic.

Fiction: Amazing Authors

These rubrics assess students' use of the five-step writing process to compose a short work of fiction that demonstrates their understanding of the interaction of plot, character, setting, and theme. The goal, or highest degree of accomplishment on the rubric, for each grade level follows:

Primary—student creates a work with a logical plot sequence, believable characters, a well-described setting, and a clear theme relevant to plot events.

Intermediate—student creates a work with a plot sequence that balances major and minor events, two to three believable characters who respond predictably to story conflict, a vivid setting relevant to plot events, and a clear theme.

Middle School—student creates a work with a compelling, complex plot with conflict or subplot, three or four believable characters whose words and actions strike a responsive chord, a vividly drawn setting integrated with the plot, and a theme relevant to readers' (classmates') lives.

High School—student creates a work with a well-paced, engaging plot with relevant subplots, a cast of four to seven believable characters who reveal inner conflicts through monologues, a setting that acts as a silent story character, and a theme relevant to readers' life experiences.

Greeting Card: It's in the (Greeting) Cards

These rubrics assess students' use of the five-step writing process to create a greeting card that demonstrates their understanding of an occasion-appropriate greeting. Students have the option of creating a birthday, holiday, thinking of you, hello, get well, sympathy, friendship, or goodbye card. The goal, or highest degree of accomplishment on the rubric, for each grade level follows:

Primary—student creates a greeting card with a two- to three-color cover, an occasion-appropriate message, and no mechanical errors.

Intermediate—student creates a greeting card with a full-color, illustrated cover design, an occasion-appropriate message, and excellent overall quality.

Middle School—student creates a greeting card with a colorful, well-illustrated, relevant cover, a poetic, occasion-appropriate message, and professional appearance.

High School—student creates a greeting card with a cover with a scanned photo or computer-generated artwork, a greeting that contains words and phrases that evoke appropriate emotion, and professional appearance.

Autobiography: It's My Life

These rubrics assess students' use of the five-step writing process to compose an autobiography of text and pictures. Students must demonstrate their understanding of appropriate autobiographical content and photos. The goal, or highest degree of accomplishment on the rubric, for each grade level follows:

Primary—student creates an autobiography with a well-designed cover that includes text and pictures, a logical sequence of events, and balance of text and pictures throughout story.

Intermediate—student creates an autobiography that has a well-designed cover with relevant text and pictures, a balance of milestones and minor events, and appropriately captioned pictures and photos.

Middle School—student creates an autobiography that has a well-designed cover with a balance of text and pictures or photos, an engaging text with a balance of milestones and personal anecdotes that brings the story to life, and appropriately captioned pictures and photos that enhance the text and introduce the author.

High School—student creates an autobiography that has a well-designed cover that includes a word/picture collage of the author, an engaging text with emphasis on major events, and appropriately captioned pictures and photos with references to outside influences (people, places, events) in the author's life.

Informational Brochure: Student for Hire

These rubrics assess students' use of the five-step writing process to produce an informational brochure promoting a service the student can provide (lawn mowing, babysitting, etc.). The goal, or highest degree of accomplishment on the rubric, for each grade level follows:

Primary—student creates a brochure that has an illustrated cover with at least one color picture, an accurate account of services and fees, and accurate contact information.

Intermediate—student creates a brochure that has an illustrated cover with full-color graphics, an accurate and appealing account of services and fees, and accurate contact information.

Middle School—student creates a brochure that has an illustrated cover with full-color graphics and a catchy title, an accurate and creative account of services and fees, and accurate contact information on a detachable portion of the brochure.

High School—student creates a brochure that has a cover with photos or computer-generated art, an accurate and reader-friendly account of services and fees, and accurate contact information with more than one contact option (phone, e-mail, fax) on a detachable portion of the brochure.

Letter: Keep in Touch

These rubrics assess students' use of the five-step writing process to compose a letter and envelope. The goal, or highest degree of accomplishment on the rubric, for each grade level follows:

Primary—the student composes a letter that has four to five sentences, a salutation and closing, an effective topic sentence, no mechanical errors, and a correctly addressed envelope.

Intermediate—the student composes a letter that has six to eight sentences, an error-free salutation and closing, an effective topic sentence that unifies the letter, no mechanical errors, and a correctly addressed envelope.

Middle School—the student composes a letter that has nine to eleven sentences, an appropriate salutation and closing, an effective topic sentence that engages the reader's attention immediately, no mechanical errors, and a correctly addressed envelope.

High School—the student composes a letter that is one full page and has an appropriate salutation and closing, an effective topic sentence that sets the tone for the letter, no mechanical errors, and a correctly addressed envelope.

How to Use the
POETRY Rubric
at the Primary Level

Introduce the Rubric

Distribute and discuss the rubric with students before they begin a poem. Review any terms, including *imagery, figurative language,* and *rhythm,* to make sure that students are clear about their meanings in relation to poetry. Focus on the rubric column that contains the highest degree of performance, and provide concrete examples of an appropriate title, complete visual imagery, correct use of figurative language, and an adequate rhythm for the poem. Be sure students know what you expect of them and understand that they must achieve these objectives to receive full credit. Incorporate the five-step process into the assignment, allowing time for each step.

Make the Assignment

Instruct students to compose a poem on the topic of their choice, or provide a variety of topics for them. Unless students have had some experience with various forms of poetry, it is best to begin with a simple rhymed poem. Again, give students at this level examples of poetry that uses rhythm so they hear that it sounds different from prose. Later, when students have exposure to specific formula poems, this rubric will still help assess their understanding. If you desire, give students a length or word count requirement for the poetry; two to three verses is appropriate at this level.

Assess Student Understanding

Title
- has appropriate title

Imagery
- uses complete images

Figurative Language
- uses figurative language correctly

Rhythm
- uses adequate rhythm

WRITING **POETRY** PRIMARY

Task: Student will use the five-step writing process to compose a poem.

Goal/Standard: Demonstrate understanding by using figurative language, imagery, and appropriate rhythm in poetry

Criteria	0	1	2	Total Points
Title	None	Present but inappropriate	Present and appropriate	_____ x 3 = _____ points
Imagery	None	Images are incomplete	Images are complete	_____ x 4 = _____ points
Figurative Language	None	Used incorrectly	Used correctly	_____ x 4 = _____ points
Rhythm	None	Uneven	Adequate	_____ x 4 = _____ points

28–30 = A 24–25 = C
26–27 = B 22–23 = D
       < 21 = F

Total score _____ /30 = _____

Keep the assessment rubric available when you read the poem. If you withhold points, refer, in writing or during a conference with the student, to specific parts of the poem where the student poet fails to demonstrate understanding of criteria listed in the poetry rubric. For example, an incomplete image does not conjure a clear picture as shown in the phrase "it was daytime" with no mention of the amount of sunlight, the smell of fresh flowers, or the tickle of grass between one's toes.

How to Use the

POETRY Rubric
at the Intermediate Level

Introduce the Rubric

Distribute and discuss the rubric with students before they begin writing a poem. Review terms, including _imagery_, _figurative language_, and _rhythm_, to make sure students are clear about their meanings in relation to poetry. Focus on the rubric column that contains the highest degree of performance, and provide concrete examples of a title that sets the mood for a poem, complete images, correct use of figurative language, and a rhythm appropriate to the poem's topic. Be sure students understand that they must achieve these objectives to receive full credit. Incorporate the five-step process into the assignment, allowing time for each step.

Make the Assignment

Students in the intermediate grades have had some exposure to a wide variety of poems, including several types of formula poems. You may wish to assign a particular type of poetry, such as a haiku or limerick. In this case, review the elements of this type of poetry with students before they begin writing. Or let students choose from the various types of poetry so their selection is the most appropriate for their topic. A three- to four-verse poem is appropriate at this level.

Assess Student Understanding

Title
- has title that sets mood for poem and captures reader interest

Imagery
- uses several complete, well-crafted images

Figurative Language
- uses several creative examples of figurative language

Rhythm
- has excellent rhythm appropriate for topic

Task: Student will use the five-step writing process to compose a poem.

Goal/Standard: Demonstrate understanding by using figurative language, imagery, and appropriate rhythm in poetry

Giving 0 points is an option—no evidence, no credit.

Criteria	1	2	3	4	Total Points
Title	Present but inappropriate	Present and appropriate	Sets mood for poem	Sets mood for poem and captures reader interest	____ x 2 = ____ points
Imagery	Images are incomplete	Few complete images	Several complete images	Several complete, well-crafted images	____ x 2 = ____ points
Figurative Language	Used incorrectly	Few present— used correctly	Several present—used correctly	Several present—used correctly and creatively	____ x 3 = ____ points
Rhythm	Uneven	Adequate	Appropriate to poem's topic	Excellent and appropriate to poem's topic	____ x 3 = ____ points

37–40 = A 31–34 = C
35–36 = B 28–30 = D
          < 28 = F

Total score ____ /40 = ____

How to Use the POETRY Rubric at the Intermediate Level

Keep the assessment rubric available as you read the poem. If you withhold points, refer, in writing or during a conference with the student, to specific words or phrases in the poem that reflect the student's lack of understanding of the rubric criteria. For example, an incomplete image does not conjure a clear picture as shown in the phrase "it was spring" with no mention of gentle breezes, blooming flowers and trees, and birds singing. Mixing metaphors is a common misuse of figurative language. Students at this level often compose a less rhythmic free verse, so the poem need not rhyme, but the rhythm students choose should be appropriate to the poem's topic.

How to Use the
POETRY Rubric
at the Middle School Level

Introduce the Rubric

Distribute and discuss the rubric with students before they begin writing a poem. Review terms, including *imagery*, *figurative language*, and *rhythm*, to make sure students understand their meanings in relation to poetry. Focus on the rubric column containing the highest degree of performance, and provide concrete examples of a title that is relevant on several levels, visually stimulating imagery, vivid comparisons with figurative language, and a rhythm that is appropriate to the poem's mood. Be sure students understand that they must achieve these objectives in the final column to receive full credit. Incorporate the five-step process into the assignment, allowing time for each step.

Make the Assignment

Students at the middle school level have been exposed to a wide variety of poetic forms, including a number of formula poems. If the purpose of the lesson is to reinforce understanding of a specific poetic form, such as free verse or cinquain, review the poem's formula with students so they have a clear understanding of its elements before they begin writing. If you prefer to let students choose the poetic form that suits their chosen topic, you can still use the poetry rubric to assess their understanding. If desired, assign a verse or word count requirement (three to five verses is appropriate), and provide students with a specified amount of time to compose the poem.

Assess Student Understanding

Title
- has title relevant on several levels

Imagery
- uses visually stimulating imagery

Figurative Language
- makes vivid comparisons

Rhythm
- uses excellent rhythm appropriate to poem's mood

How to Use the POETRY Rubric at the Middle School Level

POETRY

Task: Student will use five-step writing process to compose a poem.

Goal/Standard: Demonstrate understanding by using figurative language, imagery, and appropriate rhythm in poetry

Giving 0 points is an option—no evidence, no credit.

Criteria	1	2	3	4	Total Points
Title	Present but inappropriate	Present and appropriate	Sets mood for poem	Relevant on several levels	____ x 2 = ____ points
Imagery	Present but incomplete	A few complete images	Several complete images	Visually stimulating	____ x 2 = ____ points
Figurative Language	Used incorrectly	Used correctly	Several correct examples	Vivid comparisons	____ x 3 = ____ points
Rhythm	Uneven	Adequate	Appropriate to poem's mood	Excellent and appropriate to poem's mood	____ x 3 = ____ points

37–40 = A 31–34 = C
35–36 = B 28–30 = D
            < 28 = F

Total score ____/40 = ____

Keep the assessment rubric available as you read the poem. If you withhold points, refer, in writing or during a conference with the student, to specific words or phrases in the poem that reflect the student's lack of understanding of the rubric criteria. The title should be relevant on a literal and figurative level. The phrase "eyes that shone like diamonds against a velvet sky" is an example of a suitable vivid comparison. When assessing rhythm, remember that poetry should possess a certain cadence even when it does not rhyme. Advise students to read their poems aloud to listen to the cadence, and you should read the poem aloud when you assess it.

———

How to Use the
POETRY Rubric
at the High School Level

Introduce the Rubric

Distribute and discuss the rubric with students before they begin writing a poem. Review terms, including *imagery*, *figurative language*, or *rhythm*, to make sure students understand their meanings as they relate to poetry. Focus on the column of the rubric that contains the highest degree of performance, and provide concrete examples of a title that incorporates literary devices, stimulating sensory images, descriptive word pictures, and a rhythm appropriate to the poem's topic and mood. Be sure students understand that they must achieve these objectives in the final column to receive full credit. Incorporate the five-step process into the assignment, allowing time for each step.

Make the Assignment

Students at the high school level are capable of producing poetry of quality comparable with the works of published poets. Writing poetry provides them with an opportunity to share their understanding of symbolism, which is often present in the texts they read at this level. Presumably, they have had numerous experiences with poetry and are prepared to compose a poem by using almost any formula. Because they have this prior knowledge, give students a greater amount of freedom, allowing them to select the topic, poetic form, and length for their composition. You might review poetry and fiction titles in an anthology and ask students to identify those that use a literary device, such as metaphor, in the title.

Assess Student Understanding

Title
- has title relevant on several levels

Imagery
- uses well-developed sensory images

Figurative Language
- paints word pictures

Rhythm
- uses rhythm creatively

POETRY

Task: Student will use five-step writing process to compose a poem.

Goal/Standard: Demonstrate understanding by using figurative language, imagery, and appropriate rhythm in poetry

Giving 0 points is an option—no evidence, no credit.

Criteria	1	2	3	4	Total Points
Title	Present and adequate (e.g., first line of poem)	Sets mood for poem	Captures reader interest	Relevant on several levels	____ x 2 = ____ points
Imagery	Some images are incomplete	Several complete images	Visually stimulating	Creates sensory images	____ x 2 = ____ points
Figurative Language	1–2 images used correctly	Several examples used correctly	Vivid comparisons	Paints word pictures	____ x 3 = ____ points
Rhythm	Adequate	Appropriate to poem's mood	Appropriate to poem's mood and topic	Creative (perhaps unusual)	____ x 3 = ____ points

37–40 = A   31–34 = C
35–36 = B   28–30 = D
          < 28 = F

Total score ____/40 = ____

Chapter 4 • Assessing Student Writing with Rubrics

Keep the assessment rubric available as you read the poem. If you withhold points, refer, in writing or during a conference with the student, to specific words or phrases in the poem that reflect the student's lack of understanding of the rubric criteria. A well-defined sensory image is one that makes use of as many of the five senses as possible; for example, "strong winds scented with winter pine ripping through the rural land-scape." Assess the poem's rhythm based on the type of poem; for example, if a student writes haiku, base your assessment on the poet's adherence to the syllable count, which creates the rhythm of that poetic form. Remember that you need to assess poems based on their adherence to a standard in the case of formula poems or students' ability to convey a vivid image with language. In other words, a poem may not be to your personal taste, but if that poem manages to accomplish its objective of creating vivid images and/or following a prescribed formula, it is an acceptable poem.

How to Use the
FICTION Rubric
at the Primary Level

Introduce the Rubric

Distribute and discuss the rubric with students before they begin writing a story. Review terms, including *plot, character, setting,* and *theme,* providing concrete examples to make sure students understand their meanings. Discuss the concepts of logical plot sequence, believable character behavior, a well-described story setting, and a theme that relates to story events. Review the rubric column that contains the highest degree of mastery so students understand that they must achieve the objectives in the final column to receive full credit. Incorporate the five-step process into the assignment, allowing time for each step.

Make the Assignment

Instruct students to write a story about a character they have created doing whatever they want him or her to do. The idea here is for students to write a story about someone other than themselves and have that person do something that the author might not have the opportunity or ability to do. For example, students could make up a story about a person who flew to Mars in a '69 Mustang. The student author should control the variables in the story and be restricted only by the need for a beginning (taking off from Earth), middle (arriving on Mars), and ending (returning to Earth). At this level, students can write stories of one to two pages.

Assess Student Understanding

Plot
■ devises logical plot sequence

Character
■ creates believable character behavior

Setting
■ describes setting well

Theme
■ uses theme relevant to plot events

How to Use the FICTION Rubric at the Primary Level

FICTION

Task: Student will use the five-step writing process to compose a short work of fiction.

Goal/Standard: Demonstrate understanding of interaction of plot, character, setting, and theme

Criteria	0	1	2	Total Points
Plot	Undeveloped	Illogical sequence	Logical sequence	____ x 5 = ____ points
Character	Undeveloped	Inconsistent behavior	Believable behavior	____ x 5 = ____ points
Setting	Undeveloped	Poor description	Well described	____ x 5 = ____ points
Theme	Not present	Not well developed	Clear and relevant to plot events	____ x 5 = ____ points

37–40 = A 31–34 = C
35–36 = B 28–30 = D
    <28 = F

Total score ____/40 = ____

Keep the assessment rubric available while you read the completed story. If you withhold points, refer, in writing or during a conference with the student, to specific passages in the story that reflect an inability to understand the criteria listed in the rubric. Offer a concrete example to demonstrate what you expected relating to a particular criterion. Logical sequence is a chain of story events that follow a recognizable order rather than jumping from Point A to Point C then back to Point B. A believable character can have two heads as long as the creature's feelings are relevant to the readers, such as feelings of loneliness (during the long trip to Mars) or fear (of the unknown life forms that may live on Mars). A setting may be light years from our universe, but readers should be able to close their eyes and imagine how it feels to be in that place. If the theme of the story is "conquering your fears" and the main character never encounters anything fearsome, the story falls short of expressing its theme.

How to Use the
FICTION Rubric
at the Intermediate Level

Introduce the Rubric

Distribute and discuss the rubric with students before they begin writing a story. At this level, students have had considerable exposure to fiction, and most are familiar with the structure of a simple story. Focus on the column of the rubric that contains the highest degree of performance, providing concrete examples of a balance of major and minor plot events, character behavior and story setting that have relevance to the plot, and a clear and adequate underlying message, or theme. Make sure students understand that they must achieve the objectives in the final column to receive full credit. Incorporate the five-step process into the assignment, allowing time for each step.

Make the Assignment

Students at this level can produce a story of three to seven pages. Tell students the story should contain at least two to three characters. (You can decide and inform students whether you will base the rubric requirements on the main character only or all characters.) As students have had exposure to various types of literature, you may want to assign a specific type of story, such as a fantasy, a mystery, or science fiction. While these stories have the basic elements of fiction in common, they have very different characters and settings, and emerging authors will enjoy experimenting with the various choices.

Assess Student Understanding

Plot
- creates balance of major and minor events

Character
- creates believable characters with predictable response to story conflict

Setting
- creates vivid setting relevant to plot

Theme
- gives story clear and relevant message

FICTION

Task: Student will use the five-step writing process to compose a short work of fiction.

Goal/Standard: Demonstrate understanding of interaction of plot, character, setting, and theme

Giving 0 points is an option—no evidence, no credit.

Criteria	1	2	3	4	Total Points
Plot	Sequence not always logical	Adequate	Good plot, logical sequence	Balance of major and minor events	____ x 5 = ____ points
Character	Not always believable	Inconsistent behavior	Believable behavior	Predictable response to story conflict	____ x 5 = ____ points
Setting	Poor description	Adequate description	Good description	Vivid and relevant to plot events	____ x 5 = ____ points
Theme	Not well developed	Adequate underlying message	Relevant to plot events	Clear and relevant message	____ x 5 = ____ points

74–80 = A 62–69 = C
70–73 = B 56–61 = D
        < 56 = F

Total score ____/80 = ____

Chapter 4 • Assessing Student Writing with Rubrics

How to Use the FICTION Rubric at the Intermediate Level

Keep the assessment rubric at hand while you read the completed story. If you withhold points, refer, in writing or during a conference with the student, to specific passages in the story that reflect an inability to understand the criteria listed in the rubric. Be prepared to provide a concrete alternative example to clarify student thinking. A well-balanced tale contains a major event that drives the character response and story action and minor events that bring the story and character to life by filling in the blanks about characters. The minor events offer readers a glimpse of how the character reacts in a variety of situations, thus allowing readers to predict how that character will react to the major event in the story. The setting should exist to enhance the plot and character by providing background that can bring out the best (and worst) in characters as they move from one scene to another. The theme should be relevant to readers because it provides the main reason authors write a story in the first place.

How to Use the

FICTION Rubric

at the Middle School Level

Introduce the Rubric

Distribute and discuss the rubric with students before they begin writing a story. Focus on the rubric column that contains the highest degree of performance, reviewing such concepts as a compelling plot that draws readers from page to page, the creation of well-drawn and believable characters whose words and actions strike a responsive chord with readers, a well-drawn setting, and a theme that has relevance in the lives of readers. Be sure students know what you expect of them and understand that they must achieve the objectives in the final column to receive full credit. Incorporate the five-step process into the assignment, allowing time for each step.

Make the Assignment

Middle school students have had numerous and varied experiences with fiction, and you can expect them to produce stories of any genre that range from seven to fifteen pages. You can also expect the story to contain one or two main characters, at least two supporting characters, and one relevant subplot. (You can decide and inform students whether you will base the rubric requirements on the main character only or all characters.) One of the most effective ways to convey story theme is through the characters because readers see the story conflict through them. When student authors identify their audience (classmates) during the prewriting phase of the writing process, remind them to focus on those topics that please, frighten, and amuse their readers. Issues such as peer pressure and self-acceptance represent two major issues for young readers, and stories that contain these themes will interest them. You might instruct students to choose a genre, such as science fiction or legend, and compose a work that contains the elements associated with that type of fiction. This freedom to choose makes student authors more enthusiastic about the creative process.

WRITING   **FICTION**   MIDDLE SCHOOL

Task: Student will use the five-step writing process to compose a short work of fiction.

Goal/Standard: Demonstrate understanding of interaction of plot, character, setting, and theme

Giving 0 points is an option—no evidence, no credit.

Criteria	1	2	3	4	Total Points
Plot	Logical sequence	Interesting and logical	Good balance of major and minor events	Compelling, complex page turner with conflict and subplot	____ x 5 = ____ points
Character	Believable behavior	Predictable response to story conflict	Interesting and likable	Words and actions strike a responsive chord	____ x 5 = ____ points
Setting	Adequate description	Relevant to plot events	Good description	Vividly drawn and integrated with plot	____ x 5 = ____ points
Theme	Adequate message	Relevant to plot events	Clear and consistent	Relevant to readers' lives	____ x 5 = ____ points

75–80 = A   62–69 = C
70–73 = B   56–61 = D
            <56 = F

Total score ____/80 = ____

Assess Student Understanding

Plot

- devises compelling and complex plot sequence with subplot

Character

- creates believable characters whose words and actions strike a responsive chord in readers

Setting

- creates vividly drawn story setting(s) integrated with the plot

Theme

- creates theme relevant to lives of readers

Keep the assessment rubric at hand while you read the completed story. If you withhold points, refer, in writing or during a conference with the student, to specific passages in the story that reflect an inability to understand the criteria listed in the rubric. Offer the student concrete examples of how he or she might have demonstrated his or her understanding. While the main character deals with the central plot, other events should occur in that character's life. For example, while the character tries to help his best friend overcome a gambling addiction, he is also dealing with friction with his stepfather in his own home. The characters should possess traits readers recognize in people in the real world. The story should be set in a particular time, place, or era for a reason—the story might end differently if it had another setting. Common themes of isolation and not fitting in strike a responsive chord with young readers. The theme needs to have relevance in their lives, not the lives of their parents.

How to Use the

FICTION Rubric
at the High School Level

Introduce the Rubric

Distribute and discuss the rubric with students before they begin writing a story. Focus on the rubric column that contains the highest degree of performance, reviewing such concepts as a compelling, well-paced plot with at least one relevant subplot, characters whose thoughts reveal their inner conflicts, a clearly drawn setting that has the influence of a minor character on story events and outcome, and a theme relevant to readers. Make sure students know what you expect of them and understand that they must achieve the objectives in this final column to receive full credit. Incorporate the five-step process into the assignment, allowing time for each step.

Make the Assignment

While students at this level are familiar with the need for a solid beginning, middle, and ending for their stories, spend some time discussing how to introduce characters and story conflict to readers. Students at this level can produce a story of fifteen to twenty-five pages. Their stories should contain two to three main characters and an even larger number of supporting characters whose presence gives readers more information about the main characters. (You can decide and inform students whether you will base the rubric requirements on the main character only or all characters.) When students reflect on their potential audience during the prewriting phase of the writing process, remind them to think about issues that are important to that audience. Allow students to select the story type, such as a mystery or romance. This freedom of choice increases student interest in the project.

FICTION

Task: Student will use the five-step writing process to compose a short work of fiction

Goal/Standard: Demonstrate understanding of interaction of plot, character, setting, and theme

Giving 0 points is an option—no evidence, no credit.

Criteria	1	2	3	4	Total Points
Plot	Logical sequence	Good balance of major and minor events	Appealing to readers	Well-paced action with at least one relevant subplot	____ x 5 = ____ points
Character	Believable behavior	Predictable response to story conflict	Readers identify with character(s) easily	Demonstrate inner conflict through the use of character monologue	____ x 5 = ____ points
Setting	Described adequately	Relevant to plot events	Described vividly	Acts as a silent story character	____ x 5 = ____ points
Theme	Adequate message	Relevant to plot events	Relevant to readers' lives	Relevant in terms of character behavior and readers' prior experiences	____ x 5 = ____ points

74–80 = A	62–69 = C
70–73 = B	56–61 = D
	<56 = F

Total score ____/80 = ____

Chapter 4 • Assessing Student Writing with Rubrics

Assess Student Understanding

Plot

- devises compelling, well-paced plot with at least one relevant subplot

Character

- creates characters who reveal inner conflict through monologue (thoughts)

Setting

- creates clearly drawn setting that has the influence of a minor character on story events and outcome

Theme

- creates theme relevant to readers' prior experience

Keep the assessment rubric at hand while you read the completed story. If you withhold points, refer, in writing or during a conference with the student, to specific passages in the story that reflect an inability to understand the criteria listed in the rubric. The setting (such as urban vs. rural) should play a role in the story and make a difference to the story outcome. The story should touch on an issue important to readers. While the main character deals with the central plot, other events should occur in that character's life. For example, the main character tries to help his best friend overcome a gambling addiction; in a relevant subplot, something is stolen from the school. It turns out the gambler is not the thief, but the situation gives readers a chance to learn more about the protagonist by how he reacts to the information.

How to Use the
GREETING CARD Rubric
at the Primary Level

Introduce the Rubric

Distribute and discuss the rubric with students before they begin making a greeting card. While students at this level have probably made greetings for parents and grandparents, they may be unfamiliar with the particulars of the greeting card format: cover illustration, cover text, and inside message. Provide a sample in class while discussing the rubric criteria, noting how the use of color and an overall neat appearance enhance greeting cards. Be sure students know what you expect of them and understand that they must meet the objectives in the final column of the rubric to receive full credit. Incorporate the five-step process into the assignment, allowing time for each step.

Make the Assignment

Instruct students to assemble any supplies, such as scissors, crayons, and markers, before they begin their greeting card. The cards may be a class project or an individual project to celebrate a specific occasion. Use this opportunity to talk about some words students might use for the greeting, and write those words on the board. Instruct students to write their greetings on a "sloppy copy" first and check with a peer editor, the dictionary, and you to make sure everything is accurate. Once they have checked the greeting for accuracy, provide students with the greeting card paper.

Assess Student Understanding

Cover Design
- designs cover with two to three colors

Content
- creates appropriate message with no errors

Overall Appearance
- produces card with neat appearance and free of errors

Keep the rubric available while reviewing the card. Because the cards are likely heading for a destination beyond the classroom, show students their errors and give them a chance to try again.

WRITING **GREETING CARD** PRIMARY

Task: Student will use the five-step writing process to create a greeting card.

Goal/Standard: Demonstrate understanding with occasion-appropriate greeting card

Criteria	0	1	2	Total Points
Cover Design	No artwork	Pencil sketch	2–3 colors	_____ x 3 = _____ points
Content	None	Inappropriate message	Appropriate message with no errors	_____ x 3 = _____ points
Overall Appearance	Poor illustrations; many misspellings	Neat cover; some misspellings	Neat cover; no misspellings	_____ x 4 = _____ points

19–20 = A 16–17 = C 18 = B 14–15 = D <14 = F	Total score _____ /20 = _____

How to Use the
GREETING CARD Rubric
at the Intermediate Level

Introduce the Rubric

Distribute and discuss the rubric with students before they begin making a greeting card. Students at this level have had some experience in making bifold and quarterfold cards, so you can review these techniques quickly. Focus on the column of the rubric that contains the highest degree of performance, reminding students that they must achieve the objectives in this final column to receive full credit. Incorporate the five-step process into the assignment, allowing time for each step.

Make the Assignment

Students at this level have been making greeting cards for some time and understand that the cover design should relate to the message inside the card. To reinforce this concept, provide some commercial or handmade samples. If students are making the cards to commemorate a particular occasion like Father's Day or Valentine's Day, spend some time discussing some words they might use in the message, copying these words on the board. Instruct students to assemble their materials, such as scissors, crayons, and markers, before they begin their cards. Remind them to write their message on a "sloppy copy" and check it for spelling, grammatical, and punctuation errors before transferring it to the card. Once the card's message is accurate, provide students with the greeting card paper.

Assess Student Understanding

Cover Design
- designs cover with full color

Content
- has creative message relevant to the occasion

Overall Appearance
- produces card of excellent quality

Keep the rubric available while reviewing the card. Since the cards are likely destined for a location beyond the classroom, review errors with students and let them try again.

WRITING **GREETING CARD** INTERMEDIATE

Task: Student will use the five-step writing process to create a greeting card.

Goal/Standard: Demonstrate understanding with occasion-appropriate greeting card

Giving 0 points is an option—no evidence, no credit.

Criteria	1	2	3	4	Total Points
Cover Design	Pencil sketch	1 color	2–3 colors	Full-color illustration	_____ x 3 = _____ points
Content	Inappropriate message	Adequate message	Appropriate to occasion	Appropriate to occasion with creative language	_____ x 3 = _____ points
Overall Appearance	Neat cover; some misspellings	Neat cover; no misspellings	Good quality	Excellent quality	_____ x 4 = _____ points

37–40 = A   31–34 = C
35–36 = B   28–30 = D
            <28 = F

Total score _____/40 = _____

How to Use the
GREETING CARD Rubric
at the Middle School Level

Introduce the Rubric

Distribute and discuss the rubric with students before they begin making a greeting card. Focus attention on the column that contains the highest degree of performance. Remind students that they must achieve the objectives in this final column to receive full credit. Incorporate the five-step process into the assignment, allowing time for each step.

Make the Assignment

Students at this level have had considerable experience producing greeting cards and should have no difficulty with bifold or quarterfold cards. Instruct students to assemble any materials, such as scissors, crayons, and markers, before they begin their greeting cards. If the class has access to computers and greeting card software, students at this level should be capable of preparing a professional quality card by using this method. Instruct students to write their message on a "sloppy copy" and check it for accuracy before transferring it to their greeting cards.

Assess Student Understanding

Cover Design
■ designs full-color cover with pictures and relevant text

Content
■ has message appropriate for occasion and relevant to cover design

Overall Appearance
■ produces professional quality card

Keep the assessment rubric available while reviewing the card. Since the cards are likely heading for a destination beyond the classroom, share students' errors with them and give them a chance to try again.

WRITING **GREETING CARD** MIDDLE SCHOOL

Task: Student will use the five-step writing process to create a greeting card.

Goal/Standard: Demonstrate understanding with an occasion-appropriate greeting card

Giving 0 points is an option—no evidence, no credit.

Criteria	1	2	3	4	Total Points
Cover Design	1–2 colors	Full color	Uses photos or computer-generated image	Colorful, well illustrated, and relevant	_____ x 3 = _____ points
Content	Adequate message	Relevant to occasion and cover design	Creative	Poetic and appropriate to occasion and cover	_____ x 3 = _____ points
Overall Appearance	Neat cover; some misspellings	Neat cover; no misspellings	Good quality	Professional quality	_____ x 4 = _____ points

37–40 = A   31–34 = C
35–36 = B   28–30 = D
            <28 = F

Total score _____/40 = _____

How to Use the
GREETING CARD Rubric
at the High School Level

Introduce the Rubric

Distribute and discuss the rubric with students before they begin making a greeting card. Focus attention on the column that contains the highest degree of performance. Remind students that to receive full credit, they must achieve the objectives in this final column. Incorporate the five-step process into the assignment, allowing time for each step.

Make the Assignment

Students at this level are capable of creating professional quality cards by hand or with the aid of computer software. Their level of expertise may range from using computer clip art to scanning and arranging a photo on the covers of their cards. While students may possess the ability to design these cards with little or no assistance, it is still a good idea to have them write their message on a "sloppy copy" and check it for accuracy before transferring it to their cards.

Assess Student Understanding

Cover Design
- designs cover with high quality art, photos, or computer-generated images

Content
- has message that evokes appropriate emotions

Overall Appearance
- produces professional quality card

Keep the assessment rubric available while reviewing the card. These cards are likely destined for a location beyond the classroom, so review any errors in construction or layout with students and give them a chance to try again.

How to Use the GREETING CARD Rubric at the High School Level

GREETING CARD

Task: Student will use the five-step writing process to create a computer-generated greeting card.

Goal/Standard: Demonstrate understanding with an occasion-appropriate greeting card

Giving 0 points is an option—no evidence, no credit.

Criteria	1	2	3	4	Total Points
Cover Design	1–2 colors	Full color	Contains photograph or computer-generated image	High quality, full-color illustrations	_____ x 3 = _____ points
Content	Adequate message	Message relates to cover design	Creative language	Message evokes specific emotions	_____ x 3 = _____ points
Overall Appearance	Neat cover; no misspellings	Aesthetically pleasing cover layout and message	Good quality	Professional quality	_____ x 4 = _____ points

37–40 = A 31–34 = C
35–36 = B 28–30 = D
          <28 = F

Total score _____/40 = _____

How to Use the
AUTOBIOGRAPHY Rubric
at the Primary Level

Introduce the Rubric

Distribute and discuss the rubric with students before they begin to write. Make sure students understand the term *autobiography* and that such an account should match the chronological order of their lives. Focus attention on the rubric column that contains the highest degree of performance, reminding students that they must achieve the objectives in this final column to receive full credit. Incorporate the five-step process into the assignment, allowing time for each step.

Make the Assignment

Have students create a prewriting web to organize their information before writing. They will submit this web or outline with their manuscript. Students at this level are capable of writing one page, including pictures and photos, for each year of their lives, relating major events and interesting information about each year in the order events occurred. Instruct students to ask parents or guardians for help sifting through childhood pictures to recall events and for possible inclusion in the autobiographical account. They can include small photos or pictures on the page in newspaper-type format.

Assess Student Understanding

Cover Design
■ designs cover with picture(s) and words

Sequence
■ uses logical order of events

Content
■ balances pictures/photos and words

Keep the rubric and outline available while reviewing the account. If the autobiography contains errors in sequence, instruct the student to return to the web or outline to verify the proper order in which events occurred. This assessment focuses on appropriate format and length.

How to Use the AUTOBIOGRAPHY Rubric at the Primary Level

AUTOBIOGRAPHY

Task: Student will use the five-step writing process to compile an autobiography with text and pictures.

Goal/Standard: Demonstrate understanding with completion of autobiography

Criteria	0	1	2	Total Points
Cover Design	None	Text only	Well designed with text and pictures	____ x 3 = ____ points
Sequence	None	Omissions and reversals	Logical order of events	____ x 3 = ____ points
Content	Poor organization; all text or all pictures	Text with few pictures or photos	Appropriate balance of text and pictures or photos	____ x 4 = ____ points

19–20 = A   16–17 = C
18 = B   14–15 = D
<14 = F

Total score ____/20 = ____

How to Use the
AUTOBIOGRAPHY Rubric
at the Intermediate Level

Introduce the Rubric

Distribute and discuss the rubric with students before they begin to write. Focus attention on the rubric column that contains the highest degree of performance, reminding students that they must achieve the objectives in this final column to receive full credit. Review the importance of sequence in an autobiography as well as the need to include some supporting details to energize the life story. Incorporate the five-step process into the assignment, allowing time for each step.

Make the Assignment

Prewriting webs and outlines help students organize the information about their lives and decide what information to include in the autobiography. Instruct students to seek help from parents or guardians collecting photos to recall important events and for possible inclusion in the autobiography. Students at this level are capable of writing approximately one page for each early (preschool) year of their lives and one to two pages for school years.

Assess Student Understanding

Cover Design
- designs cover with relevant photos/pictures and words

Sequence
- balances major and minor events in author's life

Content
- uses pictures/photos with appropriate captions

Keep the assessment rubric available while reviewing the account. Have students who experience difficulty with the sequencing aspect of writing an autobiography refer to their web or outline to clarify the order of events. Make sure that all photos and pictures in the account contain appropriate, explanatory captions or commentary to help readers understand why the authors included them.

AUTOBIOGRAPHY

Task: Student will use the five-step writing process to compile an autobiography with text and pictures.

Goal/Standard: Demonstrate understanding with completion of autobiography

Giving 0 points is an option—no evidence, no credit.

Criteria	1	2	3	4	Total Points
Cover Design	Text only	Text and pictures	Relevant text and pictures	Well designed with relevant text and pictures	____ x 3 = ____ points
Sequence	Omissions and reversals	Logical order of events	Includes only major events	Sequence of major events enhanced by inclusion of minor events	____ x 3 = ____ points
Content	Text only; no pictures	Text with few pictures or photos	Appropriate balance of text with pictures or photos	Appropriately captioned photos or pictures accompany text	____ x 4 = ____ points

37–40 = A   31–34 = C
35–36 = B   28–30 = D
          <28 = F

Total score ____/40 = ____

How to Use the
AUTOBIOGRAPHY Rubric
at the Middle School Level

Introduce the Rubric

Distribute and discuss the assessment rubric with students before they begin to write. Stress the importance of sequence in writing an autobiography, and focus attention on the rubric column that contains the highest degree of performance, reminding students that they must achieve the objectives in this final column to receive full credit. Incorporate the five-step process into the assignment, allowing time for each step.

Make the Assignment

Have students create a web or an outline as a prewriting tool to organize the information they wish to include in their autobiographical account. As they group ideas and topics and place them under headings, they can easily distinguish major, milestone events and minor events and determine which events they can eliminate or reduce in size. Instruct students to ask parents or guardians for help collecting childhood photos, which they can use to recall past events and for possible inclusion in the account. They also need a picture or other graphic for their autobiography's cover that reflects their interests. Students at this level can write fairly extensive accounts, ranging from fifteen to twenty pages, including captioned pictures and photos.

Assess Student Understanding

Cover Design
■ designs cover that balances text and pictures, photos, or graphics reflecting author's interests

Sequence
■ builds anticipation from one life milestone to the next in proper order

Content
■ provides a comprehensive profile of the author

Keep the assessment rubric available while reviewing the account. Make sure students include events from more than one area in their lives; for example, the account should mention their family life, school years, and favorite pastimes to present a comprehensive portrait. The cover should reflect the author's interests.

WRITING   **AUTOBIOGRAPHY**   MIDDLE SCHOOL

Task: Student will use the five-step writing process to compile an autobiography with text and pictures.

Goal/Standard: Demonstrate understanding with completion of autobiography

Giving 0 points is an option—no evidence, no credit.

Criteria	1	2	3	4	Total Points
Cover Design	Text and pictures	Relevant text and pictures	Good design	Well designed with balance of text and pictures and photos of author's interests	_____ x 3 = _____ points
Sequence	Logical order of events	Includes only major events	Balance of milestones and everyday events	Balance of milestones and personal anecdotes bring story to life	_____ x 3 = _____ points
Content	Text with few pictures or photos	Appropriate balance of text with photos or pictures	Appropriately captioned pictures or photos accompany text	Appropriately captioned pictures or photos introduce author	_____ x 4 = _____ points

37–40 = A   31–34 = C
35–36 = B   28–30 = D
              <28 = F

Total score _____/40 = _____

How to Use the
AUTOBIOGRAPHY Rubric
at the High School Level

Introduce the Rubric

Distribute and discuss the rubric with students before they begin writing their accounts. Focus attention on the rubric column that contains the highest degree of performance, reminding students that they must achieve the objectives in this final column to receive full credit. Review the need to write an autobiography in a clear and logical order to reduce reader confusion and to make the work flow. Discuss the use of pictures to enhance the account as well as graphics to personalize the story. For example, an author who is an avid football fan might include sports-related graphic clip art in the margins of some pages to reinforce this information. Incorporate the five-step process into the assignment, allowing time for each step.

Make the Assignment

Instruct students to use a web, an outline, or another graphic organizer during the prewriting phase to help them sift through the information about their lives and decide which information merits mention in the account. Encourage students to look through early childhood photos with parents or guardians to recall specific events from their earliest years as well as for possible inclusion in the autobiography. As students move toward adulthood, it is important that they reflect on their lives and what people or places have had a major role in shaping them. They most often mention parents or guardians in this regard, but teachers, other relatives, and friends and neighbors have passed in and out of students' lives, changing them and helping them grow. And while schools, homes, and places of worship are influential locations in students' lives, athletic fields or private thinking places (a clearing near a creek, a favorite tree to climb) are also worth mentioning. Since students at this level are preparing to enter the adult world, instruct them to include any professional or personal aspirations and when they first dreamed of attaining these goals. For example, an aspiring athlete may have pictures and stories from childhood that offer evidence of this lifetime dream. Students at this level are capable of producing accounts ranging from eighteen to twenty-five pages, including photos and graphics.

WRITING **AUTOBIOGRAPHY** HIGH SCHOOL

Task: Student will use the five-step writing process to compile an autobiography with text and pictures.

Goal/Standard: Demonstrate understanding with completion of autobiography

Giving 0 points is an option—no evidence, no credit.

Criteria	1	2	3	4	Total Points
Cover Design	Text and pictures relevant to each other	Well designed but reveals little about author	Good balance of text and photos of author's interests	Well-designed word/picture and photo collage embodies spirit of author	____ x 3 = ____ points
Sequence	Emphasis on major events	Balance between milestones and everyday events	Anticipation builds from milestone to milestone throughout account	Includes supporting details to bring major events to life	____ x 3 = ____ points
Content	Appropriate balance of text with photos or pictures	Appropriate captioning on photos or pictures that accompany text	Appropriately captioned pictures or photos introduce author	Appropriately captioned pictures or photos and references to outside influences, such as people, places, or events in author's life	____ x 4 = ____ points

37–40 = A   31–34 = C
35–36 = B   28–30 = D
           <28 = F

Total score ____/40 = ____

Assess Student Understanding

Cover Design

■ designs cover that embodies the author's heart, mind, and spirit

Sequence

■ uses supporting details to enhance and clarify author's major life events

Content

■ recounts stories about influences (people and places) in author's life

Keep the assessment rubric available while reviewing the account. Make sure students emphasize major events and include details that bring these events to life. They should also refer to people and places that have had an effect on their lives. The cover should reflect the author's interests, such as a graphic representing an interest in sports, music, or art.

How to Use the
INFORMATIONAL BROCHURE Rubric
at the Primary Level

Introduce the Rubric

Distribute and discuss the rubric with students before they begin work on the brochure. Brochures of this type can advertise services the student can offer (dog walking, car washing) or announce an upcoming event in the student's life, such as an important sporting or artistic competition. Discuss reasons students might create a brochure and why they should arrange the information in a reader-friendly format. Provide concrete examples of informational brochures to allow students to examine their arrangement of information. Focus attention on the rubric column that contains the highest degree of performance, making sure students understand that they must achieve the objectives in the final column to receive full credit. Incorporate the five-step process into the assignment, allowing time for each step.

Make the Assignment

Help students decide what information they wish to share on the brochure. Discuss any services, such as car washing or garden weeding, they could perform for family and friends. Simply having students create brochures and then leave them in class is not as meaningful as a performance task of having students actually distribute the brochures in the real world. Make sure parents or guardians are aware of the type of services the student is offering and agree with the arrangement. Discuss the need to include information about how people interested in the service can contact the student. Have students use a web to organize the information and to make sure they include everything before they transfer the information to a bifold or trifold brochure.

INFORMATIONAL BROCHURE

Task: Student will use the five-step writing process to produce an informational brochure promoting a service the student can provide.

Goal/Standard: Demonstrate understanding with completed brochure

Criteria	0	1	2	Total Points
Cover Design	None	Text only	Text and at least 1 color picture	_____ x 3 = _____ points
Description of Services	None	Present with omissions	Present and accurate	_____ x 3 = _____ points
Contact Information	None	Present with omissions	Present and accurate	_____ x 4 = _____ points

19–20 = A   16–17 = C
18 = B   14–15 = D
       <14 = F

Total score _____/20 = _____

Assess Student Understanding

Cover Design

- includes text and at least one color picture or graphic

Description of Services

- describes services accurately and without error

Contact Information

- gives accurate and error-free contact information

Keep the assessment rubric available while reviewing the brochure. Note the arrangement of information in a bifold or trifold format and its ease of use for readers. At this level, the cover graphic can be a drawing. Make sure students describe the services they are offering realistically in light of their age and level of ability. For example, it is unlikely that an 8 year old would be able to walk a large, powerful dog such as a husky or an akita.

How to Use the
INFORMATIONAL BROCHURE Rubric
at the Intermediate Level

Introduce the Rubric

Distribute and discuss the assessment rubric with students before they begin work on the brochure. Focus attention on the rubric column that contains the highest degree of performance, making sure students understand that they must achieve the objectives in the final column to receive full credit. Make sure students understand that they must be able to stand behind the services or announcement the brochure describes. For example, if the student offers to weed the garden of a customer, that student must be willing and able to complete that task. If the brochure advertises an upcoming sporting event the student is taking part in, the information about the time and location of the event must be accurate. Incorporate the five-step process into the assignment, allowing time for each step.

Make the Assignment

Place students in small groups, and have them brainstorm about types of services or announcements they might place in the brochure. Remind them of the importance of an accurate and complete account of the services they are offering. For example, if a student offers lawn-mowing services, the student must consider whether the customers must provide mowers and lawn bags. This type of information helps customers make decisions about using such services. Ask them to consider what illustrations or graphics might enhance the brochure. In some instances, students may wish to work together on a brochure to offer a service jointly, such as a two-person lawn-mowing service. In those instances, check with students throughout the process to make sure both students offer input for the creation of the brochure. Discuss the importance of accurate contact information so parties interested in their services can contact them, and remind students to share the "sloppy copy" of their descriptions of services with you and with peer editors to check for clear and accurate content. Many computer software packages offer step-by-step guides for preparing a professional quality brochure, and students at this level can use them successfully with minimal teacher assistance.

WRITING **INFORMATIONAL BROCHURE** INTERMEDIATE

Task: Student will use the five-step writing process to produce an informational brochure promoting a service the student can provide (lawn mowing, babysitting, etc.).

Goal/Standard: Demonstrate understanding with completed brochure

Giving 0 points is an option—no evidence, no credit.

Criteria	1	2	3	4	Total Points
Cover Design	Text only	Text and graphics	Text, graphics, and pictures in black and white	Text, graphics, and pictures in full color	_____ x 3 = _____ points
Description of Services	Present with omissions	Complete with inaccuracies	Complete and accurate	Complete, accurate, and appealing	_____ x 3 = _____ points
Contact Information	Present with omissions	Complete with inaccuracies	Complete and accurate	Complete, accurate, and well positioned	_____ x 4 = _____ points

37–40 = A 31–34 = C
35–36 = B 28–30 = D
         <28 = F

Total score _____/40 = _____

Assess Student Understanding

Cover Design

■ includes text and full-color graphics

Description of Services

■ describes services accurately, without error, and in an appealing way

Contact Information

■ gives accurate, error-free contact information in reader-friendly format

Keep the assessment rubric available while reviewing the brochure. Make sure the brochure offers an accurate and reader-friendly account of the type of services or the announcement featured. Make sure that contact information is accurate and easy for potential customers to locate.

How to Use the
INFORMATIONAL BROCHURE Rubric
at the Middle School Level

Introduce the Rubric

Distribute and discuss the rubric with students before they begin work on the brochure. Focus attention on the rubric column that contains the highest degree of performance, making sure students understand that they must achieve the objectives in the final column to receive full credit. Discuss the types of services students can offer to customers or the type of events they might wish to announce with such brochures. Incorporate the five-step process into the assignment, allowing time for each step.

Make the Assignment

Have students work in small groups and discuss the type of services they can offer to customers or the type of events they wish to announce in the brochure. Students at this level can offer a wide variety of services, ranging from pet walking or grooming to yard work or babysitting. Remind students to offer a fair and accurate account of what they can do and accurate contact information for interested parties. Computer software can help students create a professional quality brochure with little or no teacher assistance.

Assess Student Understanding

Cover Design
- includes engaging text, full-color graphics, and a catchy title

Description of Services
- describes services in a creative and appealing way

Contact Information
- gives contact information on detachable portion of brochure

Keep the assessment rubric available while reviewing the brochure. Make sure students have arranged the words and graphics in a clear, easy-to-follow layout and have given an accurate and realistic description of services or event announcement. Contact information should appear in one location in one area of the brochure that customers can detach and retain. Students need only give the suggestion of a detachment, as in a dotted line that shows where to remove the part of the brochure with the contact information. Make sure the brochure is accurate and error-free.

INFORMATIONAL BROCHURE

Task: Student will use the five-step writing process to produce an informational brochure promoting a service the student can provide (lawn mowing, babysitting, etc.).

Goal/Standard: Demonstrate understanding with completed brochure

Giving 0 points is an option—no evidence, no credit.

Criteria	1	2	3	4	Total Points
Cover Design	Text and pictures or graphics; no color	Text, and pictures or graphics; 1 color	Text, pictures and graphics; full color	Engaging, full-color graphics and catchy title	____ x 3 = ____ points
Description of Services	Complete with inaccuracies	Complete and accurate	Accurate and easy to read	Creative salesmanship	____ x 3 = ____ points
Contact Information	Complete with inaccuracies	Complete and accurate	Complete, accurate, and easy to find	Complete and accurate on detachable portion of brochure	____ x 4 = ____ points

37–40 = A	31–34 = C
35–36 = B	28–30 = D
	<28 = F

Total score ____/40 = ____

How to Use the
INFORMATIONAL BROCHURE Rubric
at the High School Level

Introduce the Rubric

Distribute and discuss the rubric with students before they begin work on the brochure. Focus attention on the column that contains the highest degree of performance, reminding students that they must achieve those objectives to receive full credit. Stress the need for complete and accurate information as the brochure offers potential customers a first impression of the student and the services that student is prepared to offer. Incorporate the five-step process into the assignment, allowing time for each step.

Make the Assignment

Students can work in pairs or triads to discuss the types of services or announcements they wish to include on the brochure. Students at this level can offer a wide variety of services and can often provide the equipment (lawn mowers, dog grooming tools) needed to perform such tasks. Such information should appear on the brochure so customers know exactly what the student is offering. Have students exchange "sloppy copy" drafts with one another and check that the description of services or the event announcement on the brochure is clear and accurate. Students can use computer software to create eye-catching professional quality brochures to distribute to family, friends, and neighbors. Tell students to offer more than one way for potential customers to reach them such as phone, e-mail, and fax. Their accessibility makes them more marketable.

Assess Student Understanding

Cover Design
- includes eye-catching font style and full-color graphics

Description of Services
- describes services in a creative and irresistible way

Contact Information
- offers more than one method of contact (fax, phone, e-mail)

Keep the assessment rubric available while reviewing the brochure. Make sure all information is accurate, error-free, and arranged in a user-friendly format. Contact information should appear on a separate, detachable section of the brochure.

INFORMATIONAL BROCHURE

Task: Student will use the five-step writing process to produce an informational brochure promoting a service the student can provide (lawn mowing, babysitting, etc.).

Goal/Standard: Demonstrate understanding with completed brochure

Giving 0 points is an option—no evidence, no credit.

Criteria	1	2	3	4	Total Points
Cover Design	Text and pictures or graphics; no color	Text, pictures, and graphics in full color	Engaging, full-color graphics and catchy title	Relevant photographs or computer-generated art, catchy title, and appealing font style	_____ x 3 = _____ points
Description of Services	Complete and accurate	Accurate and easy to read	Accurate, easy to read, and creative	Readers will be unable to resist	_____ x 3 = _____ points
Contact Information	Complete and accurate	Complete, accurate, and easy to find	Complete and accurate on detachable portion of brochure	Complete and accurate with more than 1 contact option (fax, telephone, e-mail) on a detachable portion of brochure	_____ x 4 = _____ points

37–40 = A   31–34 = C
35–36 = B   28–30 = D
              <28 = F

Total score _____/40 = _____

How to Use the

LETTER Rubric

at the Primary Level

Introduce the Rubric

Distribute and discuss the rubric with students before they begin composing a letter. Discuss the purpose and different types of letters along with how important it is that letter writers make their thoughts clear because they will not be present to offer a detailed explanation to letter recipients. Focus attention on the rubric column that contains the highest degree of performance, making sure students understand that they must achieve the objectives in the final column to receive full credit. Review the parts of a letter, including the salutation and closing, and provide a concrete example of the proper arrangement of a completed letter on a page. Incorporate the five-step process into the assignment, allowing time for each step.

Make the Assignment

Students should write to someone they do not know with a specific request. They may wish to write letters to a favorite author with questions about his or her work, to a zookeeper with questions about animal care, or to any other person requesting information. Instruct students to decide who will receive their letters and what they want to ask before they begin writing the letter. Students at this level can produce a four- to five-sentence letter. Discuss the importance of the topic sentence, which lets the reader know almost immediately what the letter's author is talking about and sets the tone for the communication. Have students write the message on a "sloppy copy" to give to their peers to check during the editing step for spelling, grammar, and punctuation errors before they transfer it to better quality stationery. Make sure students know the full address of the recipient, including zip code, before providing them with an envelope.

LETTER

Task: Student will use the five-step writing process to compose and send a letter.

Goal/Standard: Demonstrate understanding with completed letter and envelope

Criteria	0	1	2	Total Points
Salutation and Closing	None	1 element present	2 elements present	_____ x 3 = _____ points
Topic Sentence	None	Present but not effective	Present and effective	_____ x 4 = _____ points
Body of Letter	4–5 sentences; many errors	4–5 sentences; few errors	4–5 sentences; no errors	_____ x 4 = _____ points
Envelope	None	Present with omissions	Accurate and complete	_____ x 4 = _____ points

28–30 = A   24–25 = C
26–27 = B   21–23 = D
          <21 = F

Total score _____/30 = _____

Assess Student Understanding

Salutation and Closing

- uses accurate salutation and closing

Topic Sentence

- composes an effective topic sentence

Body of Letter

- composes letter of four to five sentences with no errors

Envelope

- uses accurate and complete information

Keep the assessment rubric available while reviewing the letter. It is likely that the letter is destined for a location beyond the classroom, so review any errors with students, and give them a chance to make corrections before sending the letter. Consider giving students an extra credit point if they receive a reply to their letter.

How to Use the

LETTER Rubric

at the Intermediate Level

Introduce the Rubric

Distribute and discuss the rubric with students before they begin composing a letter. Discuss the purpose of letters and the need for their letter to request information in a way that makes the recipient happy to respond. Review the parts of a letter, including the salutation and closing, and provide a concrete example of the proper arrangement of a completed letter on a page. Focus attention on the rubric column that contains the highest degree of performance, reminding students that they must achieve the objectives in the final column to receive full credit. Incorporate the five-step process into the assignment, allowing time for each step.

Make the Assignment

With students working in pairs or triads, have them discuss who will receive their letters. The letters should request information from someone they do not know, and the tone of the letter should reflect students' reason for making contact with the letter's recipient. The recipients might range from a favorite author to a local business owner with just about anyone in between as long as the student is able to locate a name and accurate contact information. Have students draft their letters of six to eight sentences on a "sloppy copy" to give to their peers to check during the editing step for spelling, grammar, and punctuation errors before they transfer the message to appropriate stationery. During the revising phase, students reading the letter to their revision group could solicit comments about what the group thinks the letter is requesting. Have students confirm the full mailing address of the letter's recipient before providing them with an envelope.

LETTER

Task: Student will use the five-step writing process to compose and send a letter.

Goal/Standard: Demonstrate understanding with completed letter and envelope

Giving 0 points is an option—no evidence, no credit.

Criteria	1	2	3	4	Total Points
Salutation and Closing	1 element present	2 elements present with some errors	Both elements present but 1 or both inappropriate	2 appropriate elements present with no errors	_____ x 3 = _____ points
Topic Sentence	Present but ungrammatical	Present and accurate but not effective	Present, accurate, and effective	Sentence unifies letter	_____ x 3 = _____ points
Body of Letter	4–5 sentences with few errors	4–5 sentences with no errors	6–8 sentences with few errors	6–8 sentences with no errors	_____ x 5 = _____ points
Envelope	Present with omissions	Some inaccuracies	Complete with 1 or 2 misspellings	Complete and accurate	_____ x 4 = _____ points

56–60 = A   47–51 = C
52–55 = B   42–46 = D
          <42 = F

Total score _____/60 = _____

Assess Student Understanding

Salutation and Closing
- uses accurate and appropriate salutation and closing

Topic Sentence
- composes an effective topic sentence that unifies letter

Body of Letter
- composes letter of six to eight sentences with no errors

Envelope
- uses accurate and complete information

Keep the assessment rubric available while reviewing the letter. Make sure the letter meets the stated purpose of requesting information from a recipient whom the letter writer does not know. The letter is likely destined for a location beyond the classroom, so review any errors with students, and allow them to make corrections before mailing the letter.

How to Use the

LETTER Rubric

at the Middle School Level

Introduce the Rubric

Distribute and discuss the rubric with students before they begin composing a letter. Students should spend some time thinking about who will receive their letters and why they have chosen a specific individual for this type of communication. Stress to students that a letter often represents the first impression a recipient has of the sender so the letter should have a positive tone and be free of errors. Focus attention on the rubric column that contains the highest degree of performance, reminding students that they must achieve the objectives in the final column to receive full credit. Incorporate the five-step process into the assignment, allowing time for each step.

Make the Assignment

Have students work in pairs or triads to discuss who should receive their letters and why. If the students wish to send letters to a favorite author or athlete, make sure they have accurate address information and are clear about what they wish to say in their letters. Instruct students to write their message of two paragraphs (nine to eleven sentences) on a "sloppy copy" to share with their peers during the revising phase, when their revision group buddies check the letter for clarity, and during the editing step, when their peers check for spelling, grammar, and punctuation errors. Have students then transfer the letter to appropriate stationery.

Task: Student will use the five-step writing process to compose and send a letter.

Goal/Standard: Demonstrate understanding with completed letter and envelope

Giving 0 points is an option—no evidence, no credit.

Criteria	1	2	3	4	Total Points
Salutation and Closing	2 elements present with some errors	2 elements present but 1 or both inappropriate	2 elements present with no errors	2 elements present, accurate, and appropriate for recipient	____ x 3 = ____ points
Topic Sentence	Present but not effective	Present and effective	Sentence unifies letter	Sentence engages reader's attention	____ x 3 = ____ points
Body of Letter	5–7 sentences with some errors	5–7 sentences with no errors	2 paragraphs (9–11 sentences) with some errors	2 paragraphs (9–11 sentences) with no errors	____ x 5 = ____ points
Envelope	Present with omissions	Some inaccuracies	Complete with 1 or 2 misspellings	Complete and accurate	____ x 4 = ____ points

56–60 = A   47–51 = C   Total score ____ /60 = ____

52–55 = B   42–46 = D

              <42 = F

Assess Student Understanding

Salutation and Closing

■ uses accurate and appropriate salutation and closing

Topic Sentence

■ composes topic sentence that engages recipient's attention

Body of Letter

■ composes letter of two paragraphs (nine to eleven sentences) with no errors

Envelope

■ uses accurate and complete information

Keep the assessment rubric available while reviewing the letter. Check for clarity of purpose in the letter in particular. The letter is likely destined for a location beyond the classroom, so review any errors with students, allowing them to make corrections before mailing the letter.

How to Use the

LETTER Rubric

at the High School Level

Introduce the Rubric

Distribute and discuss the rubric with students before they begin composing their letters. Because a letter is, in many cases, the recipient's first impression of the sender, stress that the letter should have a positive tone. Focus attention on the rubric column that contains the highest degree of performance, reminding students that they must achieve the objectives in the final column to receive full credit. Incorporate the five-step process into the assignment, allowing time for each step.

Make the Assignment

Instruct students to write to someone they admire or from whom they wish information. Discuss the importance of an engaging topic sentence, and remind them their letter should be two paragraphs long. Have students draft a "sloppy copy" that their peers can check during the editing step for errors before they transfer the letter to appropriate stationery. Make sure students have complete and accurate address information.

Assess Student Understanding

Salutation and Closing
- uses accurate and appropriate salutation and closing

Topic Sentence
- composes topic sentence that unifies thoughts and sets tone

Body of Letter
- composes letter of two paragraphs (one full page) with no errors

Envelope
- uses accurate and complete information

Keep the assessment rubric available while reviewing the letter. Students asking for information should state their request in the first paragraph, elaborating on the need for the information in the second paragraph. Because the letter is destined for a location beyond the classroom, review any errors with students, allowing them to make corrections before they mail their letters.

WRITING   **LETTER**   HIGH SCHOOL

Task: Student will use the five-step writing process to compose and send a letter.
Goal/Standard: Demonstrate understanding with completed letter and envelope

Giving 0 points is an option—no evidence, no credit.

Criteria	1	2	3	4	Total Points
Salutation and Closing	2 elements present with some errors	2 elements present but 1 or both inappropriate	2 elements present with no errors	2 elements present, accurate, and appropriate to recipient	____ x 3 = ____ points
Topic Sentence	Present and effective	Sentence unifies letter	Sentence engages reader's attention	Sentence sets appropriate tone for letter	____ x 3 = ____ points
Body of Letter	5–7 sentences with errors	5–7 sentences with no errors	2 paragraphs with fewer than 2 errors	1 full page (2 paragraphs), no errors; conveys the message in appropriate tone	____ x 5 = ____ points
Envelope	Present with omissions	Some inaccuracies	Complete with 1 or 2 misspellings	Complete and accurate	____ x 4 = ____ points

56–60 = A   47–51 = C   Total score ____/60 = ____
52–55 = B   42–46 = D
           <42 = F

5

Using Rubrics to Assess Listening Skills

Helen, a sixth-grade teacher, noticed that many of her students experience difficulty with an assignment when she gives instructions orally. Discussing this concern in the teachers' lounge, Helen learned that the art teacher, Kathy (who also works with Helen's students), has witnessed similar problems whenever art projects involve oral step-by-step instructions. Recognizing that this deficit prevents accurate measurement of student understanding, Helen decided to design and implement some activities and rubrics to assess her students' listening skills.

THE ART AND SCIENCE OF LISTENING

Many educators share Helen's concern that their students' poor listening skills prevent accurate measurement of student understanding of various concepts. For example, students may possess grade-level knowledge in a content area but are unable to demonstrate their understanding when prompted with oral instructions.

While listening makes up a large part of students' in-class time, little formal training or assessment occurs in that area. Teachers should invest some time helping students learn how to listen as well as sharing specific strategies to maximize their listening skills.

Listening to presentations of poetry or fiction usually requires less formal instruction because a certain amount of listener interest is inherent. Nonfiction, however, contains special challenges, and listening to a lecture or a reading of a nonfiction text requires more direct instruction. Teaching students to identify the pattern (description, sequence, comparison, cause and effect, problem and solution) of an expository lecture, for example, as well as how to use titles and speaker's questions to determine purpose are only a few of the strategies that can strengthen students' listening skills.

The rubrics in this chapter cover Instructions, Stories, Guest Speakers, and Informational Speeches. The rubrics assess the number of elements present because in the case of listening, teachers are looking for the presence or absence of specific behaviors. When students in more than one age- or grade-level group should have all the skills described, the rubric and assessment guidelines have been combined.

Instructions: Step-by-Step

These rubrics assess students' ability to complete a task after receiving oral instructions. The goal, or highest degree of accomplishment on the rubric, for each grade level follows:

Primary—student recognizes and corrects any reversals, omissions, or substitutions in instructions, predicts task steps in sequence, and predicts task outcome.

Intermediate and Middle School—student recognizes and corrects any reversals or omissions in instructions, makes accurate shortcuts and substitutions, predicts task steps and task outcome, and visualizes entire process before undertaking task.

High School—student recognizes when sequence is not necessary, recognizes and makes appropriate shortcuts and substitutions, and visualizes entire process to predict outcome and see how it relates to prior knowledge of a similar task.

Stories: Tell Me a Story

These rubrics assess students' understanding of a story told to them. While the rubrics in this section cover many of the same literary elements as in chapters 2 and 3, namely, plot, character, setting, and theme, the purpose of the assessment differs. The rubrics in chapter 2 assess reading comprehension skills, the rubrics in chapter 3 assess comprehension of story structure, and the rubrics in this section assess listening skills. The goal, or highest degree of accomplishment on the rubric, for each grade level follows:

Primary—student recognizes conflict, summarizes story, identifies good and evil characters and their goals, identifies setting location, time period, and time of day, and recognizes author's message and how it applies to real life.

Intermediate—student does all the above plus predicts upcoming story events, identifies obstacles that prevent the main character from attaining a goal, recognizes influence of setting on the main character, and cites passages that embody the story theme.

Middle School—student does all the above plus recognizes story climax, predicts main character's behavior, understands the influence of setting on story outcome, and explains how the main character embodies the story theme.

High School—student does all the above plus identifies events that signal the story climax, recognizes the influence of character behavior on the story outcome, constructs profile of setting as silent story character, and explains the theme's relevance.

Guest Speaker: Be Our Guest

These rubrics assess students' comprehension of a guest speaker's presentation. The goal, or highest degree of accomplishment on the rubric, for each grade level follows:

Primary—student clears desktop before speech, does not interrupt speaker, offers appropriate questions and comments at appointed time, links prior knowledge to presentation, and clarifies familiar concepts based on the presentation.

Intermediate—student does all the above plus ignores distractions, makes eye contact with speaker, and uses presentation as a basis for further exploration of topic.

Middle School—student does all the above plus responds appropriately (applause, laughter, etc.), offers questions and comments that extend from speaker's words and ideas, and formulates new ideas on topic based on presentation.

High School—student does all the above plus demonstrates nonverbal listening behaviors (nodding, eye contact), practices active listening techniques, and formulates questions about topic based on presentation.

Informational Speech: For Your Information

These rubrics assess students' comprehension of an informational lecture. The goal, or highest degree of accomplishment on the rubric, for each grade level follows:

Primary—student uses graphic organizer appropriate to lecture structure to record information, links new information to prior knowledge, and recalls individual facts and related groups of facts.

Intermediate—student does all the above plus makes additions (not from speech) to appropriate graphic organizer, uses new information to improve related task performance, and distinguishes between fact and opinion.

Middle School—student uses graphic organizer to formulate written response, understands author's choice of text structure to convey information, and links information from visual aids to oral presentation.

High School—student uses graphic organizer as basis for multimedia response, identifies appropriate expository structure for response to presentation, and uses visual aids and oral information to construct new schema of topic.

How to Use the
INSTRUCTIONS Rubric
at the Primary Level

Introduce the Rubric

Distribute and discuss the rubric with students before they undertake the assignment, explaining that you will base the assessment on their ability to complete a project by following oral instructions. They must also recognize and follow proper instruction sequence and detect the presence of reversals, omissions, and substitutions in the instructions. Make sure students understand what you expect of them and know that to receive full credit, they must meet the objectives listed.

Make the Assignment

Students at this level are capable of completing an art project from a set of oral instructions. Make sure the instructions contain familiar words so the assessment focuses on students' ability to follow oral instructions rather than their ability to decode and comprehend the words. You should assemble all materials beforehand and instruct students to clear desks of any unnecessary items before they begin the project.

Assess Student Understanding

Reversals
- recognizes reversals
- corrects reversals

While reading the instructions to students, reverse the order of two steps in the sequence, reading the later step first. Observe student reaction to the reversal. Some students will attempt to complete the step even though it may not be possible. Students who pause and ask for some sort of clarification, such as "How can we do that?" or "Is that really the next step?," sense some interruption in the instruction sequence.

INSTRUCTIONS

Task: Student will complete a task from oral instructions.

Goal/Standard: Demonstrate understanding with error-free task performance

Criteria	0	1	2	Total Points
Reversals • recognizes reversals • corrects reversals	0 elements present	1 element present	2 elements present	_____ x 3 = _____ points
Omissions • recognizes omissions • corrects omissions	0 elements present	1 element present	2 elements present	_____ x 3 = _____ points
Substitutions • recognizes substitutions • corrects substitutions	0 elements present	1 element present	2 elements present	_____ x 4 = _____ points
Predictions • predicts next step • predicts final outcome	0 elements present	1 element present	2 elements present	_____ x 5 = _____ points

28–30 = A   24–25 = C
26–27 = B   21–23 = D
             <21 = F

Total score _____/30 = _____

Omissions
- recognizes omissions
- corrects omissions

While reading instructions to students, omit one step in the process. Observe reaction to the omission. Some students will attempt to move to the next step of the process, ignoring the omission or adding an incorrect step on their own. Students who pause and ask for some sort of clarification, such as "We can't do that without doing something else first" or "There's a step missing," demonstrate an understanding of the process sequence and the link between steps.

Substitutions
- recognizes substitutions
- corrects substitutions

While reading instructions to students, delete one step, replacing it with a step that is not part of the project sequence. Observe reaction to the substitution. Some students will attempt to complete the step even though it will not be possible. Students who pause and ask for some sort of clarification, such as "That step can't be done" or "That step doesn't belong in this project," understand the process sequence and recognize steps that are not part of that sequence.

Predictions
- predicts next step
- predicts final outcome

Pause after each step in the oral instructions, asking students to guess what they think the next step entails. Ask students to write or draw their idea for the next step. Compare students' guesses with the actual step for accuracy.

To determine whether students can guess the final outcome of a project, do not show a completed model of the art project beforehand. Tell students they will complete an art project, and at approximately the halfway point in the instructions, ask students to write or draw their guess about the appearance of the completed object. More specific responses, such as "origami tiger" or "paper holiday wreath," indicate students' ability to judge project outcome.

How to Use the
INSTRUCTIONS Rubric
at the Intermediate and Middle School Level

Introduce the Rubric

Distribute and discuss the rubric with students before they undertake the activity, explaining that you will base the assessment on their ability to follow a set of oral instructions to complete a specific project. They must also recognize and follow proper instruction sequence and detect the presence of reversals, omissions, and substitutions in the instructions. Make sure students understand what you expect of them and know that to receive full credit, they must meet the objectives listed.

Make the Assignment

Students at this level can complete a wide variety of tasks by listening to oral instructions. Their extensive vocabularies will make project selection easier. (Still, make sure they are familiar with all terms in the instructions.) Projects can range from a recipe to a classroom decoration. Select a recipe or project with very detailed instructions that lend themselves to shortcuts. Students should assemble all materials beforehand and clear their work areas of any unnecessary items before beginning the project.

Assess Student Understanding

Reversals
- recognizes reversals
- corrects reversals
- understands significance of sequence

Place students in small groups to complete a no-bake recipe. While reading the instructions, reverse two of the steps in the recipe. Observe their reaction to the reversal. Some students will attempt to complete the steps. Students who pause and ask for clarification, such as "I can't do that step before another step" or "These steps are out of order," demonstrate an understanding of the recipe sequence. After the recipe experience, ask students to write in their journals why they feel sequence is (or is not) important in following a recipe.

How to Use the INSTRUCTIONS Rubric at the Intermediate and Middle School Level

INSTRUCTIONS

Task: Student will complete a task from oral instructions.

Goal/Standard: Demonstrate understanding with error-free task performance

Giving 0 points is an option—no evidence, no credit.

Criteria	1	2	3	4	Total Points
Reversals • recognizes reversals • corrects reversals • understands significance of sequence	Evidence of 2+ incomplete elements	1 complete element present	2 complete elements present	3 complete elements present	_____ x 3 = _____ points
Omissions • recognizes omissions • corrects omissions • creates effective shortcuts	Evidence of 2+ incomplete elements	1 complete element present	2 complete elements present	3 complete elements present	_____ x 3 = _____ points
Substitutions • recognizes substitutions • corrects substitutions • offers relevant substitutions	Evidence of 2+ incomplete elements	1 complete element present	2 complete elements present	3 complete elements present	_____ x 4 = _____ points
Predictions • predicts next step • predicts final outcome • visualizes entire process beforehand	Evidence of 2+ incomplete elements	1 complete element present	2 complete elements present	3 complete elements present	_____ x 5 = _____ points

56–60 = A   47–51 = C
52–55 = B   42–46 = D
            <42 = F

Total score _____/60 = _____

Omissions

- recognizes omissions
- corrects omissions
- creates effective shortcuts

While reading the recipe, omit a vital step in the sequence. Observe reaction to the omission. Students who pause and ask for clarification, such as "Is there a step missing?" or "That comes next?," understand the need to follow every step in a recipe. After they complete the assembly portion of the recipe, ask students to think about the sequence and write down any areas where they think they could employ a shortcut without sacrificing the final outcome.

Substitutions

- recognizes substitutions
- corrects substitutions
- offers relevant substitutions

While reading the recipe, remove one step in the sequence, replacing it with a step from another recipe. Observe student reaction to the substitution. Some students will attempt to complete the step even though it is not possible. Students who pause and ask for clarification, such as "Is that from this recipe?" or "Could you read that again? I don't think we have the ingredients to do that step," demonstrate a clear understanding of the importance of having the correct and original sequence to complete the recipe. After they complete the recipe, initiate a discussion about substitutions in the sequence. Ask students what types of steps can undergo substitutions without sacrificing the final outcome. Correct responses include such statements as "You could use a spoon instead of a mixer to stir the mixture. It would take longer but it probably wouldn't affect the final product."

Predictions

- predicts next step
- predicts final outcome
- visualizes entire process beforehand

Instruct students to describe in their journals how they think the recipe goes from being a group of ingredients to a finished, edible product, asking them to focus on those steps they think are most important in that transition. For example, cake batter will remain cake batter until heat (the oven) is introduced into the recipe. Once students have worked with an actual recipe, the hope is that they can extrapolate the logic with other recipes. Take a new recipe. Write each step on a separate index card, number the cards randomly, and post them in random order on a bulletin board. Instruct students to use the numbers on the cards to list the proper order of the cards.

INSTRUCTIONS Rubric

at the High School Level

Introduce the Rubric

Distribute and discuss the rubric with students before they undertake the assignment, explaining that you will base the assessment on their ability to complete a project by following oral instructions. They must also recognize and follow proper instruction sequence and detect the presence of reversals, omissions, and substitutions in the instructions. Make sure students understand what you expect of them and know that to receive full credit, they must meet the objectives listed.

Make the Assignment

Students at this level are capable of following instructions for almost any type of project, ranging from all forms of needlecraft to carpentry. Their vocabulary is sufficient to comprehend steps so their performance reflects their ability to follow directions rather than decode specific terms. Select a project that the student has not completed previously. For example, if a student is an avid knitter, select a different project since that student will have extensive background knowledge in that field, making the assessment less accurate. Such crafts as candle making or batik are interesting activities with generally low student expertise. Have students assemble all materials beforehand, and instruct them to clear any unnecessary items from the work area.

Assess Student Understanding

Reversals

- recognizes and corrects reversals
- understands significance of sequence
- recognizes when sequence is not essential

While reading instructions to students, switch the order of two steps, noting the reaction of this action by students. Students who pause and ask for clarification, such as "Are you sure about the order of those steps?" or "You can't do the first one without doing something else first," have a clear understanding of the need for proper sequence. After they complete the project, ask students to summarize the instructions in their journals, focusing on the proper sequence of the instructions and highlighting those steps (if any) that can be reversed without compromising the final outcome.

Task: Student will complete a task from oral instructions.
Goal/Standard: Demonstrate understanding with error-free task performance

Giving 0 points is an option—no evidence, no credit.

Criteria	1	2	3	4	Total Points
Reversals • recognizes and corrects reversals • understands significance of sequence • recognizes when sequence is not essential	Evidence of 2+ incomplete elements	1 complete element present	2 complete elements present	3 complete elements present	____ x 3 = ____ points
Omissions • recognizes and corrects omissions • creates effective shortcuts • recognizes when shortcuts are useful	Evidence of 2+ incomplete elements	1 complete element present	2 complete elements present	3 complete elements present	____ x 3 = ____ points
Substitutions • recognizes and corrects substitutions • offers relevant substitutions • completes task despite substitutions	Evidence of 2+ incomplete elements	1 complete element present	2 complete elements present	3 complete elements present	____ x 4 = ____ points
Predictions • predicts final outcome • visualizes entire process beforehand • relates sequence to outcome of other tasks	Evidence of 2+ incomplete elements	1 complete element present	2 complete elements present	3 complete elements present	____ x 5 = ____ points

56–60 = A 47–51 = C
52–55 = B 42–46 = D
          <42 = F

Total score ____/60 = ____

Omissions

- recognizes and corrects omissions
- creates effective shortcuts
- recognizes when shortcuts are useful

In some situations, such as interior painting or woodworking, shortcuts are not only acceptable but useful since there is often a time frame, referred to as open time, when the materials are easier to use. For example, when constructing a pegboard shelf, it is logical to let the first coat of stain dry on the shelf while moving to a different part of the work area to begin sanding the pegs for insertion later. Ask students to review the instruction sequence and identify any areas where they might make shortcuts.

Substitutions

- recognizes and corrects substitutions
- offers relevant substitutions
- completes task despite substitutions

Students at this level possess a broad base of knowledge that allows them to make substitutions when specific materials are not available. For example, a high school student would know that if butter were unavailable for a recipe, some forms of margarine could be substituted without sacrificing the final outcome. Remove one of the elements from students' materials, replacing it with an acceptable substitute, and note student reaction. Students who pause and ask for clarification, such as "I can't go any further without having _____," have a clear understanding of the need for proper materials, while the student who examines remaining supplies and identifies the element that can be used as a substitute has a higher level of understanding of how to complete the project with the alternate element.

Predictions

- predicts final outcome
- visualizes entire process beforehand
- relates sequence to outcome of other tasks

Present students with the project materials, and read the entire sequence to them before they start the project. Ask students to write their prediction of the final outcome based on the materials assembled and the instruction sequence. Collect these predictions and begin the project. At the completion, ask students to write the names of any other projects with a sequence similar to the one they performed in class. Students who are able to make a connection between the sequence they followed constructing a quilt with a set of instructions for constructing a patchwork crocheted afghan are able to see the connection between the sequence of the two projects.

How to Use the
STORIES Rubric
at the Primary Level

Introduce the Rubric

Distribute and discuss the rubric with students before they listen to the story, explaining that you will base the assessment on their understanding of the literary elements plot, character, setting, and theme while listening to a work of fiction. Make sure students understand what you expect of them and know that to receive full credit, they must meet the objectives listed.

Make the Assignment

Have students clear their work areas before the listening activity. Share the cover illustration with them, brainstorming as a group about possible story events or outcome. Then remind students to listen carefully, and read the story.

Assess Student Understanding

Plot

■ recognizes conflict
■ summarizes story events

Work with students in small groups after the listening activity, asking them to vote (in secret) about the type of conflict they believe takes place in the story. Then, moving around the group, ask the first student to provide the first story event, the second student to provide the second story event, and so on until they complete the story.

Character

■ identifies good and evil characters
■ identifies main character's goal

With students still in their small groups, provide them with drawing supplies. Instruct them to divide a sheet of paper in half, drawing good characters on one side and evil characters on the other side. On the side with the good character(s), instruct students to draw something that shows what the character was trying to do in the story, such as a young Abe Lincoln trying to read books to prepare himself for law school.

How to Use the STORIES Rubric at the Primary Level

STORIES

Task: Student will listen to an oral retelling of a story.

Goal/Standard: Demonstrate understanding through verbal, visual, or written response

Criteria	0	1	2	Total Points
Plot • recognizes conflict • summarizes story events	0 elements present	1 element present	2 elements present	____ x 4 = ____ points
Character • identifies good and evil characters • identifies main character's goal	0 elements present	1 element present	2 elements present	____ x 4 = ____ points
Setting • identifies location • identifies time period/time of day	0 elements present	1 element present	2 elements present	____ x 3 = ____ points
Theme • knows author's message • applies message to real life	0 elements present	1 element present	2 elements present	____ x 4 = ____ points

28–30 = A   24–25 = C
26–27 = B   21–23 = D
          <21 = F

Total score ____/30 = ____

SkyLight Professional Development

Setting

- identifies location
- identifies time period/time of day

Provide students in their small groups with drawing materials and instruct them to draw the primary or main setting of the story, including location and time of day. Tell them to use character dress or buildings to indicate the time period.

Theme

- knows author's message
- applies message to real life

Instruct students to write the message the author is trying to convey. In the case of less mature readers, provide students with a group of cards stating a variety of story themes and ask them to pick the one that fits the story they just heard. Next, have students tell about a time when they felt like the story character. Students who identify how the main character feels by finding a comparable event in their own lives or the life of a close friend have a clear idea of the theme.

How to Use the
STORIES Rubric
at the Intermediate Level

Introduce the Rubric

Distribute and discuss the rubric with students before they listen to the story, explaining that you will base the assessment on their understanding of the literary elements plot, character, setting, and theme while listening to a work of fiction. Make sure students understand what you expect of them and know that to receive full credit, they must meet the objectives listed.

Make the Assignment

Instruct students to clear their work area before listening to the story. Share the cover illustration with them, discussing as a group possible story events and outcome. Then remind students to listen carefully, and read the story.

Assess Student Understanding

Plot

- recognizes conflict
- summarizes story events
- predicts upcoming events

While reading the story to students, pause after a number of paragraphs or pages and ask students what they think will happen next in the story. When students respond, ask them to explain their response. At the completion of the reading, review the types of conflict (man vs. man, man vs. nature, man vs. self, man vs. society) and instruct students to write a journal entry in which they identify and describe the type of conflict in the story as well as write a brief (fewer than fifty words) summary of the story.

Task: Student will listen to an oral retelling of a story.

Goal/Standard: Demonstrate understanding through verbal, visual, or written response

Giving 0 points is an option—no evidence, no credit.

Criteria	1	2	3	4	Total Points
Plot • recognizes conflict • summarizes story events • predicts upcoming events	Evidence of 2+ incomplete elements	1 complete element present	2 complete elements present	3 complete elements present	____ x 4 = ____ points
Character • identifies good and evil characters • identifies main character's goal • lists obstacles to goal	Evidence of 2+ incomplete elements	1 complete element present	2 complete elements present	3 complete elements present	____ x 4 = ____ points
Setting • identifies location • identifies time period/time of day • recognizes positive/ negative locations	Evidence of 2+ incomplete elements	1 complete element present	2 complete elements present	3 complete elements present	____ x 3 = ____ points
Theme • knows author's message • applies message to own life • cites story passages that embody theme	Evidence of 2+ incomplete elements	1 complete element present	2 complete elements present	3 complete elements present	____ x 4 = ____ points

56–60 = A 47–51 = C
52–55 = B 42–46 = D
          <42 = F

Total score ____/60 = ____

Character

- identifies good and evil characters
- identifies main character's goal
- lists obstacles to goal

After the story reading, have students identify in their journals the story's main good and evil characters and explain the reasons for their choices. Next, have them identify the main character's goal. Finally, they should list three obstacles to the attainment of that goal that the character faces during the story.

Setting

- identifies location
- identifies time period/time of day
- recognizes positive/negative locations

After the story reading, provide students with art supplies and instruct them to divide a sheet of paper into quarters, sketching, in pencil, the four main story locations, including information that indicates time period and time of day. Next, use a specified color (red) to shade in those settings that represent negative experiences for the main character and a second color (blue) for settings that represent positive experiences for the main character.

Theme

- knows author's message
- applies message to own life
- cites specific passages that embody theme

After the story reading, instruct students to use their journals to explain, in their own words, what they think the author is trying to tell readers. Then have them link this message to something in their own lives. For example, if the author is encouraging people to trust one another, students should relate a story in their own lives where they chose to reach out to someone and demonstrate trust in that person. Next, have students list specific scenes in the story that demonstrate the theme of trusting someone.

How to Use the
STORIES Rubric
at the Middle School Level

Introduce the Rubric

Distribute and discuss the rubric with students before they hear the story or story passage, explaining that you will base the assessment on their understanding of the literary elements plot, character, setting, and theme while listening to a work of fiction. Make sure students understand what you expect of them and know that to receive full credit, they must meet the objectives listed.

Make the Assignment

Students at this level are capable of dealing with longer stories with more complex plots and themes. If you read regularly to your middle school students (such as at the end of the day to help them both develop listening skills and wind down), you might read a chapter every day or two from a longer book. Then, for this activity, use the last chapter of a book you have read to the entire class. If the activity is primarily a listening skills exercise, you might wish to use a short story or short chapter in a longer work.

Assess Student Understanding

Plot
- summarizes story events
- predicts upcoming events
- recognizes story climax

While students listen to the story, pause at specified intervals and ask them what they think happens next. After they give their response, ask students what makes them think this way. When you finish the reading, have students summarize (fewer than 100 words) the main events of the story in a journal entry, identifying the climax, the point at which the resolution of the story became apparent to them.

How to Use the STORIES Rubric at the Middle School Level

STORIES

Task: Student will listen to an oral retelling of a story.

Goal/Standard: Demonstrate understanding through verbal, visual, or written response

Giving 0 points is an option—no evidence, no credit.

Criteria	1	2	3	4	Total Points
Plot • summarizes story events • predicts upcoming events • recognizes story climax	Evidence of 2+ incomplete elements	1 complete element present	2 complete elements present	3 complete elements present	_____ x 4 = _____ points
Character • identifies main character's goal • lists obstacles to goal • predicts main character's behavior	Evidence of 2+ incomplete elements	1 complete element present	2 complete elements present	3 complete elements present	_____ x 4 = _____ points
Setting • identifies time period/time of day • recognizes positive/negative locations • explains influence of setting on story outcome	Evidence of 2+ incomplete elements	1 complete element present	2 complete elements present	3 complete elements present	_____ x 3 = _____ points
Theme • applies author's message to own life • cites specific passages that embody theme • explains how main character embodies theme	Evidence of 2+ incomplete elements	1 complete element present	2 complete elements present	3 complete elements present	_____ x 4 = _____ points

56–60 = A   47–51 = C
52–55 = B   42–46 = D
              <42 = F

Total score _____/60 = _____

Character

- identifies main character's goal
- lists obstacles to goal
- predicts main character's behavior

Instruct students to write in their journals what they think is the main character's goal as well as three obstacles to that goal that the character faces during the story. Next, provide students with a scenario, such as the main character moving to a new city, and ask them to predict, based on the character's behavior in the story, how they think the character might react and why they think that way.

Setting

- identifies time period/time of day
- recognizes positive/negative locations
- explains influence of setting on story outcome

After the reading, instruct students to write in their journals a one-week diary as the main character. Each day's entry should identify the time of day, including time period—the calendar year or a close approximation. Tell students to make sure the entries contain information about the places the character travels to in the story, with reflection on whether the places were positive or negative. To assess student understanding of influence of setting on story outcome, have them include in the final entry the main character's reflection on how the story might have turned out differently if he or she had been somewhere else.

Theme

- applies author's message to own life
- cites specific passages that embody theme
- explains how main character embodies theme

After the reading, have students write in their journals about the relevance of the story theme to their lives. Correct responses demonstrate an ability to connect the author's message to their own lives. The journal entry should include specific passages from the story that embody the theme, including references to the main character's words, thoughts, and actions that convey the author's message.

How to Use the
STORIES Rubric
at the High School Level

Introduce the Rubric

Distribute and discuss the rubric with students before the reading, explaining that you will base the assessment on their understanding of the literary elements plot, character, setting, and theme while listening to a work of fiction. Make sure students understand what you expect of them and know that to receive full credit, they must meet the objectives listed.

Make the Assignment

Students at this level are less accustomed to listening to a story, so it is a good idea to review good listening behaviors. Instruct students to remove all materials from their work area so they can focus their attention on the story. Since the selections for this age/grade level are longer, discussions and journal writing exercises may take place on more than one day. For example, after reading a chapter to students, instruct them to make predictions in writing or during a discussion about what they think is coming next and why. These activities can be part of the read-aloud sessions.

Assess Student Understanding

Plot
- predicts upcoming events
- recognizes story climax
- identifies events that signal story climax

Since the reading of an age-appropriate selection will likely take more than one or two days, stop at critical points in the plot and ask students what they think happens next. Record the responses, and begin the next day's reading by reviewing them. Then begin reading the story, and at the end of that day's session, refer to the previous day's predictions to refute or validate them. Next, have students make new predictions based on the information from that day's reading. Near the end of the story, have students offer their opinion of when the story climax occurs. Students can respond orally or by writing their opinions in their journals or on paper to hand in at the end of a day's reading. Their response should include reference to specific scenes and events in the reading that told them the climax was approaching.

STORIES

Task: Student will listen to an oral retelling, such as a historic monologue.

Goal/Standard: Demonstrate understanding through verbal, visual, or written response

Giving 0 points is an option—no evidence, no credit.

Criteria	1	2	3	4	Total Points
Plot • predicts upcoming events • recognizes story climax • identifies events that signal story climax	Evidence of 2+ incomplete elements	1 complete element present	2 complete elements present	3 complete elements present	____ x 4 = ____ points
Character • identifies obstacles to main character's goal • predicts main character's behavior • recognizes influence of character's behavior on story outcome	Evidence of 2+ incomplete elements	1 complete element present	2 complete elements present	3 complete elements present	____ x 4 = ____ points
Setting • recognizes positive/negative locations • explains effect of setting on story outcome • constructs profile of setting as silent character	Evidence of 2+ incomplete elements	1 complete element present	2 complete elements present	3 complete elements present	____ x 3 = ____ points
Theme • cites specific passages that embody theme • explains how main character embodies theme • explains theme's relevance to listeners	Evidence of 2+ incomplete elements	1 complete element present	2 complete elements present	3 complete elements present	____ x 4 = ____ points

56–60 = A   47–51 = C
52–55 = B   42–46 = D
            <42 = F

Total score ____/60 = ____

Character

- identifies obstacles to main character's goal
- predicts main character's behavior
- recognizes influence of character's behavior on story outcome

After the reading, instruct students to divide a paper into three columns. In the first column, have students list the obstacles facing the main character. In the second column, they should explain the character's response to the obstacle based on that character's behavior throughout the story. For example, in *Romeo and Juliet*, Romeo's reaction to facing life without Juliet is to commit suicide. Students should see this response as predictable given that Romeo is a sensitive, brooding, and somewhat romantic youth. They should cite examples of the character's behavior that explain why he or she reacts in a certain way. In the final column, students should write about how the story might have ended differently if the main character had a different personality, such as less aggressive or more fearful. Correct responses link the actual story outcome to an alternate outcome based on the character's altered behavior patterns.

Setting

- recognizes positive/negative locations
- explains effect of setting on story outcome
- constructs profile of setting as silent character

Students should be able to express that the setting and the author's choice of placing a story in a specific setting (urban vs. rural, present day vs. past) has an effect on character behavior and, ultimately, story outcome. After the reading, instruct students to use their journals to write a compare-and-contrast entry regarding the story settings that had a negative or positive effect on the main character. In the entry, students should be able to relate the influence these settings had on the story outcome.

Theme

- cites specific passages that embody story theme
- explains how main character embodies story theme
- explains theme's relevance to listeners

After the reading, instruct students to identify in their journals the story's theme by restating it in a brief sentence. Students should cite specific passages from the story that embody the theme, such as a conversation between two characters or the main character's response to the situation. Finally, the journal entry should explain the relevance of the story's theme to the student's life. For example, if the theme encourages readers/ listeners to follow dreams despite objections from others, students should write about how this story caused them to reflect on the pursuit of their dreams.

How to Use the
GUEST SPEAKER Rubric
at the Primary Level

Introduce the Rubric

Distribute and discuss the rubric with students before the guest speaker arrives, and explain that you will base the assessment primarily on observation of their behavior during the guest speaker's visit. Make sure students understand what you expect of them and know that to receive full credit, they must meet the objectives listed.

Make the Assignment

Discuss the specified topic with students before the speaker's arrival, providing them with an opportunity to formulate some questions they wish the speaker to answer during the visit. Review the behaviors of a good listener, including sitting up with eyes on the speaker and feet on the floor. Instruct students to clear their work area so they are not distracted during the speaker's presentation.

Assess Student Understanding

Listening Behaviors

- clears desktop before speech
- does not interrupt speaker

You can assess both these elements during the guest speaker's entire visit. Make notes about student behaviors before, during, and after the presentation in these areas.

Questions and Comments

- offers appropriate questions and comments
- waits for appointed time to ask questions/offer comments

Assess these behaviors during the guest speaker's entire visit. Make notes about student behaviors during and after the presentation in these areas.

LISTENING   **GUEST SPEAKER**   PRIMARY

Task: Student will listen to a guest speaker's presentation.

Goal/Standard: Demonstrate understanding through verbal or written response

Criteria	0	1	2	Total Points
Listening Behaviors • clears desktop before speech • does not interrupt speaker	0 elements present	1 element present	2 elements present	_____ x 3 = _____ points
Questions and Comments • offers appropriate questions and comments • waits for appointed time to ask questions/offer comments	0 elements present	1 element present	2 elements present	_____ x 3 = _____ points
Extension of Ideas • links prior knowledge to presentation • uses presentation to clarify familiar concepts	0 elements present	1 element present	2 elements present	_____ x 4 = _____ points

19–20 = A   16–17 = C
18 = B   14–15 = D
   <14 = F

Total score _____/20 = _____

Extension of Ideas

- links prior knowledge to presentation
- uses presentation to clarify familiar concepts

Before the guest speaker's presentation, instruct students to list, orally or in writing, three things they know about the specified topic. After the presentation, instruct students to add to the list three things they learned about the topic from the presentation. Instruct students to reflect, orally or in writing, on how the new information fits with what they already knew about the topic.

How to Use the
GUEST SPEAKER Rubric
at the Intermediate Level

Introduce the Rubric

Distribute and discuss the rubric with students before the arrival of the guest speaker, reminding students of effective listening behaviors. Explain that you will base the assessment primarily on observation of their behavior before, during, and after the speaker's visit. Make sure students understand that to receive full credit, they must meet the objectives listed.

Make the Assignment

Discuss the topic before the speaker's arrival, providing students with an opportunity to think about questions or comments they have related to that topic. Instruct students to clear their work area so they can focus their full attention on the speaker's presentation. Require each student to respond to the speaker with a question or comment.

Assess Student Understanding

Listening Behaviors

- clears desktop before speech
- does not interrupt speaker
- ignores distractions

Assess these behaviors by means of observation throughout the guest speaker's visit, making notes of student behavior in these specific areas before, during, and after the speaker's presentation.

Questions and Comments

- offers appropriate questions and comments
- waits for appointed time to ask questions/offer comments
- makes eye contact with speaker

Assess these behaviors through observation throughout the guest speaker's visit, making notes of student behavior in these specific areas during and after the speaker's presentation.

GUEST SPEAKER

Task: Student will listen to a guest speaker's presentation.

Goal/Standard: Demonstrate understanding through verbal, visual, or written response

Giving 0 points is an option—no evidence, no credit.

Criteria	1	2	3	4	Total Points
Listening Behaviors • clears desktop before speech • does not interrupt speaker • ignores distractions	Evidence of 2+ incomplete elements	1 complete element present	2 complete elements present	3 complete elements present	_____ x 3 = _____ points
Questions and Comments • offers appropriate questions and comments • waits for appointed time to ask questions/offer comments • makes eye contact with speaker	Evidence of 2+ incomplete elements	1 complete element present	2 complete elements present	3 complete elements present	_____ x 3 = _____ points
Extension of Ideas • links prior knowledge to presentation • uses presentation to clarify familiar concepts • uses presentation as a basis for further exploration of concept	Evidence of 2+ incomplete elements	1 complete element present	2 complete elements present	3 complete elements present	_____ x 4 = _____ points

37–40 = A   31–34 = C
35–36 = B   28–30 = D
          <28 = F

Total score _____/40 = _____

Extension of Ideas

- links prior knowledge to presentation
- uses presentation to clarify familiar concepts
- uses presentation as a basis for further exploration of concept

Before the speaker's arrival, discuss the specified topic with students, instructing them to list three to five facts they already know about the topic. Instruct students to illustrate how the facts relate to one another by using a web, an outline, or another graphic organizer. After the presentation, instruct students to refer to this graphic organizer and add three to five new facts they learned during the speaker's presentation and how these facts relate to that information they already had before the speech. Finally, have students write one question that the presentation did not answer and where they could look, such as the Internet or an encyclopedia, to find the answer.

How to Use the
GUEST SPEAKER Rubric
at the Middle School Level

Introduce the Rubric

Distribute and discuss the rubric with students before the speaker arrives, and explain that you will base this assessment mostly on observation of their behavior before, during, and after the speaker's presentation. Make sure students understand what you expect of them and know that to receive full credit, they must meet the objectives listed.

Make the Assignment

Before the speaker's arrival, discuss the specified topic, providing students with an opportunity to clarify any questions or comments they may wish to share during the speaker's visit. Instruct students to clear their work areas so they can give the speaker their full attention.

Assess Student Understanding

Listening Behaviors

- does not interrupt speaker
- ignores distractions
- responds appropriately (applause, laughter)

Observe and make notes about student behavior in these areas throughout the guest speaker's visit.

Questions and Comments

- waits for appointed time to ask questions/offer comments
- makes eye contact with speaker
- uses speaker's words as basis for questions and comments

Assess these behaviors through observation during and after the guest speaker's presentation. Make notes about student behavior to evaluate these areas.

LISTENING **GUEST SPEAKER** MIDDLE SCHOOL

Task: Student will listen to a guest speaker's presentation.

Goal/Standard: Demonstrate understanding through verbal or written response

Giving 0 points is an option—no evidence, no credit.

Criteria	1	2	3	4	Total Points
Listening Behaviors • does not interrupt speaker • ignores distractions • responds appropriately (applause, laughter)	Evidence of 2+ incomplete elements	1 complete element present	2 complete elements present	3 complete elements present	____ x 3 = ____ points
Questions and Comments • waits for appointed time to ask questions/ offer comments • makes eye contact with speaker • uses speaker's words as basis for questions and comments	Evidence of 2+ incomplete elements	1 complete element present	2 complete elements present	3 complete elements present	____ x 3 = ____ points
Extension of Ideas • uses presentation to clarify familiar concepts • uses presentation as a basis for further exploration of concept • uses presentation to formulate new ideas	Evidence of 2+ incomplete elements	1 complete element present	2 complete elements present	3 complete elements present	____ x 4 = ____ points

37–40 = A   31–34 = C
35–36 = B   28–30 = D
              <28 = F

Total score ____/40 = ____

Extension of Ideas

- uses presentation to clarify familiar concepts
- uses presentation as basis for further exploration of concept
- uses presentation to formulate new ideas

Before the speaker's presentation, instruct students to list in their journals five to seven items of information they already know about the topic. After the presentation, instruct students to reflect on that list. Tell them to select four of the items and add depth to their entries by using information they gained during the presentation. Then ask students to highlight a single item and list two questions they still have about those areas and where they might go to find the answers. Finally, instruct students to reflect, orally or in writing, on a new question or comment that has come into their heads since the speaker's departure—what else would they like to know about the topic?

How to Use the

GUEST SPEAKER Rubric

at the High School Level

Introduce the Rubric

Distribute and discuss the rubric with students before the speaker arrives. Remind students about positive listening behaviors, and explain that you will base the majority of the assessment on observation of their behavior before, during, and after the speaker's presentation. Make sure students understand what you expect of them and know that to receive full credit, they must meet the objectives listed.

Make the Assignment

Discuss the specified topic with students before the speaker's arrival, providing them with an opportunity to share information they already possess about the topic as well as any questions or concerns they wish the speaker to address during the visit. If the speaker has time and the class is not too large, require students to ask a question or make an appropriate comment during the speaker's visit. Instruct students to clear their work areas so they can give the speaker their undivided attention.

Assess Student Understanding

Listening Behaviors

- does not interrupt speaker
- responds appropriately (applause, laughter)
- demonstrates nonverbal listening behaviors

Assess these behaviors by means of observation throughout the guest speaker's visit, making notes of student behavior in these specific areas during and after the speaker's presentation.

GUEST SPEAKER

Task: Student will listen actively to a guest speaker's presentation.

Goal/Standard: Demonstrate understanding through verbal or written response

Giving 0 points is an option—no evidence, no credit.

Criteria	1	2	3	4	Total Points
Listening Behaviors • does not interrupt speaker • responds appropriately • demonstrates nonverbal listening behaviors	Evidence of 2+ incomplete elements	1 complete element present	2 complete elements present	3 complete elements present	_____ x 3 = _____ points
Questions and Comments • makes eye contact with speaker • uses speaker's words as a basis for questions and comments • practices active listening techniques	Evidence of 2+ incomplete elements	1 complete element present	2 complete elements present	3 complete elements present	_____ x 3 = _____ points
Extension of Ideas • uses presentation to clarify familiar concepts • uses presentation as basis for further exploration of concept • uses presentation to formulate new ideas	Evidence of 2+ incomplete elements	1 complete element present	2 complete elements present	3 complete elements present	_____ x 4 = _____ points

37–40 = A   31–34 = C
35–36 = B   28–30 = D
　　　　　　　<28 = F

Total score _____/40 = _____

Questions and Comments

- makes eye contact with speaker
- uses speaker's words as a basis for questions and comments
- practices active listening techniques

Assess these behaviors by means of observation throughout the guest speaker's visit, making notes of student behavior before and after students ask their required questions or make their required comments.

Extension of Ideas

- uses presentation to clarify familiar concepts
- uses presentation as basis for further exploration of concept
- uses presentation to formulate new ideas

Before the speaker's presentation, instruct students to list in their journals five to seven items of information they already know about the topic. After the presentation, instruct students to reflect on that list. Tell them to select four of those items and add depth to their entries with information they gained during the presentation. Then ask students to highlight a single item and list two more questions they have about the item and where they might go to find the information. Finally, instruct students to reflect, orally or in writing, on a question or comment related to the topic they developed while listening to the speaker that the presentation did not cover.

How to Use the
INFORMATIONAL SPEECH Rubric
at the Primary Level

Introduce the Rubric

Distribute and discuss the rubric with students before the speeches. Review text structure (description, sequence, comparison, cause and effect, problem and solution) with students, using graphic organizers to reinforce those concepts. (See chapter 2 for examples of appropriate graphic organizers for each of the text structures, such as description, a web; sequence, a list; comparison, a Venn diagram; cause and effect, one cause with several effects radiating from it; and problem and solution, two boxes linked together.) Make sure students understand what you expect of them and know that they will not receive full credit unless they achieve the objectives listed.

Make the Assignment

Students at this level are capable of listening to basic informational speeches, particularly those that use demonstrations or illustrations to help them grasp the material. Show and tell is a familiar informational speech. You might also use primary level videos from National Geographic for this activity. The speech should be relatively brief (5 to 8 minutes) because attention span is still an issue at this level. The speech or show and tell topic should build on their own prior knowledge of the topic. Students at this level can relate the topic to other experiences or objects they have encountered in the past. If you choose to use student speeches, evaluate just five or six listening students at a time.

Assess Student Understanding

Structure

- recognizes lecture structure
- uses graphic aids to organize information

After the speech, work with students in a large group, asking them to think about the type of information they received in the speech. Did the speech describe something? Did the speech tell them how to do something? Did the speech compare two things? Did the speech tell why something happened? Did the speech tell about how to solve a problem? Once the discussion group establishes which type of lecture structure the speech employed, present the appropriate graphic organizer and have students offer information they recall from the speech to fill in the organizer. Display the completed graphic organizer in the room, and refer to it to review the speech information with students.

How to Use the INFORMATIONAL SPEECH Rubric at the Primary Level

INFORMATIONAL SPEECH

Task: Student will listen to an informational (expository) speech with (optional) visual aids.

Goal/Standard: Demonstrate understanding through verbal, visual, or written response

Criteria	0	1	2	Total Points
Structure • recognizes lecture structure • uses graphic aids to organize information	0 elements present	1 element present	2 elements present	____ x 3 = ____ points
Application • links new information to daily life • links new information to prior knowledge of topic	0 elements present	1 element present	2 elements present	____ x 4 = ____ points
Recall • recalls individual facts • recalls related groups of information	0 elements present	1 element present	2 elements present	____ x 3 = ____ points

19–20 = A 16–17 = C
18 = B 14–15 = D
<14 = F

Total score ____/20 = ____

Application

- links new information to daily life
- links new information to prior knowledge

Before the speech, ask students to discuss, in a large group, the information they already have about the topic. Then after the speech, ask students what new information they gained from the speech. Work with students in a large group, helping them use this prior knowledge and new information to write a brief paragraph about the speech's topic and how they can use this information in their own lives.

Recall

- recalls individual facts
- recalls related groups of information

After the speech, instruct students to write down all the information they can recall from the speech. Next, instruct students to draw lines between the facts to show which ones relate to one another. For example, if the speech dealt with the solar system, they should draw lines between all information they recall about a specific planet.

How to Use the
INFORMATIONAL SPEECH Rubric
at the Intermediate Level

Introduce the Rubric

Distribute and discuss the rubric with students before they listen to the speech. Review text structure (description, sequence, comparison, cause and effect, problem and solution) with the students before the speech, instructing them to think about those structures as they listen to the speech. Make sure students understand what you expect of them and know that to receive full credit, they must meet the objectives listed.

Make the Assignment

For this activity, have students give oral reports based on content area subjects, such as science and social studies, or show them a videotape of a speech by a well-known person. Since information appropriate for students at this level may be somewhat technical, permit students to take notes during the presentation. Speeches for this level can range from 10 to 15 minutes and should include visual aids to clarify the concept for listeners. If you choose to use student speeches, evaluate just five or six listening students at a time.

Assess Student Understanding

Structure

- recognizes lecture structure
- uses graphic aids to organize information
- makes additions to the graphic organizer

After the speech, initiate a large-group discussion about the type of information the speech conveyed. Did the speech describe something? Did the speech explain how to do something? Did the speech compare two or more things? Did the speech tell why something has happened? Did the speech offer a solution to a problem? Once the class determines the type of speech it was, provide students with blank copies of the appropriate graphic organizer, instructing them to use a blue marker to fill in the information they received during the speech. Next, instruct students to use a red marker to add information to the graphic organizer that was not in the speech but is related to the topic. *Note:* you may wish to combine the structure and application assignments and assessment.

INFORMATIONAL SPEECH

Task: Student will listen to an informational (expository) speech with (optional) visual aids.

Goal/Standard: Demonstrate understanding through verbal, visual, or written response

Giving 0 points is an option—no evidence, no credit.

Criteria	1	2	3	4	Total Points
Structure • recognizes lecture structure • uses graphic aids to organize information • makes additions to graphic organizer	Evidence of 2+ incomplete elements	1 complete element present	2 complete elements present	3 complete elements present	_____ x 3 = _____ points
Application • links new information to daily life • links new information to prior knowledge of topic • uses new information to improve related task performance	Evidence of 2+ incomplete elements	1 complete element present	2 complete elements present	3 complete elements present	_____ x 4 = _____ points
Recall • recalls individual facts • recalls related groups of information • distinguishes between fact and opinion	Evidence of 2+ incomplete elements	1 complete element present	2 complete elements present	3 complete elements present	_____ x 3 = _____ points

37–40 = A   31–34 = C
35–36 = B   28–30 = D
            <28 = F

Total score _____/40 = _____

Chapter 5 • Using Rubrics to Assess Listening Skills

Application

- links new information to daily life
- links new information to prior knowledge of topic
- uses new information to improve related task performance

Before the speech, instruct students to write in their journals any information they already possess about the topic, leaving spaces between the writing to make additions after the speech. After the speech, instruct students to return to their journals and add new information, linking it (in the blank spaces) to what they already knew about the topic. Instruct students to tell at the end of the entry how they will use the information in their daily lives to improve the way they currently do things. For example, if the speech was about using natural resources wisely, acceptable responses would include a stronger commitment to using recycling centers and conserving water and electricity.

Recall

- recalls individual facts
- recalls related groups of information
- distinguishes between fact and opinion

After the speech, instruct students to divide a sheet of paper into two columns. In the first column, they should write down all the facts they already knew about the topic. In the second column, they should write all the new facts they learned from the speech. Next, instruct students to draw lines linking the facts based on their relationship. For example, if the speech concerns how a bill becomes a law, students would link all information about a particular step. Next, refer to specific passages from the speech, asking students to identify the passages as fact or opinion along with their reasons for that identification.

How to Use the
INFORMATIONAL SPEECH Rubric
at the Middle School Level

Introduce the Rubric

Distribute and discuss the rubric with students before they hear the speech. Review text structure (description, sequence, comparison, cause and effect, problem and solution) with the students before the speech, instructing them to think about those structures as they listen to the speech. Make sure students understand what you expect of them and know that to receive full credit, they must meet the objectives listed.

Make the Assignment

Students at this level should be able to put on an effective news format speech with two or more students taking places at a long desk or table in front of the room and presenting world, local, state, and school news to classmates. While they are capable of dealing with more complex information conveyed in an oral format, permit them to take notes during the speech to help them organize their responses. The speech can last from 20 to 30 minutes, and it should use at least one visual aid to help reinforce a concept or simply enhance student comprehension. If you choose to use student speeches, evaluate just five or six listeners at a time.

Assess Student Understanding

Structure

- uses graphic aid to organize information
- makes additions to graphic organizer
- uses organizer as a basis for written response

Since the speeches at this level will require students to process more technical and detailed information, discuss the lecture structure beforehand and provide students with a matching graphic organizer. Students can use this aid for taking notes and organizing information. (See chapter 2 for examples of appropriate graphic organizers for each of the text structures, such as description, a web; sequence, a list; comparison, a Venn diagram; cause and effect, one cause with several effects radiating from it; and problem and solution, two boxes linked together.) After the speech, examine students' graphic organizers for accurate information. Then instruct students to add new information from their own prior experiences to the graphic organizer. *Note:* you may wish to combine the activities and the assessment of the structure and application elements.

How to Use the INFORMATIONAL SPEECH Rubric at the Middle School Level

INFORMATIONAL SPEECH

Task: Student will listen to an informational (expository) speech with (optional) visual aids.

Goal/Standard: Demonstrate understanding through verbal, visual, or written response

Giving 0 points is an option—no evidence, no credit.

Criteria	1	2	3	4	Total Points
Structure • uses graphic aid to organize information • makes additions to graphic organizer • uses organizer as a basis for written response	Evidence of 2+ incomplete elements	1 complete element present	2 complete elements present	3 complete elements present	____ x 3 = ____ points
Application • links new information to prior knowledge of topic • uses new information to improve related task performance • sees significance of structure for conveying information	Evidence of 2+ incomplete elements	1 complete element present	2 complete elements present	3 complete elements present	____ x 4 = ____ points
Recall • recalls related groups of information • distinguishes between fact and opinion • links visual aid and verbal information	Evidence of 2+ incomplete elements	1 complete element present	2 complete elements present	3 complete elements present	____ x 3 = ____ points

37–40 = A 31–34 = C
35–36 = B 28–30 = D
       <28 = F

Total score _____/40 = _____

Application

■ links new information to prior knowledge of topic
■ uses new information to improve related task performance
■ sees significance of structure for conveying information

After the speech, instruct students to divide a page in their journals into two columns. In the left column, instruct students to write five to eight facts they knew about the topic before the speech, leaving room to write after each fact. (They can perform this segment of the activity before the speech.) Next, instruct students to write a relative fact they learned during the speech below that fact. For example, if the student already knew that Saturn has rings, he would write that fact in the left column of the journal entry. If, during the speech, the student learns that the rings are made of, among other elements, chunks of ice, he would write that fact below the first fact concerning the existence of Saturn's rings. Finally, instruct students to write in the second column three to four reasons why they think the text structure the speech employed was (or was not) the best way to convey the information.

Recall

■ recalls related groups of information
■ distinguishes between fact and opinion
■ links visual aid with verbal information

After the speech, instruct students to write a list of ten to twenty items they learned during the informational speech. Next, have students draw a circle around those items that are opinion rather than fact. Then instruct students to draw lines connecting those facts that relate directly to one another. Finally, instruct students to relate how the information in the speech's visual aid connects to the verbal information. For example, if the speech on the solar system used a three-dimensional model, students should be able to explain why that sort of visual aid made it easier to understand the relationship between planets based on their sizes and their orbits around the sun.

How to Use the
INFORMATIONAL SPEECH Rubric
at the High School Level

Introduce the Rubric

Distribute and discuss the rubric with students before the speech. Review text structure (description, sequence, comparison, cause and effect, problem and solution) with the students before the speech, instructing them to think about those structures as they listen to the speech. Make sure students understand what you expect of them and know that to receive full credit, they must meet the objectives listed.

Make the Assignment

These students should have adult-level public speaking skills and may even surpass adults with their ability to convey information. Students at this level have attention spans comparable with the attention spans of adults. News program formats and demonstration speeches (how to use something or how to do something) are two possible avenues for this level. Because the material in the speech is likely to be somewhat technical, permit students to take notes to organize their thinking for responses after the presentation. Informational speeches at this level can last from 30 to 45 minutes and should include at least one visual aid. If you choose to use student speeches, evaluate just five or six listeners at a time.

Assess Student Understanding

Structure

- constructs graphic organizer to clarify information
- uses organizer as basis for response
- uses organizer as basis for multimedia response

Students at this level are capable of giving complex responses after an informational speech. Since students are familiar with text structure and should have organized notes in a specific format (for example, for a comparison lecture, they divide their notebook paper in half; for a sequence lecture, they number the notes; and so on), they can use the appropriate graphic organizer to offer a response. The response should be student-directed and could take the form of a verbal response accompanied by a poster highlighting important information for others to read debating the virtues of the information conveyed in the speech.

INFORMATIONAL SPEECH

Task: Student will listen to an informational (expository) speech with (optional) visual aids.

Goal/Standard: Demonstrate understanding through verbal, visual, or written response

Giving 0 points is an option—no evidence, no credit.

Criteria	1	2	3	4	Total Points
Structure • constructs graphic organizer to clarify information • uses organizer as basis for response • uses organizer as basis for multimedia response	Evidence of 2+ incomplete elements	1 complete element present	2 complete elements present	3 complete elements present	____ x 3 = ____ points
Application • uses new information to improve related task performance • sees significance of expository structure for conveying information • identifies appropriate expository structure for response	Evidence of 2+ incomplete elements	1 complete element present	2 complete elements present	3 complete elements present	____ x 4 = ____ points
Recall • distinguishes between fact and opinion • links visual aids and verbal information • uses visual aids and verbal information to construct new schema of topic	Evidence of 2+ incomplete elements	1 complete element present	2 complete elements present	3 complete elements present	____ x 3 = ____ points

37–40 = A   31–34 = C
35–36 = B   28–30 = D
          <28 = F

Total score ____ /40 = ____

For example, if the speech dealt with the issue of capital punishment, students should be able to construct a visual aid detailing the pros and cons of that issue to accompany a verbal response.

Application

- uses new information to improve related task performance
- sees significance of expository structure for conveying information
- identifies appropriate expository structure for response

When students receive new information regarding a task they already have performed (outlining, building a birdhouse), the speaker's information may allow them to improve their performance. To assess the first element, "uses new information to improve related task performance," have students explain in a journal entry how the new information will help them next time they undertake this task. After the speech, initiate a group discussion about the presentation of the information and whether the format and structure of the speech was the most effective method available. For example, if the speech dealt with how a bill becomes a law and the speaker used a descriptive format, students should be able to recognize that a sequence format would have been more effective. Likewise, students should also be able to organize a response to the information in the speech by using the most effective structure. For example, if the speech dealt with solutions to pollution, students might organize a response in a comparison format to contrast two or more of the solutions with one another.

Recall

- distinguishes between fact and opinion
- links visual aids and verbal information
- uses visual aids and verbal information to construct new schema of topic

Students at this level are capable of going beyond recalling information from an informational speech. They should be able to organize the concepts presented in the speech, relegating opinions to a level of less importance than facts. Next, instruct students to relate how the information in the speech's visual aid connects to the verbal information. Finally, instruct students working in small groups to use what they have learned from the verbal and visual presentation to present the information from a new perspective. For example, if the speech focused on the need for sweeping reforms in education, students should be able to organize the information to present a viewpoint not represented in the informational speech.

6

Assessment Rubrics and Oral Language

To prepare her students for the challenges of high school, eighth-grade teacher Michelle designs and teaches a wide variety of oral language activities in her social studies classes. Reflecting on the types of classroom exercises (discussion, oral reports) and extracurricular experiences (debates, theater, storytelling) her students will face during the next four years, Michelle develops assessment rubrics for each type of activity. She shares these rubrics with her students as they participate in each exercise. By creating these forms of assessment, Michelle enables her students to take control of their performance by focusing on strengths and weaknesses in each area of oral language presentation.

ORAL PRESENTATIONS: BEYOND WORDS

Michelle's students are fortunate that she invests time and energy to help them maximize their future high school experience. In many cases, grade school teachers assess students' oral performances solely on content, disregarding such categories as eye contact and enunciation. When students reach ninth grade and are judged on these and other presentation-related skills, their limited prior experience often makes them self-conscious about giving speeches or engaging in debates. Their reluctance can escalate if students remain confused about what they are doing incorrectly. Michelle's efforts to help students identify and refine their public speaking skills will yield positive effects in the lives of these students long after they have moved beyond classroom walls into the real world.

The rubrics in this chapter cover five areas related to oral language skills: Debate, Oral Report, Storytelling, Dramatic Presentation, and Discussion. These rubrics list full-credit responses to provide teachers with concrete examples of what they may see in student work. A summary of expectations for each age and grade level follows. For areas not suitable for primary grades, no rubric appears at that level.

Debates: That's Debatable

These rubrics assess students' participation in a formal or informal debate. The goal, or highest degree of accomplishment on the rubric, for each grade level follows:

Intermediate—student speaks in a well-modulated voice, stays focused on debate topic, maintains eye contact with audience and opponent(s), and observes debating rules.

Middle School—student speaks in a clear, persuasive tone, fields unanticipated questions and comments with ease, uses facial gestures to emphasize arguments, and acts as a positive debating role model for peers.

High School—student uses tone that engages listeners immediately, displays no gaps in logic or accuracy of content, uses facial expressions to emphasize arguments, and sets a positive tone and pace for the debating session.

Oral Report: What's News?

These rubrics assess students' ability to present an oral news report with visual aids. The goal, or highest degree of accomplishment on the rubric, for each grade level follows:

Primary—student addresses and organizes topic adequately, speaks with adequate volume and pace, looks at notes and at audience, and uses adequately constructed, relevant visual aids.

Intermediate—student addresses and organizes topic well, speaks with appropriate emphasis, maintains eye contact with audience, and uses well-constructed, relevant visual aids.

Middle School—student selects topic that captures and holds audience interest with easy-to-follow organization of ideas, uses effective speaking voice and facial expressions to engage audience, and uses relevant, well-constructed visual aids that enhance report.

High School—student selects topic that stimulates audience interest, uses professional quality public speaking voice, uses facial expressions to emphasize specific statements, and uses visual aids that stimulate audience interest at the onset of the presentation.

Storytelling: It's Story Time!

These rubrics assess students' ability to tell a fictional story with props or costumes. The goal, or highest degree of accomplishment on the rubric, for each grade level follows:

Primary—student selects story appropriate for intended audience, tells story with no omissions or reversals in story sequence, and uses adequate vocal tone and pace and appropriate props or costumes.

Intermediate—student selects story that encourages audience interaction with storyteller, emphasizes major events in story sequence, and uses vocal inflection and props or costumes that enhances retelling.

Middle School—student selects story that engages audience immediately and throughout retelling, involves audience in predicting upcoming story events, uses distinct voices for characters and narrator to enhance retelling, and uses props or costumes to immerse audience in story events.

High School—student selects story that delights audience and connects with their previous experiences, tells story in a way that heightens audience interest while building to climax, creates unique voices to enhance retelling, and uses props or costumes that blend the story and storyteller into a single entity.

Dramatic Presentation: The Play's the Thing

These rubrics assess students' participation in a dramatic presentation. The goal, or highest degree of accomplishment on the rubric, for each grade level follows:

Primary—student has vocal delivery, gestures, and movements appropriate for characters and story and uses props and costumes relevant to the story.

Intermediate—student uses vocal delivery that engages audience attention and interest, gestures and movements that enhance verbal delivery, and props and costumes that provide additional information about character.

Middle School—student uses vocal delivery that brings character to life, gestures and movements that give depth to story character, and props and costumes that enhance the character and story.

High School—student uses vocal delivery that makes him or her become character, gestures and movement that give depth to story character, and props and costumes that create stunning visual image of character.

Discussion: Let's Talk About It

These rubrics assess students' participation in a group discussion. The goal, or highest degree of accomplishment on the rubric, for each grade level follows:

Primary—student waits for appropriate time to speak and stays focused on topic.

Intermediate—student encourages other group members to participate in discussion and uses information to draw conclusions about topic.

Middle School—student demonstrates leadership skills and shares a wealth of prior knowledge of topic.

High School—student sets positive pace and tone for discussion and brings unexplored knowledge of topic to discussion.

How to Use the

DEBATE Rubric

at the Intermediate Level

Introduce the Rubric

Distribute and discuss the rubric with students before they begin the debate, focusing attention on the column that contains the highest level of performance. Remind students that to receive full credit, they must achieve the objectives listed in this column.

Use this opportunity to review the rules of debating with students and relate those rules to the objectives in the rubric. For example, debating rules cite the need for debaters to stay on topic, and the rubric mentions this need under the Content heading.

Make the Assignment

Students at this level perform best with a debate format that has a balance of research presentation and the students' opinions. For example, a debate about the most and least effective solutions to pollution should contain information on studies conducted on that topic as well as some input from students about why they believe certain methods are more or less effective than others. Choose a topic of interest and importance to students. Ask for student input because the more passionately individuals feel about a topic, the more likely they will invest time and energy in researching and presenting a debate. They should conduct their research in publications or at Internet sites designed for their age group. At this level, have students debate one-on-one or in teams of two students. Set some time limits for presentation (about 1 to 2 minutes per student), rebuttal (about 1 minute per student), and closing arguments (about 3 minutes—in a team format, one student from each team gives the closing argument), and appoint a timekeeper to make sure students adhere to those guidelines. Place the rules of the debate on a checklist, making a copy for each debater.

Assess Student Understanding

Vocal Delivery
- has well-modulated, clear, and strong delivery

Content
- stays focused on topic

Eye Contact
- maintains eye contact with opponent(s) and audience

Procedure
- observes all debate rules

DEBATE

Task: Student will participate in a formal or informal debate.

Goal/Standard: Debate performance meets stated criteria

Giving 0 is an option—no evidence, no credit.

Criteria	1	2	3	Total Points
Vocal Delivery	Erratic volume	Adequate volume	Well modulated, clear, and strong	____ x 5 = ____ points
Content	Drifts from topic	Drifts from topic, but catches drift and refocuses	Stays on topic	____ x 5 = ____ points
Eye Contact	Looks at notes too much	Balances looking at notes with making eye contact	Maintains eye contact to connect with audience and opponent(s)	____ x 5 = ____ points
Procedure	Seems uncertain of debate rules	Observes some debate rules	Observes all debate rules	____ x 5 = ____ points

37–40 = A   31–34 = C
35–36 = B   28–30 = D
           < 28 = F

Total score ____/40 = ____

How to Use the DEBATE Rubric at the Intermediate Level

Because you will conduct this assessment during the actual debate, keep the rubric at hand during that time. Sit near the rear of the room to ensure that the entire audience can hear the debaters' voices. Take note of participants who drift continually from the specified topic and those who read from their notes without looking at opponent(s) or audience. During the debate, check those areas where the debater performs at or above age-appropriate expectations as well as those areas where the debater needs improvement.

How to Use the
DEBATE Rubric
at the Middle School Level

Introduce the Rubric

Distribute and discuss the rubric with students before they begin the debate, focusing attention on the column that contains the highest level of performance. Remind students that to receive full credit, they must achieve the objectives listed in that column.

Take this opportunity to review the rules of debating with students and relate those rules to the objectives stated in the rubric. For example, many debating guidelines cite the need for debaters to act as a positive role model, and this item appears under the Procedure heading in the rubric.

Make the Assignment

Students at this level are capable of debating with a format that uses significantly more research presentation than students' opinions. For example, a debate about the most and least effective methods of controlling environmental damage should contain the results of studies conducted on that topic as well as some input from students about why they believe certain methods are more or less effective than others. Choose a topic of interest and importance to students, making sure that it is a topic with sufficient resources for students to examine and include in their debate presentation. In addition, ask for student input because the more passionately individuals feel about a topic, the more likely they will invest time and energy in researching and presenting a debate. At this level, have students debate in teams of two to four students. Set some time limits for presentation (about 2 to 4 minutes per student), rebuttal (about 2 minutes per student), and closing arguments (about 4 minutes—one student from each team gives the closing argument), and appoint a timekeeper to make sure students adhere to those guidelines.

Assess Student Understanding

Vocal Delivery
- has a clear, persuasive tone

Content
- fields questions with ease

Eye Contact
- uses facial gestures to emphasize arguments

Procedure
- acts as a positive debating role model for peers

How to Use the DEBATE Rubric at the Middle School Level

DEBATE

Task: Student will participate in a formal or informal debate.
Goal/Standard: Debate performance meets stated criteria

Giving 0 points is an option—no evidence, no credit.

Criteria	1	2	3	4	Total Points
Vocal Delivery	Erratic volume	Adequate volume	Well modulated	Clear, persuasive tone	____ x 5 = ____ points
Content	Drifts from topic	Stays on topic	Presents topic clearly and knowledgeably	Fields questions with ease	____ x 5 = ____ points
Eye Contact	Looks at notes frequently	Looks at notes and makes eye contact	Maintains eye contact to connect with audience and opponent(s)	Uses facial gestures to emphasize arguments	____ x 5 = ____ points
Procedure	Asks questions about debate rules	Observes some debate rules	Observes all debate rules	Acts as a positive debating role model for peers	____ x 5 = ____ points

74–80 = A   62–69 = C
70–73 = B   56–61 = D
            <56 = F

Total score ____/80 = ____

Because you will conduct the assessment during the debate, keep the rubric at hand during that time. Debaters should speak in a clear voice easily heard from anywhere in the room. The tone should be firm enough to persuade audience members but not overly aggressive, a situation that often causes otherwise competent debaters to lose support for their position. Debaters should make consistent eye contact with his or her opponent(s) and audience members as well as use facial gestures, such as a raised eyebrow, to emphasize a significant remark in their presentation. The debaters' overall demeanor should stand as a positive role model for those in the audience who will, in time, have an opportunity to try their hand at debating.

———

How to Use the

DEBATE Rubric
at the High School Level

Introduce the Rubric

Distribute and discuss the rubric with students before they begin the debate, focusing attention on the column that contains the highest level of performance. Remind students that to receive full credit, they must achieve the objectives listed in that column. Take this opportunity to review the rules of debating with students and relate those rules to the objectives stated in the rubric. For example, the need for debaters to demonstrate no gaps in logic or accuracy appears under the Content heading in the rubric as well as in many debating guidelines.

Make the Assignment

Students at this level are capable of debating with a format that uses significantly more research presentation than actual students' opinions. For example, a debate about the most and least effective methods of controlling environmental damage should contain the results of studies conducted on that topic as well as some input from students about why they believe certain methods are more or less effective than others. Students should also be able to debate effectively on a topic from a standpoint that differs from their personal opinion on the topic. For example, a student who is a devoted environmentalist should be able, within the framework of a debate, to make a believable case for drilling for oil in Alaska. Choose a topic of interest and importance to students, making sure that it is a topic with sufficient resources for students to examine and include in their debate presentation. Ask for student input because the more passionately individuals feel about a topic, the more time and energy they will invest in researching and presenting a debate. At this level, have students debate in teams of three to five students. Set some time limits for presentation (about 3 to 5 minutes per student), rebuttal (about 2 minutes per student), and closing arguments (about 5 to 6 minutes—one student from each team gives the closing argument), and appoint a timekeeper to make sure students adhere to those guidelines.

Task: Student will participate in a formal or informal debate.

Goal/Standard: Debate performance meets stated criteria

Giving 0 points is an option—no evidence, no credit.

Criteria	1	2	3	4	Total Points
Vocal Delivery	Adequate volume	Well modulated	Clear, persuasive tone	Tone engages audience immediately	____ x 5 = ____ points
Content	Stays on topic	Presents topic clearly and knowledgeably	Fields unanticipated questions with ease	Demonstrates no gaps in logic or accuracy of content	____ x 5 = ____ points
Eye Contact	Looks at notes frequently	Maintains eye contact with audience and opponent(s)	Uses facial gestures to emphasize arguments	Facial expression, body language, and eye contact demonstrate confidence	____ x 5 = ____ points
Procedure	Observes some debate rules	Observes all debate rules	Acts as a positive debating role model for peers	Sets a positive tone and pace for debate	____ x 5 = ____ points

74–80 = A	62–69 = C
70–73 = B	56–61 = D
	<56 = F

Total score ____/80 = ____

Assess Student Understanding

Vocal Delivery

- engages listeners immediately

Content

- demonstrates no gaps in logic or accuracy of content

Eye Contact

- demonstrates confidence through facial expressions, body language, and eye contact

Procedure

- sets a positive tone and pace for the debate

Because you will conduct the assessment during the debate, keep the rubric at hand during that time. The debater's voice should be clear and persuasive, yet warm and inviting enough to engage audience members. The debater should present well-documented research containing no gaps in logic or accuracy. This element is particularly important because some debaters attempt to alter the truth to make their argument stronger. The time limit should prompt astute debaters to use facial gestures to emphasize their statements. Their facial expressions, eye contact, and body language exude confidence. They should not, however, employ facial gestures to undermine their opponents' remarks. Finally, the debater's entire demeanor should reflect a positive tone and pace for the debate setting. Courteous and professional behavior encourages audience members to give their attention to the debater.

How to Use the
ORAL REPORT Rubric
at the Primary Level

Introduce the Rubric

Distribute and discuss the rubric with students before they begin their oral reports. Focus attention on the rubric column containing the highest levels of performance, reminding students that to receive full credit, they must achieve these objectives. Students at this level can handle some reporting of factual information, although the majority of student presentations will revolve around the student's ideas and opinions.

Make the Assignment

Students at this level can engage in such oral reports as show and tell or group or circle sharing time. Their participation in these activities should follow the guidelines in the rubric because these primary activities are the foundation for future oral presentations. For early primary grades, begin with a simple show and tell presentation. Older primary students (grades 2 and 3) may feel more comfortable with a group or circle time activity when they can share an event they experienced, such as a special vacation or celebration. Set a time limit, approximately 3 to 5 minutes, to help students plan their presentations more effectively. To enhance the presentation for visual learners, instruct students to bring some sort of relevant visual aid to accompany their oral report. (This instruction is not necessary for show and tell because students already bring some item to share with classmates.)

Assess Student Understanding

Vocal Delivery
- uses adequate volume and pace

Content
- addresses and organizes topic adequately

Eye Contact
- reads from notes and makes eye contact with audience

Visual Aids
- uses well-constructed visual aid relevant to topic

SPEAKING **ORAL REPORT** PRIMARY

Task: Student will present an oral news report with visual aids.

Goal/Standard: Oral report meets stated criteria

Criteria	0	1	2	Total Points
Vocal Delivery	Inaudible	Erratic volume and pace	Adequate volume and pace	_____ x 5 = _____ points
Content	Unclear topic and report organization	Some weak links connecting ideas	Addresses and organizes topic adequately	_____ x 5 = _____ points
Eye Contact	Little or none	Infrequent	Looks at notes and at audience	_____ x 5 = _____ points
Visual Aids	Little or none	Poorly made	Adequately constructed and relevant	_____ x 5 = _____ points

37–40 = A 31–34 = C
35–36 = B 28–30 = D
<28 = F

Total score _____/40 = _____

Because you will conduct the assessment during the oral presentation, keep the rubric at hand during that time. Consider the speaker's volume and pace throughout the presentation. An excessively slow or rapid pace diminishes the impact of the speaker's words. While speakers at this level may need to rely on notes to make the presentation, they should also be able to make eye contact with audience members, preferably while emphasizing an important part of the oral presentation. The visual aid should enhance the presentation and be relevant to the topic and adequately constructed.

———

How to Use the
ORAL REPORT Rubric
at the Intermediate Level

Introduce the Rubric

Distribute and discuss the rubric with students before they begin the activity. Focus attention on the rubric column containing the highest levels of performance, reminding students that to receive full credit, they must achieve these objectives. While the majority of these presentations will revolve around the student's ideas and opinions, students at this level are able to present brief informational presentations.

Make the Assignment

Students at this level have taken classes in a number of content area subjects, such as social studies or science, and these areas can provide ample topics for students preparing an oral report. Compile a list of acceptable topics in either of these or other areas (such as health, math, art, or music), instructing students to select from the list. Students who wish to prepare a report on another topic should share their reasons for choosing that topic as well as demonstrate their ability to gather and present a sufficient amount of relevant material.

Students at this level are capable of presenting a 5- to 10-minute oral report that includes relevant visual aids to clarify and enhance the information presented.

Assess Student Understanding

Vocal Delivery
- uses volume and pace effectively for emphasis

Content
- presents topic well and in a well-organized format

Eye Contact
- maintains eye contact with audience members

Visual Aids
- uses well-made visual aids relevant to oral report

ORAL REPORT

Task: Student will present an oral news report with visual aids.

Goal/Standard: Oral report meets stated criteria

Giving 0 points is an option—no evidence, no credit.

Criteria	1	2	3	4	Total Points
Vocal Delivery	Erratic volume and pace	Adequate volume and pace	Good, even volume and pace	Uses volume and pace to emphasize statements	____ x 5 = ____ points
Content	Weak links connecting ideas	Addresses and organizes topic adequately	Topic is clear; organization is logical	Addresses and organizes topic well	____ x 5 = ____ points
Eye Contact	Infrequent	Looks at notes and at audience	Looks more at audience than at notes	Maintains eye contact with audience	____ x 5 = ____ points
Visual Aids	Poorly made	Relevant but not well constructed	Adequately constructed and relevant	Relevant and well made	____ x 5 = ____ points

74–80 = A   62–69 = C
70–73 = B   56–61 = D
         <56 = F

Total score ____/80 = ____

Chapter 6 • Assessment Rubrics and Oral Language

Because you will conduct the assessment during the oral presentation, keep the rubric at hand during that time. Reflect on the speaker's volume and pace throughout the presentation. These factors should vary as the student emphasizes important information in the oral report. Students speaking at an excessively slow or rapid pace diminish the impact of their words. Speakers at this level should not need to rely on notes to make the presentation. They should make eye contact with audience members, especially while emphasizing an important part of the oral presentation. Their visual aid should enhance the presentation and be relevant to the topic and well constructed.

How to Use the
ORAL REPORT Rubric
at the Middle School Level

Introduce the Rubric

Distribute and discuss the rubric with students before they begin the activity. Focus attention on the rubric column containing the highest levels of performance, reminding students that to receive full credit, they must achieve these objectives. Students at this level may participate in a wide variety of oral reporting activities that extend beyond simply sharing their ideas and opinions with classmates. They are capable of presenting oral reports from an objective, journalistic standpoint, sharing facts without including their personal bias.

Make the Assignment

Middle school students can do a capable job of reporting on current events to their classmates. These students are able to gather and share information from news stories about which they have not yet formed an opinion. Younger students tend to share their parents' opinions while older (high school) students are developing strong ideas of their own. Using the newspaper in the classroom, help students select local, national, and world event stories that interest their classmates. Set time limits, such as 10 to 15 minutes, and encourage students to practice the oral report beforehand to learn about pacing themselves under a time limit.

Assess Student Understanding

Vocal Delivery
- uses professional quality volume and pace—news anchor potential!

Content
- presents topic in well-organized format—standing ovation time!

Eye Contact
- uses eye contact for emphasis

Visual Aids
- uses visual aids that enhance the presentation

How to Use the ORAL REPORT Rubric at the Middle School Level

ORAL REPORT

Task: Student will present an oral news report with visual aids.
Goal/Standard: Oral report meets stated criteria

Giving 0 points is an option—no evidence, no credit.

Criteria	1	2	3	4	Total Points
Vocal Delivery	Adequate volume and pace	Good, even volume and pace	Uses volume and pace to emphasize statements	Uses professional quality volume and pace	____ x 5 = ____ points
Content	Addresses and organizes topic adequately	Topic is clear; organization is logical	Addresses and organizes topic well	Presentation and organization of topic engage audience	____ x 5 = ____ points
Eye Contact	Looks at notes and at audience	Looks more at audience than at notes	Maintains eye contact with audience	Uses eye contact to emphasize statements	____ x 5 = ____ points
Visual Aids	Relevant but not well constructed	Adequately constructed and relevant	Relevant and well made	Enhance oral news report	____ x 5 = ____ points

74–80 = A	62–69 = C
70–73 = B	56–61 = D
	<56 = F

Total score ____/80 = ____

Because you will conduct the assessment during the oral report, keep the rubric at hand during that time. The speaker's sentences should link to one another and construct a comprehensive portrait of the topic without distracting asides that fail to enhance the report. The speaker should use a voice loud enough for classmates to hear in all parts of the classroom and an even delivery style that lets listeners focus on the information rather than on any erratic vocal inflections. Well-constructed visual aids should enhance and clarify the information presented orally.

How to Use the
ORAL REPORT Rubric
at the High School Level

Introduce the Rubric

Distribute and discuss the rubric with students before they begin the activity. Focus attention on the rubric column containing the highest level of performance, reminding students that to receive full credit, they must achieve those objectives. Students at this level are capable of dealing with a wide variety of oral presentation formats. In addition to informational speeches, high school students can present persuasive speeches, seeking to convince classmates to share their opinion regarding a particular product or idea. Speeches they make during student government elections are one example of student speakers attempting to sell their point of view to a listening audience.

Make the Assignment

Students at this level are capable of finding a topic for their oral report. Instruct students to submit their topic idea before they begin researching it to avoid needless repetition by several students or the selection of a topic below the student's ability level. Provide time limits, 15 to 30 minutes, and encourage students to practice their speeches before the presentation date to learn correct pacing and to eliminate distracting verbal tics. Students can work alone to get pacing down correctly and with another student during independent time in a quiet corner of the room or outside of school to deal with such aspects as verbal tics.

Assess Student Understanding

Vocal Delivery
- uses professional quality volume and pace—news anchor potential!

Content
- presents topic superbly in well-organized format—standing ovation time!

Eye Contact
- uses eye contact and facial expressions for emphasis

Visual Aids
- uses visual aids that stimulate audience interest at onset of presentation

ORAL REPORT

Task: Student will present an oral news report with visual aids.

Goal/Standard: Oral report meets stated criteria

Giving 0 points is an option—no evidence, no credit.

Criteria	1	2	3	4	Total Points
Vocal Delivery	Adequate volume and pace	Good volume and pace	Uses volume and pace to emphasize statements	Uses professional quality volume and pace	____ x 5 = ____ points
Content	Addresses and organizes topic well	Gears topic to audience interest and previous experience	Topic and organization capture and maintain audience interest	Superb presentation and organization of topic	____ x 5 = ____ points
Eye Contact	Looks at notes and at audience	Looks at audience more than notes	Maintains eye contact with audience	Uses eye contact and facial expressions to emphasize statements	____ x 5 = ____ points
Visual Aids	Relevant and constructed adequately	Relevant and well made	Enhance oral news report	Stimulates audience interest at onset of presentation	____ x 5 = ____ points

74–80 = A	62–69 = C
70–73 = B	56–61 = D
	<56 = F

Total score ____/80 = ____

Chapter 6 • Assessment Rubrics and Oral Language

Because you will conduct the assessment during the oral report, keep the rubric at hand during that time. The speaker's sentences should link to one another and construct a comprehensive portrait of the topic without distracting asides that fail to enhance the report. The speaker should use a voice loud enough for classmates to hear in all parts of the classroom and an even delivery style that lets listeners focus on the information rather than on any erratic vocal inflections. Quality and relevant visual aids should enhance and clarify the information presented orally.

———————

How to Use the
STORYTELLING Rubric
at the Primary Level

Introduce the Rubric

Distribute and discuss the rubric with students before they begin the activity. Focus attention on the column containing the highest level of performance, reminding students that to receive full credit, they must achieve these objectives. Make sure students understand the difference between storytelling and reading aloud. Unlike the reader, a storyteller must know the story with little or no aid from index cards or other cuing devices.

Make the Assignment

Students at this level might tell incredible stories due to their unbridled imaginations. For this assignment, however, it is important that their stories have a clear beginning, middle, and ending. Begin by having students retell one of their favorite stories from a work of children's literature. They can refer to the book as a guide while practicing their retelling, and teachers can recognize almost immediately if gaps or reversals occur in the story sequence. Set time guidelines (3 to 6 minutes) to help students who might stray from the purpose of telling the story. Props and costumes are an excellent way to enhance the retelling and give storytellers something on which to build their storyteller persona. Discuss the types of props students can use, such as hats, shawls, or puppets, and limit students at this level to one to two props or costume items.

Assess Student Understanding

Selection
■ chooses story appropriate for audience

Sequence
■ has no omissions or reversals in sequence

Vocal Delivery
■ uses adequate tone and pace for retelling

Props or Costumes
■ uses neat and appropriate props or costumes

How to Use the STORYTELLING Rubric at the Primary Level

STORYTELLING

Task: Student will tell a fictional story with props and/or costumes.

Goal/Standard: Performance meets stated criteria

Criteria	0	1	2	Total Points
Selection	Too long or complex for retelling	Not appropriate for audience	Appropriate for intended audience	____ x 5 = ____ points
Sequence	Illogical	Omissions and reversals in retelling	No omissions or reversals in retelling	____ x 5 = ____ points
Vocal Delivery	Flat or inaudible tone	Erratic tone and pace	Adequate tone and pace	____ x 5 = ____ points
Props or Costumes	None	Sloppy; not relevant	Neat and appropriate	____ x 5 = ____ points

37–40 = A   31–34 = C
35–36 = B   28–30 = D
           <28 = F

Total score ____/40 = ____

Because you will conduct the assessment during the retelling, keep the rubric at hand during that time. Join other audience members in the story circle because, unlike reading aloud, storytellers use their voice as a tool in the retelling and may choose to use a soft voice at times to heighten suspense in a particular part of the story. Know the story beforehand. If you permit students to tell an original story, have a hard copy available to check for omissions or reversals in the sequence. Any story that is of interest to the specific age group is appropriate. For example, a fairy tale is generally appropriate for primary-level storytelling. Props and costumes should enhance not detract from the retelling.

How to Use the
STORYTELLING Rubric
at the Intermediate Level

Introduce the Rubric

Distribute and discuss the rubric with students before they begin the activity. Focus attention on the column containing the highest level of performance, reminding students that to receive full credit, they must achieve these objectives. Make sure students understand the difference between storytelling and reading aloud. Unlike the reader, a storyteller must know the story with little or no aid from index cards or other cuing devices.

Make the Assignment

Students at this level are capable of telling stories with multiple characters. They can retell a popular children's story or compose a tale of their own. If they choose the latter, make sure you receive a hard copy of the story so during assessment you can determine whether any omissions or reversals occur. Set time guidelines (5 to 8 minutes) to help storytellers focus on telling only the story without venturing into asides that may detract from the tale. Instruct students to select a tale appropriate for their audience and one that gets the audience actively involved in the retelling through such devices as repetition of certain lines or gestures. So you can assess their ability to emphasize major events, instruct them to select a story with three to four major events and one to two minor details to go with each event. Discuss the types of props they can use, such as hats, shawls, or puppets, but limit students at this level to two to three props or costume items.

Assess Student Understanding

Selection
- chooses story that encourages audience interaction with storyteller

Sequence
- emphasizes major events

Vocal Delivery
- uses vocal inflection appropriate to the retelling

Props or Costumes
- props or costumes that enhance the retelling

STORYTELLING

Task: Student will tell a fictional story with props and/or costumes.

Goal/Standard: Performance meets stated criteria

Giving 0 points is an option—no evidence, no credit.

Criteria	1	2	3	4	Total Points
Selection	Not appropriate for audience	Appropriate for audience but too long	Appropriate for audience in content and length	Encourages audience interaction with storyteller	____ x 5 = ____ points
Sequence	Difficult to follow	1–2 omissions and reversals in retelling	No omissions or reversals in retelling	Emphasizes major story events	____ x 5 = ____ points
Vocal Delivery	Erratic tone and pace	Adequate tone and pace	Good, even tone and pace	Uses appropriate vocal inflection	____ x 5 = ____ points
Props or Costumes	Sloppy or not relevant	Present, but do not enhance story	Neat and appropriate	Enhance retelling	____ x 5 = ____ points

74–80 = A   62–69 = C
70–73 = B   56–61 = D
            <56 = F

Total score ____/80 = ____

Chapter 6 • Assessment Rubrics and Oral Language

How to Use the STORYTELLING Rubric at the Intermediate Level

Because you will conduct the assessment during the retelling, keep the rubric at hand during that time. Join other audience members in the story circle because, unlike reading aloud, storytellers use their voices as a tool in the retelling and may choose to use a soft voice at times to heighten suspense in a particular part of the story. Know the story beforehand. Again, if you permit students to tell an original story, keep a hard copy available to check for omissions or reversals in the sequence. Any story that is of interest to the specific age group is appropriate. Intermediate-level storytellers gravitate toward stories of people in their age group. Look for the storyteller's emphasis on major events. Props and costumes should enhance not detract from the retelling.

How to Use the
STORYTELLING Rubric
at the Middle School Level

Introduce the Rubric

Distribute and discuss the rubric with students before they begin the activity. Focus attention on the column containing the highest level of performance, reminding students that to receive full credit, they must achieve these objectives. Students at this level are capable of extending the storytelling experience beyond language arts into content area subjects, such as science or social studies. In these cases, students might assume the identity of a person who lived in another time to tell the story of a famous person. For example, a student storyteller might assume the fictitious identify of one of Ben Franklin's neighbors to tell about all the "crazy experiments" that interested young Ben in his early years. Distinct voices for story characters as well as props and costumes are particularly helpful with this sort of retelling, but students should use them sparingly so they do not detract from the effect of the storyteller's voice and gestures.

Make the Assignment

Students at this level are capable of telling stories with multiple characters. They can retell a popular children's story or compose a tale of their own. If they choose the latter option, make sure they supply you with a hard copy of the story so you can determine whether any omissions or reversals occur in the retelling. Set time guidelines (8 to 10 minutes) to help storytellers focus on telling only the story and avoid asides that detract from the tale. Instruct students to select a tale that involves the audience in the retelling through such devices as asking the audience prediction questions ("Then what do you suppose happened?") and by using repetition of certain lines or gestures throughout the retelling. Discuss the types of props they can use, such as hats, shawls, or puppets. Limit students to two to three props or costume items.

How to Use the STORYTELLING Rubric at the Middle School Level

STORYTELLING

Task: Student will tell a fictional story using props and/or costumes.

Goal/Standard: Performance meets stated criteria

Giving 0 points is an option—no evidence, no credit.

Criteria	1	2	3	4	Total Points
Selection	Appropriate for audience, but too long	Appropriate for audience in content and length	Encourages audience interaction with storyteller	Engages and pleases audience	____ x 5 = ____ points
Sequence	1–2 omissions and reversals in retelling	No omissions or reversals in retelling	Emphasizes major story events	Uses predicting to involve audience in retelling	____ x 5 = ____ points
Vocal Delivery	Adequate tone and pace	Good, even tone and pace	Uses appropriate vocal inflection	Creates unique voices for story characters and narrator	____ x 5 = ____ points
Props or Costumes	Present, but do not enhance story	Neat and appropriate	Enhance retelling	Immerse storyteller and audience in story events	____ x 5 = ____ points

74–80 = A	62–69 = C
70–73 = B	56–61 = D
	<56 = F

Total score ____/80 = ____

Assess Student Understanding

Selection
- engages and pleases audience

Sequence
- uses prediction questions to involve audience in retelling

Vocal Delivery
- creates unique, distinct voices for story characters and narrator

Props or Costumes
- uses props or costumes that immerse storyteller and audience in story events

Because you will conduct the assessment during the retelling, keep the rubric at hand during that time. Join other audience members in the story circle because, unlike reading aloud, storytellers use their voices as a tool in the retelling and may choose to use a soft voice at times to heighten suspense in a particular part of the story. Know the story beforehand. If you permit students to tell an original story, keep a hard copy available to check for omissions or reversals in the sequence. Any story that is of interest to the specific age group is appropriate. For example, many middle school storytellers find behind-the-scene stories from historical events, such as what happened before or after Paul Revere's famous ride, fun to share. Students at this level are capable of creating distinct voices for story characters in addition to their narration voice. Observe how the storyteller involves the audience. Look for techniques such as use of prediction questions. Props and costumes should enhance not detract from the retelling.

How to Use the
STORYTELLING Rubric
at the High School Level

Introduce the Rubric

Distribute and discuss the rubric with students before they begin the activity. Focus attention on the column containing the highest level of performance, reminding students that to receive full credit, they must achieve these objectives. Students at this level are capable of extending the storytelling experience beyond language arts into content area subjects, such as science or social studies. In these cases, students might assume the identity of a person who lived in another time to tell the story of a famous person. For example, a student storyteller might assume the fictitious identify of one of Ben Franklin's neighbors to tell about all the "crazy experiments" that interested young Ben in his early years. Distinct voices for story characters as well as props and costumes are particularly helpful with this sort of retelling, but students should use them sparingly so they do not detract from the impact of the storyteller's voice and gestures.

Make the Assignment

Students at this level are capable of telling stories containing multiple characters. They can retell a popular children's story or compose a tale of their own. If they choose the latter option, make sure they supply you with a hard copy of the story so you can determine whether any omissions or reversals occur in the retelling. Set time guidelines (10 to 15 minutes) to help storytellers focus on telling only the story and avoid asides that may detract from the tale. Instruct students to involve the audience in the retelling through such devices as guessing or predicting what will happen next as well as by using vocal inflection to heighten drama as the story nears its climax. A softer or tenser voice indicates significant change ahead for listeners. Discuss the types of props they can use, such as hats, shawls, or puppets. Limit students to four to five props or costume items. Instruct students to choose an article of clothing or personal effect that will represent the character in the minds of audience members. For example, a student might portray a pure, innocent character with an article of white or pastel clothing, such as a scarf, while conveying a sinister character by using a cape to obscure facial features.

STORYTELLING

Task: Student will relate a historical event using props and/or costumes.

Goal/Standard: Performance meets stated criteria

Giving 0 points is an option—no evidence, no credit.

Criteria	1	2	3	4	Total Points
Selection	Appropriate for intended audience	Encourages audience interaction	Connects with previous experiences of audience	Engages and delights audience	___ x 5 = ___ points
Sequence	No omissions or reversals in retelling	Emphasizes major story events	Uses predicting to involve audience in retelling	Engages audience interest with a dramatic build up to climax	___ x 5 = ___ points
Vocal Delivery	Good tone and pace	Uses appropriate vocal inflection	Rhythmic flow of voice engages audience	Creates unique voices for story characters and narrator	___ x 5 = ___ points
Props or Costumes	Neat and appropriate	Enhance retelling	Immerse storyteller and audience in story events	Story and storyteller become one	___ x 5 = ___ points

74–80 = A 62–69 = C
70–73 = B 56–61 = D
          <56 = F

Total score ___/80 = ___

Assess Student Understanding

Selection
- engages and delights audience

Sequence
- engages audience interest with dramatic tension building to story climax

Vocal Delivery
- creates unique, distinct voices for story characters and narrator

Props or Costumes
- uses props and costumes that allow story and storyteller to become one

Because you will conduct the assessment during the retelling, keep the rubric at hand during that time. Join other audience members in the story circle because, unlike reading aloud, storytellers use their voice as a tool in the retelling and may choose to use a soft voice at times to heighten suspense in a particular part of the story. Know the story beforehand. If you permit students to tell an original story, keep a hard copy available to check for omissions or reversals in the sequence. Any story that is of interest to the specific age group is appropriate. For example, high school storytellers might capture the attention of classmates with an urban myth. Students at this level are capable of creating distinct voices for story characters in addition to their narration voice. Observe how the storyteller involves the audience. Look for techniques such as use of prediction questions, where the storyteller asks audience members, "Then what do you suppose happened?" Storytellers should also use the tone and volume of their voice to set the stage for a dramatic story climax. Students should use props and costumes in a manner that blurs the line between story and storyteller and allows the audience to become totally immersed in the experience.

How to Use the
DRAMATIC PRESENTATION Rubric
at the Primary Level

Introduce the Rubric

Distribute and discuss the rubric with students before they begin the activity. Focus attention on the column containing the highest level of performance, reminding students that to receive full credit, they must achieve those objectives. Review the criteria for dramatic performance, including use of voice and gestures to create a memorable character, making sure students understand the difference between this type of exercise and other oral presentations such as show and tell or an oral report.

Make the Assignment

Students at this level are capable of memorizing a small amount of dialogue (fewer than ten lines) in preparation for their appearance in a dramatic presentation. The play can be teacher-composed or a published play suitable for the grade level. (Suitable published plays are available in libraries or through children's magazines.) Students can work together as a group on a play. For example, one of the students might take the role of a high school graduate who does not know what career to follow. One by one, the other students in the class tell their classmate, the high school student, about their chosen profession. Each character may have only a few lines, but the entire play might take about 15 to 20 minutes because the entire class participates.

Before the dramatic performance activity, make sure students know their lines well so they focus on effective delivery and do not simply recite the dialogue. While most students at this level do not possess the ability to display a wide range of emotions in the context of a dramatic presentation, they are able to "act" happy or sad based on the nature of their character's situation. Ask students what they do when they are happy or sad or frightened or embarrassed and have them show you by using their hands, arms, and face. If they will perform the play before an audience beyond their classmates, provide time for students to prepare their lines and practice delivery, preferably in a room comparable with the one housing the actual performance. As the class makes preparations for the play, hold a group discussion about the type of props and costumes that would work with each character. Solicit help from parents or friends in acquiring the props necessary for the play.

DRAMATIC PRESENTATION

Task: Student will participate in a dramatic presentation.

Goal/Standard: Performance meets stated criteria

Criteria	0	1	2	Total Points
Vocal Delivery	Forgets lines; inaudible tone	Lacks expression; barely audible tone	Appropriate tone and pace for character	_____ x 4 = _____ points
Gestures and Movements	None	Stilted and unnatural	Appropriate for character	_____ x 3 = _____ points
Props or Costumes	None	Present but not related to story	Present and relevant to story	_____ x 3 = _____ points

19–20 = A   16–17 = C
18 = B   14–15 = D
<14 = F

Total score _____/20 = _____

Assess Student Understanding

Vocal Delivery

- uses tone and pace appropriate for character

Gestures and Movements

- uses gestures and movements appropriate for character

Props or Costumes

- uses props or costumes appropriate to the story and character

Because the assessment will take place during the dramatic presentation, keep the rubric at hand during that time. Students should speak in a clear voice so audience members can hear them, pacing their lines so they convey the intended emotion. Observe how students use hand and facial gestures as well as how they move about the performance area. Note whether these gestures and movements are consistent with the character. For example, if the character is supposed to be happy or sad, gestures and movements should convey the appropriate emotion. Note whether costumes or any props the student uses are consistent with the character and do not distract the audience from the performer's words or actions.

DRAMATIC PRESENTATION Rubric

at the Intermediate Level

Introduce the Rubric

Distribute and discuss the rubric with students before they begin the activity. Focus attention on the column containing the highest level of performance, reminding students that to receive full credit, they must achieve those objectives. Review the criteria for dramatic performance, including use of voice and gestures to create a memorable character, making sure students understand the difference between this type of exercise and other oral presentations such as show and tell or an oral report.

Make the Assignment

Students at this level are capable of memorizing a moderate amount of dialogue (ten to twenty lines) in preparation for their appearance in a dramatic presentation. The play can be teacher-composed or a published play suitable for the grade level. (Suitable published plays are available in libraries or through children's magazines.) Students can work together as a group on a play.

Before the oral performance activity, make sure students know their lines well so they focus on effective delivery and do not simply recite the dialogue. While some students at this level do not possess the ability to display a wide range of emotions in the context of a dramatic presentation, most students are able to "act" happy or sad based on the nature of their character's situation. (You may want to prompt them by asking them what they do when they feel happy or sad or embarrassed or surprised.) In the area of props and costumes, talk to students about the character and what he or she might do with a particular article of clothing. A shady person might try to use a cape to obscure his facial features, while a proud person might continually fluff her dress to make it look more pleasing. If they are to perform before an audience beyond their classmates, provide time for students to prepare their lines and practice delivery, preferably in a room comparable with the one housing the actual performance.

DRAMATIC PRESENTATION

Task: Student will participate in a dramatic presentation.

Goal/Standard: Performance meets stated criteria

Giving 0 points is an option—no evidence, no credit.

Criteria	1	2	3	4	Total Points
Vocal Delivery	Forgets lines or lacks expression	Adequate tone and pace	Appropriate tone and pace for character	Engages audience attention	____ x 4 = ____ points
Gestures and Movements	Stilted or unnatural (overdone)	Adequate gestures and movement	Appropriate for character	Enhance verbal delivery	____ x 3 = ____ points
Props or Costumes	Present but not related to story or sloppy	Present and relevant to story	Neat, clever, and relevant to story	Provide information about character	____ x 3 = ____ points

37–40 = A   31–34 = C
35–36 = B   28–30 = D
          <28 = F

Total score ____ /40 = ____

Assess Student Understanding

Vocal Delivery
- uses tone and pace that engage audience attention

Gestures and Movements
- uses gestures and movements that enhance verbal delivery

Props or Costumes
- uses props and costumes that provide information about the character

Because the assessment will take place during the dramatic presentation, keep the rubric at hand during that time. Students should speak clearly so audience members can hear them, pacing their lines so they convey the intended emotion. Observe how students use hand and facial gestures as well as how they move about the performance area, and determine whether these gestures and movements are consistent with the character. Note whether the costumes or any props students use are consistent with the character. These visual aids should offer additional information about the character, such as a bold-colored scarf or hat to identify the character as an outgoing person, but they should not distract the audience from the performer's words or actions.

How to Use the
DRAMATIC PRESENTATION Rubric
at the Middle School Level

Introduce the Rubric

Distribute and discuss the rubric with students before they begin the activity. Focus attention on the column containing the highest level of performance, reminding students that to receive full credit, they must achieve those objectives. Review the criteria for dramatic performance, including use of voice and gestures to create a memorable character, making sure students understand the difference between this type of exercise and other oral presentations such as a debate or an oral report.

Make the Assignment

Students at this level are capable of memorizing a significant amount of dialogue (thirty to fifty lines) in preparation for their appearance in a dramatic presentation. Middle school students can compose and present short plays working in groups of four to seven students. Give students a topic, such as friendship, new beginnings, or bullying, and allow them the freedom to construct the play, each group creating a vignette based on this topic that all the groups can then compile into a single performance.

Before the oral performance activity, make sure students know their lines well so they focus on effective delivery and do not simply recite the dialogue. Students at this level possess the ability to display a wide range of emotions in the context of a dramatic presentation based on the nature of their character's situation. Remind students that dramatic interpretation differs from reading a story aloud and their voices are among their strongest tools for conveying the personality and plight of the character to audience members. Encourage students to offer input into the type of costumes and props that will help bring their characters to life. For example, students may wish to portray an eccentric character by wearing outdated clothes or unexpected combinations of current clothing trends. If they are to perform the play before an audience beyond their classmates, provide time for students to prepare their lines and practice delivery, preferably in a room comparable with the one housing the actual performance.

How to Use the DRAMATIC PRESENTATION Rubric at the Middle School Level

DRAMATIC PRESENTATION

Task: Student will participate in a dramatic presentation.

Goal/Standard: Performance meets stated criteria

Giving 0 points is an option—no evidence, no credit.

Criteria	1	2	3	4	Total Points
Vocal Delivery	Adequate tone and pace	Appropriate for tone and pace for character	Engages audience attention	Superior quality	____ x 4 = ____ points
Gestures and Movements	Adequate	Appropriate for character	Enhance verbal delivery	Bring character to life	____ x 3 = ____ points
Props or Costumes	Present and relevant to story	Neat, clever, and relevant to story	Provide information about character	Help audience become involved in story	____ x 3 = ____ points

37–40 = A 31–34 = C
35–36 = B 28–30 = D
        <28 = F

Total score ____/40 = ____

Assess Student Understanding

Vocal Delivery

- has superior quality vocal delivery

Gestures and Movements

- uses gestures and movements that bring the character to life

Props or Costumes

- uses props and costumes that help the audience become involved in the story

Because you will conduct the assessment during the dramatic performance, keep the rubric at hand during that time. Students at this level are capable of turning in a high quality performance demonstrating a range of emotions that extend beyond happy and sad. While you may have suggested some of the facial gestures and body movements, students at this level often add subtle gestures of their own. For example, students playing characters who are disgusted with events going on around them may add a gesture of exasperation, such as rolling their eyes or exhaling loudly to underscore character feelings. Observe how students use costumes and props to draw audience members into the story.

How to Use the
DRAMATIC PRESENTATION Rubric
at the High School Level

Introduce the Rubric

Distribute and discuss the rubric with students before they begin the activity. Focus attention on the column containing the highest level of performance, reminding students that to receive full credit, they must achieve those objectives. Review the criteria for dramatic performance, including use of voice and gestures to create a memorable character, making sure students understand the difference between this type of exercise and other oral presentations.

Make the Assignment

Students at this level are capable of memorizing a significant amount of dialogue (fifty to eighty lines) in preparation for their appearance in a dramatic presentation. High school students can compose and present short plays working in groups of four to seven students. Give students a topic, such as friendship, new beginnings, or bullying, and allow them the freedom to construct the play, each group creating a vignette based on this topic that all the groups can then compile into a single performance.

Before the oral performance activity, make sure students know their lines well so they focus on effective delivery and do not simply recite the dialogue. Students at this level possess the ability to display a wide range of emotions in the context of a dramatic presentation based on the nature of their character's situation. For example, students playing characters unhappy about their lot in life should add subtle touches to underscore these feelings, such as slumped shoulders or a distracted manner when talking with others. Remind students that dramatic interpretation differs from reading a story aloud and their voices are among their strongest tools for conveying the personality and plight of the character to audience members. Encourage students to offer input into the type of costumes and props that will help bring their characters to life. For example, students may wish to portray an eccentric character by wearing outdated clothes or unexpected combinations of current clothing trends. If they are to perform the play before an audience beyond their classmates, provide time for students to prepare their lines and practice delivery, preferably in a room comparable with the one housing the actual performance.

DRAMATIC PRESENTATION

Task: Student will participate in a dramatic presentation.

Goal/Standard: Performance meets stated criteria

Giving 0 points is an option—no evidence, no credit.

Criteria	1	2	3	4	Total Points
Vocal Delivery	Even tone and pace	Appropriate tone and pace for character	Engages audience attention	Superior quality	____ x 4 = ____ points
Gestures and Movements	Appropriate for character	Enhance vocal delivery	Bring character to life	Student becomes the character	____ x 3 = ____ points
Props or Costumes	Neat, clever, and relevant to story	Provide information about character	Help audience get involved in story	Create a stunning visual image of character	____ x 3 = ____ points

37–40 = A   31–34 = C
35–36 = B   28–30 = D
        <28 = F

Total score ____/40 = ____

Chapter 6 • Assessment Rubrics and Oral Language

Assess Student Understanding

Vocal Delivery

- has superior quality vocal delivery

Gestures and Movements

- uses gestures and movements to become the character

Props or Costumes

- uses props and costumes that create a stunning visual image of the character

Because you will conduct the assessment during the dramatic performance, keep the rubric at hand during that time. Students at this level are capable of turning in a high quality performance that demonstrates a range of emotions. While you may suggest some of the facial gestures and body movements, students at this level often add subtle gestures based on what characters say at the time. Observe how students use costumes and props to draw audience members into the story.

How to Use the
DISCUSSION Rubric
at the Primary Level

Introduce the Rubric

Distribute and discuss the rubric with students before they begin the activity. Focus attention on the column containing the highest level of performance, reminding students that to receive full credit, they must achieve those objectives. While a discussion is less formal than a debate or dramatic presentation, students must understand that guidelines exist for taking part in a discussion, and these guidelines, contained in the rubric, are the basis for the assessment of their performance.

Make the Assignment

Discussion groups should consist of four to five students. Larger groups invite domination by an outgoing member, and smaller groups often fail to generate enough diversity in opinions among group members. Set a time limit (5 to 8 minutes) and provide students with a topic that is familiar to all group members. This step is important because group members not familiar with the topic are less likely to participate. Discussion groups at the primary level may need a few questions to stimulate the discussion. Provide those questions at the onset of the discussion. For example, if the student discussion concerns a favorite holiday, the discussion could begin with members stating their favorite holiday and why they feel that way. Early in the year, students may require more teacher involvement in the form of open-ended questions, but as they progress and gain a greater understanding of the give and take of discussion, they will need less teacher direction.

Assess Student Understanding

Behavior
- waits for appropriate time to begin speaking

Content
- stays focused on topic

Because you will conduct the assessment during the discussion, keep the rubric at hand during that time. Take note of students who continually interrupt other speakers or attempt to dominate the discussion. Listen to students' comments, noting whether they relate to the topic or whether their verbal excursions are irrelevant to the discussion.

How to Use the DISCUSSION Rubric at the Primary Level

SPEAKING

DISCUSSION

PRIMARY

Task: Student will participate in a group discussion.

Goal/Standard: Participation meets stated criteria

Criteria	0	1	2	Total Points
Behavior	Interrupts others	Fails to make contributions	Waits for appropriate time before speaking	____ x 5 = ____ points
Content	No topic-related comments	Drifts from topic	Stays focused on topic	____ x 5 = ____ points

19–20 = A
18= B
16-17 = C
14–15 = D
<14 = F

Total score ____/20 = ____

SkyLight Professional Development

How to Use the
DISCUSSION Rubric
at the Intermediate Level

Introduce the Rubric

Distribute and discuss the rubric with students before they begin the activity. Focus attention on the column containing the highest level of performance, reminding students that to receive full credit, they must achieve those objectives. While a discussion is less formal than a debate or dramatic presentation, it is important for students to understand that guidelines exist for taking part in a discussion, and these guidelines, contained in the rubric, are the basis for assessment of their performance.

Make the Assignment

Discussion groups should consist of four to five students. Larger groups invite domination by an outgoing member, and smaller groups often fail to generate enough diversity in opinions among group members. Set a time limit (8 to 12 minutes) and provide students with a topic familiar to all group members. This step is important because group members not familiar with the topic are less likely to participate. Less seasoned discussion groups may need a few questions to stimulate the discussion. For example, if the student discussion concerns a current news event, opening questions could reflect on what group members think about the event as well as how it has affected their daily lives. Early in the year, students may require more teacher involvement in the form of open-ended questions, but as they progress and gain a greater understanding of the give and take of discussion, they will need less teacher direction.

Assess Student Understanding

Behavior
- encourages other group members to participate

Content
- uses information from discussion to draw conclusions about topic

Because you will conduct the assessment during the discussion, keep the rubric at hand during that time. Note how individual students interact with group members. Do one or two students attempt to dominate the discussion, or do group members encourage one another to participate? Do students simply discuss until the end of the time period, or do they draw some conclusions regarding their topic?

How to Use the DISCUSSION Rubric at the Intermediate Level

DISCUSSION

Task: Student will participate in a group discussion.

Goal/Standard: Participation meets stated criteria

Giving 0 points is an option—no evidence, no credit.

Criteria	1	2	3	4	Total Points
Behavior	Makes minimal contributions	Contributes, but tends to hog the floor	Waits for appropriate time before speaking	Encourages other group members to participate	_____ x 5 = _____ points
Content	Drifts from topic	Stays focused on topic, but speaks too long	Stays focused on topic; speaks briefly and succinctly	Uses information to draw conclusions about topic	_____ x 5 = _____ points

37–40 = A 31–34 = C
35–36 = B 28–30 = D
          <28 = F

Total score _____/40 = _____

How to Use the
DISCUSSION Rubric
at the Middle School Level

Introduce the Rubric

Distribute and discuss the rubric with students before they begin the activity. Focus attention on the column containing the highest level of performance, reminding students that to receive full credit, they must achieve those objectives. While a discussion is less formal than a debate or dramatic presentation, it is important for students to understand that guidelines exist for taking part in a discussion, and these guidelines, contained in the rubric, are the basis for assessment of their performance.

Make the Assignment

Discussion groups should consist of four to five students. Larger groups invite domination by an outgoing member, and smaller groups often fail to generate enough diversity in opinions among group members. Set a time limit (12 to 20 minutes) and provide students with a topic familiar to all group members. This step is important because group members not familiar with the topic are less likely to participate. You might stimulate discussion with a question. Students at this level have participated in a number of class discussions, but they should understand that a small-group discussion requires them to participate more openly and contribute to any conclusions the group draws about the topic. Limit your involvement to keeping groups focused on the topic or noting if any one individual holds the floor for a disproportionate amount of time.

Assess Student Understanding

Behavior
■ demonstrates leadership qualities

Content
■ shares a wealth of prior knowledge on the topic

Because you will conduct the assessment during the discussion, keep the rubric at hand during that time. While one student may emerge as the group's leader, it is possible for more than one student to demonstrate leadership qualities, such as encouraging other members to participate and setting an appropriate tone and pace for the discussion. Note which students are able to support their comments and which students simply offer their unsubstantiated opinion.

How to Use the DISCUSSION Rubric at the Middle School Level

DISCUSSION

Task: Student will participate in a group discussion.

Goal/Standard: Participation meets stated criteria

Giving 0 points is an option—no evidence, no credit.

Criteria	1	2	3	4	Total Points
Behavior	Contributes, but tends to dominate floor	Waits for appropriate time before speaking	Encourages other group members to participate	Demonstrates leadership qualities	_____ x 5 = _____ points
Content	Stays focused on topic, but speaks too long	Stays focused on topic; speaks briefly and succinctly	Uses information to draw conclusions about topic	Shares a wealth of prior knowledge of topic	_____ x 5 = _____ points

37–40 = A	31–34 = C
35–36 = B	28–30 = D
	<28 = F

Total score _____/40 = _____

How to Use the
DISCUSSION Rubric
at the High School Level

Introduce the Rubric

Distribute and discuss the rubric with students before they begin the activity. Focus attention on the column containing the highest level of performance, reminding students that to receive full credit, they must achieve those objectives. While a discussion is less formal than a debate or dramatic presentation, it is important for students to understand that guidelines exist for taking part in a discussion, and these guidelines, contained in the rubric, are the basis for assessment of their performance.

Make the Assignment

Discussion groups should consist of four to five students. Larger groups invite domination by an outgoing member, and smaller groups often fail to generate enough diversity in opinions. Set a time limit (20 to 30 minutes) and provide students with a topic familiar to all group members. Stimulate discussion with a question that asks students to draw conclusions about the topic. Students at this level have participated in a number of class discussions, but they should understand that a small-group discussion requires them to participate more openly as well as listen and respect the opinions of other group members. Students at this level need very little teacher intervention. Move among the groups, helping students remain focused on the topic and watching for individuals monopolizing the discussion.

Assess Student Understanding

Behavior
- sets positive tone and pace for the discussion

Content
- introduces unexplored point or perspective about topic

Because you will conduct the assessment during the discussion, keep the rubric at hand during that time. Note how students use their speaking time. Do they set a positive tone by referring to the ideas and opinions of others in a way that encourages more participation? Note how long students spend explaining their ideas and opinions. Observe the type of information students share. Is the knowledge familiar to group members, or do students bring new perspectives on the topic to the discussion?

How to Use the DISCUSSION Rubric at the High School Level

DISCUSSION

Task: Student will participate in a group discussion.

Goal/Standard: Participation meets stated criteria

Giving 0 points is an option—no evidence, no credit.

Criteria	1	2	3	4	Total Points
Behavior	Waits for appropriate time before speaking	Encourages other group members to participate	Demonstrates leadership qualities	Sets positive tone and pace for discussion	____ x 5 = ____ points
Content	Stays focused on topic; speaks briefly and succinctly	Uses information to draw conclusions about topic	Shares a wealth of prior knowledge about topic	Introduces unexplored point or perspective about topic	____ x 5 = ____ points

37–40 = A   31–34 = C
35–36 = B   28–30 = D
          <28 = F

Total score ____/40 = ____

Rubrics and the Research Process

While explaining a long-term research project to his seventh-graders, Peter discovers that a significant number of students lack basic knowledge regarding how to use reference materials and other research tools, such as interviewing or field experiences. Realizing that this deficit would translate into low quality written reports, Peter opts to shelve the research project until he can remedy the situation. Before teaching a mini-unit on using research tools, Peter prepares assessment rubrics for each tool, listing the skills students should possess to use that tool effectively. Creating a rubric before teaching a unit of study offers Peter a chance to reflect on what he wants his students to learn. Sharing these rubrics with the students at the beginning of the unit helps them identify critical skills necessary for conducting research.

INVESTIGATE THE POSSIBILITIES

Each year, as they attempt to prepare their students for upper grades, intermediate and middle school teachers share Peter's discovery that students lack research skills. Knowing how to use research tools effectively is an invaluable skill because it allows student authors to build on their experiences and observations by using the existing body of knowledge on a specific topic. For example, with the topic *wildflowers,* student authors unfamiliar with research tools are limited to their own knowledge about the topic. By using research tools, including a dictionary and an encyclopedia, student authors can gather and include information in their reports about how these natural beauties touch our lives, healing us, feeding us, and creating a more balanced ecosystem. Understanding where to find information and how to incorporate it into oral or written reports represent solid first steps in the development of effective research skills.

Although the World Wide Web is an innovative avenue for conducting research, basic reference materials, such as the dictionary, encyclopedia, or atlas, remain essential tools students use to compile meaningful research projects.

RESEARCH RUBRICS

The rubrics in this chapter cover the following areas related to good research skills: Reference Materials, First-Hand Experiences, Written Report, and Collaboration. The reference rubrics list required elements in the first column, and teachers note whether a certain behavior is present or absent, while the remaining rubrics in the chapter list full-credit responses to provide teachers with specific examples of what they may see in student work. A summary of the expectations for the age and grade level follows. In cases when students in more than one age- or grade-level group should have all the skills described, the rubric and assessment guidelines have been combined. In the case of areas not suitable for primary grades, no rubric appears at that level.

Reference Materials: Tools of the Trade

These rubrics assess students' use of reference materials. The goal, or highest degree of accomplishment on the rubric, for each grade level follows:

Primary—student uses dictionary and encyclopedia guide words to locate words and topics independently and uses an atlas to locate states and countries, capitals, and major cities independently.

Intermediate—student does all the above plus understands dictionary abbreviations (for noun, adjective, preposition, etc.), uses a compass rose and map key in an atlas, and distinguishes between major and minor details in encyclopedia entries.

Middle School—student does all the above plus chooses appropriate definition from a dictionary entry with multiple definitions, translates information from an atlas map to a globe, and paraphrases an encyclopedia entry.

High School—student does all the above plus adds suffixes accurately, understands significance of latitude and longitude, and identifies additional encyclopedia entries related to topic.

First-Hand Experiences: Let's Make Contact

These rubrics assess students' participation in three information-gathering experiences—a field trip, an interview, and an experiment. The goal, or highest degree of accomplishment on the rubric, for each grade level follows:

Primary—student records observations during a field trip, asks an interview subject three to five relevant questions, and participates in an experiment or field trial.

Intermediate—student uses observations and notes from a field trip to formulate questions, uses an interview subject's responses to formulate new questions, and conducts an experiment or field trial.

Middle School—student uses observations and notes from a field trip to draw conclusions about a topic, confirms credibility of an interview subject through available knowledge on the topic, and initiates a question and answer session before and after conducting an experiment or field trial.

High School—student uses observations and notes to form generalizations about a topic, contrasts an interview subject's information with other experts to confirm credibility, and constructs an overview of an experiment or field trial, including predicted outcome of experience.

Written Report: The "Write" Stuff

These rubrics assess students' ability to produce a written research project. The goal, or highest degree of accomplishment on the rubric, for each grade level follows:

Intermediate—student responds adequately to topic question, demonstrates grasp of topic's concepts, presents accurate information and proof of accuracy, and prepares an accurate and mostly current bibliography.

Middle School—student addresses topic question creatively, uses appropriate quotes to reinforce concepts presented, documents accuracy of information and quotations, and prepares accurate bibliography from a variety of sources.

High School—student employs a text structure that enhances presentation of the topic, uses appropriate quotes to reinforce concepts presented, documents accuracy of information and quotations, and prepares accurate multimedia bibliography.

Collaboration: Let's Get Together

These rubrics assess students' ability to participate in a collaborative research project. The guidelines for assessment are the same at all levels because the instructions for group work—wait your turn before speaking, hear and respect the opinions of others, complete the tasks assigned to you in the group, and work as a unit to complete the project—are the same no matter what the student age or grade. The goal, or highest degree of accomplishment on the rubric, for each grade level follows:

Primary—student shares information with most group members, makes occasional eye contact with speakers, asks relevant questions, exhibits positive gestures and facial expressions, and distributes tasks for projects evenly.

Intermediate/Middle School—student shares information with all group members, makes full eye contact with speakers, asks relevant, open-ended questions, makes encouraging gestures and facial expressions, and distributes tasks logically based on level of difficulty.

High School—student shares information, including source, with all group members, models active listening behaviors for other group members, makes encouraging gestures and facial expressions, and distributes tasks logically based on interrelatedness of subtopics.

How to Use the
REFERENCE MATERIALS Rubric
at the Primary Level

Introduce the Rubric

Distribute and discuss the rubric with students before they begin the assignment, focusing attention on the column containing the highest level of performance. Remind students that to receive full credit they must achieve these objectives. Because this rubric contains a wide variety of skills, teachers may prefer to conduct a series of activities that specifically test student proficiency with reference materials rather than simply observing their use of the materials to complete another assignment.

Make the Assignment

Dictionary: provide students with a set of guide words from the top of a page spread in the dictionary such as *scene* and *seat,* and tell them to list ten words one can find between those guide words. Next, provide students with a list of five to eight words, instructing them to locate those words in the dictionary within 6 to 10 minutes.

Atlas: provide students with their own copy of a map and a list of five to eight locations, such as specific states or countries. Number the locations students must identify, and instruct them to circle the state or country and write the correct number within the circle. For example, if the third state on the student list is *Wyoming,* students should be able to circle the state of Wyoming and write a number *3* within that circle. Discuss the use of a map key to denote capital and major cities with students. They should be able to distinguish between the symbols representing both types of cities. Next, instruct students to return to their maps and underline the capital city of each circled state or country, then draw a box around two major cities within that state or country.

Encyclopedia: provide students with a set of guide words from the encyclopedia, instructing them to list four topics that appear between those guide words. Next, provide students with a list of four topics, instructing them to identify the letter and number of the volume where each topic appears, then the page number(s) and guide words for the actual location of the topic.

How to Use the REFERENCE MATERIALS Rubric at the Primary Level

REFERENCE MATERIALS

Task: Student will use reference materials to complete assignments.

Goal/Standard: Participation meets stated criteria

Criteria	0	1	2	Total Points
Dictionary • uses guide words • locates words independently	0 elements present	1 element present	2 elements present	____ x 3 = ____ points
Atlas • locates states or countries • locates capitals and major cities	0 elements present	1 element present	2 elements present	____ x 3 = ____ points
Encyclopedia • uses guide words • locates topics independently	0 elements present	1 element present	2 elements present	____ x 4 = ____ points

19–20 = A   16–17 = C
18 = B   14–15 = D
<14 = F

Total score ____/20 = ____

Assess Student Understanding

Dictionary

- uses guide words
- locates words independently

Have students use the dictionary to check the list of words they created from the guide words you supplied. Errors may be the result of students misspelling the words on their list. On the timed portion of the activity, reduce the number of words for those students unable to locate every word on the list, gradually working back to the desired number of words within the specified time frame. Dropping back temporarily on the number of words allows students to build up some expertise and experience some success while they gradually work back up to the requirements of the original assignment.

Atlas

- locates states or countries
- locates capitals and major cities

Check student maps for accurate responses, reviewing with students the symbols for capital and major cities when necessary. Point out errors and provide time for students to correct their errors until they have 100 percent accuracy.

Encyclopedia

- uses guide words
- locates topics independently

Provide students with the appropriate encyclopedia volume, instructing them to check their answers. Give credit for a topic that would appear within the guide words but is not contained in the encyclopedia. For example, if a student states that the topic shoes appears between encyclopedia guide words shark and skiing, but the encyclopedia refers users to footwear, the student has still demonstrated the ability to specify topics one might find between those guide words. Next, provide students access to a full set of encyclopedias to check their responses to the second activity. A complete response gives the volume number in which the information appears as well as the page number(s) and guide words where the topic appears.

How to Use the
REFERENCE MATERIALS Rubric
at the Intermediate Level

Introduce the Rubric

Distribute and discuss the rubric with students before they begin the assignment, focusing attention on the column containing the highest level of performance. Remind students that to receive full credit, they must achieve these objectives. Because this rubric contains a wide variety of skills, teachers may prefer to conduct a series of activities that specifically test student proficiency with reference materials rather than simply observing their use of the materials to complete another assignment.

Make the Assignment

Dictionary: provide students with a set of guide words from the top of a page spread in the dictionary such as *scene* and *seat,* and tell them to list ten words one can find between those guide words. Next, provide students with a list of eight to fifteen words, instructing them to locate those words in the dictionary within 5 to 8 minutes. Finally, make a list of common dictionary abbreviations, instructing students to list the complete term. For example, students should be able to convert */adj/* to *adjective.*

Atlas: provide students with their own copy of a map and a list of five to eight locations, such as specific states or countries. Number the locations students must identify and instruct them to circle the state or country and write the correct number within the circle. For example, if the third state on the student list is *Ohio,* students should be able to circle the state of Ohio and write a number *3* within that circle. Discuss the use of a map key to denote capital and major cities with students. They should be able to distinguish between the symbols representing both types of cities. Next, instruct students to return to their maps and underline the capital city of each circled state or country, then draw a box around two major cities within that state or country. Finally, provide students with a list of state or country names, instructing them to use the compass rose to identify the states or countries that are north, south, east, and west of each state or country on the list.

Encyclopedia: provide students with a set of guide words from the encyclopedia, instructing them to list four topics one might find between those guide words. Next, provide students with a list of four topics, instructing them to identify the letter and number of the volume where that topic appears, then give the page number(s) and guide words of the actual location of the topic. Finally, ask students to explain, in their own words, how they can tell the difference between a major topic and a supporting detail in an encyclopedia entry.

REFERENCE MATERIALS

Task: Student will use reference materials to complete assignments.
Goal/Standard: Participation meets stated criteria

Giving 0 points is an option—no evidence, no credit.

Criteria	1	2	3	4	Total Points
Dictionary • uses guide words • locates words independently • understands dictionary abbreviations	Evidence of 2+ incomplete elements	1 complete element present	2 complete elements present	3 complete elements present	____ x 3 = ____ points
Atlas • locates states or countries • locates capitals and major cities • uses compass rose and atlas map key	Evidence of 2+ incomplete elements	1 complete element present	2 complete elements present	3 complete elements present	____ x 3 = ____ points
Encyclopedia • uses guide words • locates topic independently • distinguishes between major and minor details in entry	Evidence of 2+ incomplete elements	1 complete element present	2 complete elements present	3 complete elements present	____ x 4 = ____ points

37–40 = A   31–34 = C
35–36 = B   28–30 = D
          <28 = F

Total score ____/40 = ____

Assess Student Understanding

Dictionary

- uses guide words
- locates words independently
- understands dictionary abbreviations

Have students check their list of words in the dictionary to determine how many of the words actually appear between the specified guide words. Errors may be the result of students misspelling the words. On the timed portion of the activity, reduce the number of words for those students unable to locate every word on the list, gradually working back to the desired number of words within the specified time frame. Finally, review student responses for converting dictionary abbreviations to their full-length form. Discuss incorrect responses with students, exploring the reason behind their choices.

Atlas

- locates states or countries
- locates capitals and major cities
- uses compass rose and atlas map key

Check student maps for accurate responses, reviewing the symbols for capital and major cities when necessary. Finally, examine student responses to the compass rose activity. Discuss incorrect responses with students, exploring the reason for their choices.

Encyclopedia

- uses guide words
- locates topic independently
- distinguishes between major and minor details in entry

Provide students with the appropriate encyclopedia volume, instructing them to check their answers. Give credit for a topic that would appear between the guide words but is not in the encyclopedia. For example, if a student states that one might find the topic *shoes* between encyclopedia guide words *shark* and *skiing,* but the encyclopedia refers users to *footwear,* the student has still demonstrated the ability to specify topics that might appear between those guide words. Next, provide students access to a full set of encyclopedias to check their responses to the second activity. A complete response includes the volume number in which the information appears as well as the page number(s) and guide words associated with that topic. Finally, examine student responses regarding distinguishing between a major topic and a supporting detail in encyclopedia entries. Correct responses may include reference to the type of print encyclopedias use such as **bold** for major topics and *italic* for subheadings and details.

How to Use the
REFERENCE MATERIALS Rubric
at the Middle School Level

Introduce the Rubric

Distribute and discuss the rubric with students before they begin the assignment, focusing attention on the column containing the highest level of performance. Remind students that to receive full credit, they must achieve these objectives. Because this rubric contains a wide variety of skills, teachers may prefer to conduct a series of activities that specifically test student proficiency with reference materials rather than simply observing their use of the materials to complete another assignment.

Make the Assignment

Dictionary: provide students with a list of eight to fifteen words, instructing them to locate those words in the dictionary within 5 to 8 minutes. Then make a list of common dictionary abbreviations, instructing students to list the complete term. For example, students should be able to convert /adj/ to adjective. Finally, select a word with multiple meanings and instruct students to use each of the meanings in a sentence, demonstrating the various uses for a single word. For example, the word chair can be a verb, as in to chair a meeting. It can also be a noun that identifies a piece of furniture or the person holding a senior position in an organization, as in the chair of a department.

Atlas: provide students with their own copy of a map and a list of five to eight locations, such as specific states or countries. Number the locations students must identify and instruct them to circle the state or country and write the correct number within the circle. For example, if the third state on the student list is Illinois, students should be able to circle the state of Illinois and write a number 3 within that circle. Discuss the use of a map key to denote capital and major cities. They should be able to distinguish between the symbols representing both types of cities. Next, instruct students to return to their maps and underline the capital city of each circled state or country, then draw a box around two major cities within that state or country. Then provide students with a list of state or country names, instructing them to use the compass rose to identify the states or countries that are north, south, east, and west of each state or country on the list. Finally, provide students with a world map and globe and the name of a place they must locate on the map and the globe.

Encyclopedia: provide students with a list of four topics, instructing them to identify the letter and number of the volume where that topic appears and give the page number(s) and guide words of the entry. Then ask students to explain, in their own words,

How to Use the REFERENCE MATERIALS Rubric at the Middle School Level

REFERENCE MATERIALS

Task: Student will use reference materials to complete assignments.

Goal/Standard: Participation meets stated criteria

Giving 0 points is an option—no evidence, no credit.

Criteria	1	2	3	4	Total Points
Dictionary • locates words independently • understands dictionary abbreviations • chooses appropriate definition from multiple meanings	Evidence of 2+ incomplete elements	1 complete element present	2 complete elements present	3 complete elements present	____ x 3 = ____ points
Atlas • locates capitals and major cities • uses compass rose and atlas map key • translates information from atlas map to globe	Evidence of 2+ incomplete elements	1 complete element present	2 complete elements present	3 complete elements present	____ x 3 = ____ points
Encyclopedia • locates topic independently • distinguishes between major idea and detail • paraphrases topic entry	Evidence of 2+ incomplete elements	1 complete element present	2 complete elements present	3 complete elements present	____ x 4 = ____ points

37–40 = A   31–34 = C
35–36 = B   28–30 = D
               <28 = F

Total score ____/40 = ____

how they can tell the difference between a major topic and a supporting detail in an encyclopedia entry. Finally, instruct students to paraphrase the encyclopedia information found about a particular topic. The topic may be one either you or the student chooses.

Assess Student Understanding

Dictionary

- locates words independently
- understands dictionary abbreviations
- chooses appropriate definition from multiple meanings

On the timed portion of the activity, reduce the number of words for those students unable to locate every word on the list, gradually working back to the desired number of words within the specified time frame. Next, review student responses for converting dictionary abbreviations to their original form. Discuss incorrect responses with students, exploring the reason behind their choice. Finally, review student sentences, requiring verbal explanations for incorrect responses.

Atlas

- locates capitals and major cities
- uses compass rose and atlas map key
- translates information from atlas map to globe

Check student maps for accurate responses, reviewing with students the symbols for capital and major cities when necessary. Then examine student responses to the compass rose activity. Discuss incorrect responses with students, exploring the reason for their choices. Finally, observe as students point out the location you gave them in the map and globe exercise.

Encyclopedia

- locates topic independently
- distinguishes between major idea and detail
- paraphrases topic entry

Provide students access to a full set of encyclopedias to check their responses to the first activity. A complete response includes the volume number in which the information appears as well as the page number(s) and guide words for the actual topic. Then examine student responses regarding distinguishing between a major topic and supporting detail in encyclopedia entries. Correct responses may include reference to the type of print (**bold** for major topics; *italic* for subheadings and details). Finally, review the student-authored passage, noting whether the student includes important information about the topic while limiting the number of supporting details.

How to Use the

REFERENCE MATERIALS Rubric

at the High School Level

Introduce the Rubric

Distribute and discuss the rubric with students before they begin the assignment, focusing attention on the column containing the highest level of performance. Remind students that to receive full credit, they must achieve these objectives. Because this rubric contains a wide variety of skills, teachers may prefer to conduct a series of activities that specifically test student proficiency with reference materials rather than simply observing their use of the materials to complete another assignment.

Make the Assignment

Dictionary: make a list of common dictionary abbreviations, instructing students to list the complete term. For example, students should be able to convert */adj/* to *adjective.* Then select a word with multiple meanings and instruct students to use each of the meanings in a sentence, demonstrating the various uses for a single word. For example, the word *chair* can be a verb, as in to chair a meeting. It can also be a noun that identifies a piece of furniture or the person holding a senior position in an organization, as in the chair of a department. Finally, review the definition of *suffix,* then provide students with a list of words, instructing them to add a suffix to each to create another word. Tell them to check their responses in the dictionary.

Atlas: provide students with a list of state or country names, instructing them to use the compass rose to identify the states or countries that are north, south, east, or west of each state or country on the list. Then provide students with a world map and globe and the name of a place they must locate on the map *and* the globe. Finally, instruct students to write a brief explanation of the terms *latitude* and *longitude* and describe their usage and purpose.

Encyclopedia: ask students to explain, in their own words, how they can tell the difference between a major topic and a supporting detail in an encyclopedia entry. Then instruct students to paraphrase the encyclopedia information found about a particular topic. The topic may be one you or the student chooses. Finally, instruct students to compile a list of other entries in the encyclopedia that might provide additional information about their topic. For example, they might find more information about the topic *pollution* under *environment* or *urban problems.*

REFERENCE MATERIALS

Task: Student will use reference materials to complete assignments.

Goal/Standard: Participation meets stated criteria

Giving 0 points is an option—no evidence, no credit.

Criteria	1	2	3	4	Total Points
Dictionary • understands dictionary abbreviations • chooses appropriate definition from multiple meanings • adds suffixes with 100% accuracy	Evidence of 2+ incomplete elements	1 complete element present	2 complete elements present	3 complete elements present	____ x 3 = ____ points
Atlas • uses compass rose and atlas map key • translates information from map to globe • understands significance of latitude and longitude	Evidence of 2+ incomplete elements	1 complete element present	2 complete elements present	3 complete elements present	____ x 3 = ____ points
Encyclopedia • distinguishes between major and minor details • paraphrases topic entry • identifies additional entries relevant to topic	Evidence of 2+ incomplete elements	1 complete element present	2 complete elements present	3 complete elements present	____ x 4 = ____ points

37–40 = A   31–34 = C
35–36 = B   28–30 = D
              <28 = F

Total score ____/40 = ____

Assess Student Understanding

Dictionary

- understands dictionary abbreviations
- chooses appropriate definition from multiple meanings
- adds suffixes with 100 percent accuracy

Review student responses for converting dictionary abbreviations to their original form. Discuss incorrect responses with students, exploring the reason behind their choices. Next, review student sentences, again requiring verbal explanations for incorrect responses. Finally, review the students' suffix word lists to make sure they have not invented any new words.

Atlas

- uses compass rose and atlas map key
- translates information from map to globe
- understands significance of latitude and longitude

Examine student responses to the compass rose activity. Discuss incorrect responses with students, exploring the reason for their choices. Next, observe as students point out the location you gave them in the map and globe exercise. Finally, review students' written statements about latitude and longitude, requesting verbal clarification for incorrect or vague responses that fail to address the question.

Encyclopedia

- distinguishes between major and minor details
- paraphrases topic entry
- identifies additional entries relevant to topic

Examine student responses regarding distinguishing between a major topic and supporting detail in encyclopedia entries. Correct responses may include reference to the type of print (**bold** for major topics; *italic* for subheadings and details). Next, review the student-authored passage, noting whether the student has included important information about the topic while keeping supporting details to a minimum. Finally, review the students' lists of entries related to the topic, requiring verbal or written clarification for incorrect or vague responses.

How to Use the
FIRST-HAND EXPERIENCE Rubric
at the Primary Level

Introduce the Rubric

Distribute and discuss the rubric with students before they begin the assignment. Focus attention on the column containing the highest level of performance, reminding students that to receive full credit, they must achieve these objectives. This rubric is well suited for a science unit. Because it deals with three different types of first-hand experience—Observation, Interview, and Participation—you need not complete the rubric at a single session but may use it to monitor student understanding over the duration of a unit of study that includes all three experiences. It is also beneficial to keep informal records during observation periods (such as field trips) that you can then transfer to the rubric at a more convenient time.

Make the Assignment

Observation: during a class field trip, instruct students to make written notes or sketches of what they experience. They will use this written record later for a response extension activity, such as compiling a list of attractions at a local planetarium.

Interview: instruct students to work in pairs developing three to five questions they can ask each other that will provide important information. Questions should require more than a yes or no response. Then have students interview each other.

Participation: instruct students working in pairs to participate in a field experience, such as a math measuring exercise or science experiment. Both members of the team should take an active role in the exercise.

How to Use the FIRST-HAND EXPERIENCE Rubric at the Primary Level

FIRST-HAND EXPERIENCE

Task: Student will participate in experiences (field trip, interview, experiment) to gather information.
Goal/Standard: Participation meets stated criteria

Criteria	0	1	2	Total Points
Observation (Field trip)	Fails to observe presentation	Observes presentation and takes notes	Uses notes as basis for creative response	____ x 3 = ____ points
Interview (Expert on subject)	Fails to conduct interview	Asks subject 3–5 random questions	Asks subject 3–5 pertinent questions	____ x 3 = ____ points
Participation (Experiment or field trial)	Fails to participate in experiment or field trial	Observes experiment or field trial	Participates in experiment or field trial	____ x 4 = ____ points

19–20 = A   16–17 = C
18 = B   14–15 = D
       <14 = F

Total score ____/20 = ____

Assess Student Understanding

Observation

■ uses notes as basis for creative response

Develop an activity that allows students to use the recorded notes, such as a brochure listing attractions at the field trip site. Review the list for accuracy.

Interview

■ develops and asks three to five pertinent questions

Students should be able to produce some evidence of the interview subject's responses, either a written or verbal account. Review the questions and responses, noting whether each question required more than a yes or no answer and whether the questions sought information that revealed more about the person than his or her favorite color or TV show.

Participation

■ participates in an experiment or field trial

Because you will conduct this assessment during the experiment or field trial, keep the rubric at hand during those times. Note student cooperation and active participation in the experiment.

How to Use the
FIRST-HAND EXPERIENCE Rubric
at the Intermediate Level

Introduce the Rubric

Distribute and discuss the rubric with students before they begin the assignment. Focus attention on the column containing the highest level of performance, reminding students that to receive full credit, they must achieve these objectives. This rubric is well suited for a science unit. Because it deals with three different types of first-hand experience—Observation, Interview, and Participation—you need not complete the rubric at a single session but may use it to monitor student understanding over the duration of a unit of study that includes all three experiences. It is also beneficial to keep informal records during observation periods (such as field trips) that you can then transfer to the rubric at a more convenient time.

Make the Assignment

Observation: instruct students to make notes and sketches during a field trip, then to use those tools to develop three to four questions relating to the experience.

Interview: instruct students to develop three to four open-ended (requiring more than a yes or no response) questions before conducting an interview with an adult relative. Then have them use the interview subject's responses to develop three additional questions that occurred to them during the interview.

Participation: instruct students to select an experiment in a content area subject to conduct for the class or for a small group of classmates.

FIRST-HAND EXPERIENCE

Task: Student will participate in experiences (field trip, interview, experiment) to gather information.

Goal/Standard: Participation meets stated criteria

Giving 0 points is an option—no evidence, no credit.

Criteria	1	2	3	4	Total Points
Observation (Field trip)	Observes presentation satisfactorily	Observes presentation actively	Records notes about experience	Uses notes and observations to ask relevant questions	_____ x 3 = _____ points
Interview (Expert on subject)	Asks subject 1–2 random questions	Asks subject 3–5 random questions	Asks subject 3–5 pertinent questions	Uses subject's responses to formulate new questions	_____ x 3 = _____ points
Participation (Experiment or Field trial)	Participates in experiment or field trial satisfactorily	Participates in experiment or field trial actively	Participates in experiment or field trial	Conducts experiment or field trial	_____ x 4 = _____ points

37–40 = A   31–34 = C
35–36 = B   28–30 = D
           <28 = F

Total score _____ /40 = _____

Chapter 7 • Rubrics and the Research Process

Assess Student Understanding

Observation

- uses notes and observations to ask relevant questions

Review questions for relevance to student notes and field experience and require verbal clarification for vague responses.

Interview

- uses subject's responses to formulate new questions

Review additional questions for relevance to interview subject's responses and require verbal clarification for vague responses.

Participation

- conducts experiment or field trial

Observe student-conducted experiment for student's ability to conduct the trial and convey information. The emphasis here is on getting students involved in the process rather than insisting that they conduct an experiment or field trial that is a total success. The purpose of the rubric element is to get students out of their seats and actively participating.

How to Use the
FIRST-HAND EXPERIENCE Rubric
at the Middle School Level

Introduce the Rubric

Distribute and discuss the rubric with students before they begin the assignment. Focus attention on the column containing the highest level of performance, reminding students that to receive full credit, they must achieve these objectives. This rubric is well suited for science classes. Because it deals with three different types of first-hand experience—Observation, Interview, and Participation—you need not complete the rubric at a single session but may use it to monitor student understanding over the duration of a unit of study that includes all three experiences. It is also beneficial to keep informal records during observation periods (such as field trips) that you can then transfer to the rubric at a more convenient time.

Make the Assignment

Observation: instruct students to use their recorded notes from a field experience to draw three conclusions about the experience.

Interview: instruct students to interview an individual considered an expert in his or her field. The interview should consist of three to six initial questions, plus any questions the student develops based on the interview subject's responses. After the interview, instruct students to compare the subject's responses with other sources (Internet, encyclopedia, other experts) to confirm or refute the subject's credibility.

Participation: instruct students to conduct an experiment for classmates that includes a three- to five-question discussion before or after the experiment. Have students conduct this experiment for the whole class, or have them work in small groups and conduct the experiment just for the other group members. The discussion takes place between the student conducting the experiment and the group watching it. Assume the role of a facilitator watching the groups.

How to Use the FIRST-HAND EXPERIENCE Rubric at the Middle School Level

FIRST-HAND EXPERIENCE

Task: Student will participate in experiences (field trip, interview, experiment) to gather information.

Goal/Standard: Participation meets stated criteria

Giving 0 points is an option—no evidence, no credit.

Criteria	1	2	3	4	Total Points
Observation (Field trip)	Observes presentation actively	Records notes about experience	Uses notes and observations to ask relevant questions	Uses notes and observations to draw conclusions about topic	____ x 3 = ____ points
Interview (Expert on subject)	Asks subject 3–5 random questions	Asks subject 3–5 pertinent questions	Uses subject's responses to formulate new questions	Confirms credibility of subject with existing knowledge on topic	____ x 3 = ____ points
Participation (Experiment or field trial)	Participates in experiment or field trial actively	Participates in experiment or field trial	Conducts experiment or field trial	Initiates Q and A session before and after experiment or field trial	____ x 4 = ____ points

37–40 = A   31–34 = C
35–36 = B   28–30 = D
            <28 = F

Total score ____/40 = ____

Assess Student Understanding

Observation

- uses notes and observations to draw conclusions about topic

Review conclusions for accuracy and relevance to notes and observations, and require verbal clarification for vague responses.

Interview

- confirms credibility of subject with existing knowledge on topic

Have students confirm or refute the subject's credibility by comparing the information they received from the subject with existing knowledge on the topic (written material from another source on the topic) and present the existing knowledge (photocopies or computer printouts) to support their conclusions.

Participation

- initiates question and answer session before and after experiment

Observe question and answer session for relevance to experiment, and require verbal clarification for vague responses.

How to Use the
FIRST-HAND EXPERIENCE Rubric
at the High School Level

Introduce the Rubric

Distribute and discuss the rubric with students before they begin the assignment. Focus attention on the column containing the highest level of performance, reminding students that to receive full credit, they must achieve these objectives. This rubric is well suited for science classes. Because it deals with three different types of first-hand experience—Observation, Interview, and Participation—you need not complete the rubric at a single session but may use it to monitor student understanding over the duration of a unit of study that includes all three experiences. It is also beneficial to keep informal records during observation periods (such as field trips) that you can then transfer to the rubric at a more convenient time.

Make the Assignment

Observation: instruct students to use their notes and observations from the field experience to form two generalizations about the experience. To guide their responses, you might provide students with sentences to complete, such as "Based on the observation at the _____, one can say that all _____ are _____."

Interview: instruct students, first, to interview an individual considered an expert in his or her field and then, after the interview, to gather information from other sources, including other experts, to confirm or refute the interview subject's credibility.

Participation: instruct students to devise an experiment to conduct for the class or for group members if you place students in small groups. The presentation should include a pre-experiment explanation of the anticipated outcome.

FIRST-HAND EXPERIENCE

Task: Student will participate in experience (field trip, interview, experiment) to gather information.

Goal/Standard: Participation meets stated criteria

Giving 0 points is an option—no evidence, no credit.

Criteria	1	2	3	4	Total Points
Observation (Field trip)	Records notes about experience	Uses notes and observations to ask relevant questions	Uses notes and observations to draw conclusions about experience	Uses notes and observations to form generalizations about experience	____ x 3 = ____ points
Interview (Expert on subject)	Asks subject 3–5 pertinent questions	Uses subject's responses to formulate new questions	Confirms credibility of subject using existing knowledge of topic	Contrasts subject's information with other experts in field to confirm credibility	____ x 3 = ____ points
Participation (Experiment or Field trial)	Participates in experiment or field trial	Conducts experiment or field trial	Initiates Q and A session before and after experiment or field trial	Constructs an overview that includes predicted outcome of experience	____ x 4 = ____ points

37–40 = A   31–34 = C
35–36 = B   28–30 = D
            <28 = F

Total score ____/40 = ____

Chapter 7 • Rubrics and the Research Process

Assess Student Understanding

Observation

■ uses notes and observations to form generalizations about experience

Review generalizations for accuracy and relevance to experience, and require verbal clarification for vague responses.

Interview

■ contrasts interview subject's information with other field experiences and experts to test credibility

Ask students to document the individual's credibility, or lack of credibility, and provide tangible proof to support their claims.

Participation

■ constructs an overview that indicates predicted outcome of experiment

Observe students' pre-experiment overviews for accuracy, and require verbal clarification for any vague responses.

How to Use the
WRITTEN REPORT Rubric
at the Intermediate Level

Introduce the Rubric

Distribute and discuss the rubric with students before they begin the assignment, focusing attention on the column containing the highest level of performance. Remind students that to receive full credit, they must achieve these objectives.

Make the Assignment

Instruct students to select and get your OK on a topic question and write a report that answers the question by using available resources. The paper should be four to six pages, excluding any illustrations or graphics, and the bibliography should have at least three entries. Remind students that they must not plagiarize, and require photocopies or computer printouts of sources with information they used highlighted. To ensure accuracy, you might limit choice of topics to those you have covered in that year's curriculum.

Assess Student Understanding

Topic
■ answers topic question adequately

Depth of Understanding
■ grasps concepts well

Accuracy
■ presents accurate information and proof of accuracy

Bibliography
■ prepares accurate bibliography with appropriate publishing dates

Determine whether students have addressed the topic question adequately. The report should reflect the student's grasp of concepts the report covers. The bibliography, with at least three entries, should contain accurate author names, titles, and publishing information. The bibliography should consist primarily of recent references (not older than five years), although a small number of older references is acceptable, depending on the topic. (A paper on Abraham Lincoln can use older references; a paper on the Internet cannot.)

How to Use the WRITTEN REPORT Rubric at the Intermediate Level

WRITTEN REPORT

Task: Student will produce a written research project.

Goal/Standard: Project meets stated criteria

Giving 0 points is an option—no evidence, no credit.

Criteria	1	2	3	Total Points
Topic	Has minor gaps in answer to topic question	Answers topic question, but includes too much irrelevant material	Answers topic question adequately	____ x 3 = ____ points
Depth of Understanding	Grasps some concepts	Grasps concepts adequately	Grasps concepts well	____ x 4 = ____ points
Accuracy	Errors in accuracy and incomplete documentation of accuracy	Accurate information, but incomplete documentation of accuracy	Accurate information with complete documentation of accuracy	____ x 4 = ____ points
Bibliography	Some inaccurate or outdated references	Accurate with some outdated references	All accurate and all appropriate dates	____ x 4 = ____ points

42–45 = A   35–38 = C
39–41 = B   32–34 = D
             <32 = F

Total score ____/45 = ____

SkyLight Professional Development

How to Use the
WRITTEN REPORT Rubric
at the Middle School Level

Introduce the Rubric

Distribute and discuss the rubric with students before they begin the assignment, focusing attention on the column containing the highest level of performance. Remind students that to receive full credit, they must achieve these objectives.

Make the Assignment

Instruct students to select and get your OK on a topic question and write a report answering that question by using available resources. The paper should be six to twelve pages, excluding any illustrations or graphics and the bibliography, and it should have at least four quotes. The bibliography should have at least five entries from varied sources. Remind students that they must not plagiarize and require photocopies of sources with information they used highlighted in one color and quotes they used highlighted in another color. Review the proper way to incorporate quotes in a text.

Assess Student Understanding

Topic
- addresses topic question in innovative, entertaining way

Depth of Understanding
- uses appropriate quotes to reinforce concepts

Accuracy
- has accurate information and quotations and provides clear documentation for them

Bibliography
- prepares accurate bibliography from a variety of sources

Review the report to determine how well students address their initial question. The report should reflect a genuine understanding of topic concepts. The bibliography should contain mostly recent references (not older than five years) and should include various sources such as weekly newsmagazines, books, professional journals, and the Internet.

How to Use the WRITTEN REPORT Rubric at the Middle School Level

WRITTEN REPORT

Task: Student will produce a written research project.

Goal/Standard: Project meets stated criteria

Giving 0 points is an option—no evidence, no credit.

Criteria	1	2	3	4	Total Points
Topic	Answers topic question, but includes too much irrelevant material	Addresses topic question adequately	Addresses topic question well	Addresses topic question in innovative and entertaining way	____ x 3 = ____ points
Depth of Understanding	Grasps some concepts	Grasps concepts adequately	Grasps concepts well	Uses appropriate quotes to reinforce concepts	____ x 4 = ____ points
Accuracy	Accurate information, but incomplete documentation of accuracy	Accurate information and complete documentation of accuracy, but inaccurate or too few quotes	Accurate information, correct quotes, but incomplete documentation of accuracy	Accurate information, quotes, and documentation	____ x 4 = ____ points
Bibliography	A few inaccurate references	Accurate with some outdated references	All accurate, but not varied enough	Accurate and varied	____ x 4 = ____ points

56–60 = A   47–51 = C
52–55 = B   42–46 = D
        <42 = F

Total score ____/60 = ____

How to Use the
WRITTEN REPORT Rubric
at the High School Level

Introduce the Rubric

Distribute and discuss the rubric with students before they begin the assignment, focusing attention on the column containing the highest level of performance. Remind students that to receive full credit, they must achieve these objectives.

Make the Assignment

Instruct students to select and get your OK on a topic question and write a report answering that question by using available resources. The paper should be twelve to twenty pages, excluding illustrations, graphics, and bibliography, and it must contain six to ten quotes. The multimedia bibliography should have a minimum of seven entries. Review nonfiction text structures—description, sequence, comparison, cause and effect, and problem and solution. Remind students that they must not plagiarize, and require photocopies of sources with information they used highlighted in one color and quotes they used highlighted in another color. Review the proper way to incorporate quotes in a text.

Assess Student Understanding

Topic
- uses text structure that enhances presentation of topic

Depth of Understanding
- uses appropriate quotes to reinforce concepts

Accuracy
- has accurate information and quotes and provides clear documentation for them

Bibliography
- prepares accurate, multimedia bibliography with mostly recent references

How to Use the WRITTEN REPORT Rubric at the High School Level

WRITTEN REPORT

Task: Student will produce a written research project.
Goal/Standard: Project meets stated criteria

Giving 0 points is an option—no evidence, no credit.

Criteria	1	2	3	4	Total Points
Topic	Addresses topic question adequately	Addresses topic question well	Addresses topic question in innovative, entertaining way	Text structure enhances presentation of topic	____ x 3 = ____ points
Depth of Understanding	Grasps concepts adequately	Grasps concepts well	Adds own prior knowledge of topic	Uses appropriate quotes to reinforce concepts	____ x 4 = ____ points
Accuracy	Accurate information, but incomplete documentation of accuracy	Accurate information and complete documentation of accuracy, but too few or inaccurate quotes	Accurate information, correct quotes, but incomplete documentation of accuracy	Accurate information, quotes, and documentation	____ x 4 = ____ points
Bibliography	1–2 inaccurate references	Accurate with some outdated references	Accurate with current references	Accurate with current multimedia references	____ x 4 = ____ points

56–60 = A 47–51 = C 52–55 = B 42–46 = D <42 = F	Total score ____/60 = ____

The report should reflect a genuine understanding of topic concepts. Be sure students have included six to ten quotes and provided highlighted pages that document quotes and other information. Determine whether the text structure strengthens or weakens its presentation. For example, the most effective organization for a report on two methods of organic gardening is the comparison format. Finally, the multimedia bibliography should include Web sites, videos, or other nonprint information.

How to Use the
COLLABORATION Rubric
at the Primary Level

Introduce the Rubric

Distribute and discuss the rubric with students before they begin the assignment, focusing attention on the column containing the highest level of performance. Remind students that to receive full credit, they must achieve these objectives. You might also have students complete the rubric for their group members to give them practice in using rubrics and help them focus on their own performance in the group.

Make the Assignment

Students can complete this assignment through a variety of group projects, ranging from an oral in-class presentation to a writers' collaboration. The emphasis is on student cooperation with the group. While this rubric presumes students have some experience working in cooperative groups, you may want to review the rules of group work, including respecting others' opinions, waiting for their turn to speak, completing the task the group assigns them, and working as a unit to complete the project. Once they have the assignment, give students a time frame (1 to 2 days) to complete the project.

Assess Student Understanding

Sharing Information
- shares information with most group members

Listening
- makes occasional eye contact with speaker and asks relevant questions

Nonverbal Communication
- exhibits positive gestures and facial expressions

Division of Tasks
- distributes tasks evenly

Because you will conduct this assessment while observing students in the group setting, keep the rubric at hand during those times. Make notes about individual behaviors and overall group cooperation. Intervene only when the group's collapse seems inevitable. Otherwise, allow students to work through conflicts independently.

COLLABORATION

Task: Student will participate in a collaborative research project.
Goal/Standard: Participation meets stated criteria

Criteria	0	1	2	Total Points
Sharing Information	Does not share information	Shares information with a few group members	Shares information with most group members	____ x 5 = ____ points
Listening	Does not acknowledge speaker or ask questions	Looks at speaker; asks questions	Makes occasional eye contact with speaker; asks relevant questions	____ x 5 = ____ points
Nonverbal Communication	Exhibits inappropriate or negative gestures or facial expressions	Exhibits no gestures and blank facial expression	Exhibits positive gestures and facial expressions	____ x 5 = ____ points
Division of Tasks	No cooperation among group members	Uneven distribution of tasks	Even distribution of tasks	____ x 5 = ____ points

37–40 = A   31–34 = C
35–36 = B   28–30 = D
            <28 = F

Total score ____/40 = ____

How to Use the
COLLABORATION Rubric
at the Intermediate and Middle School Level

Introduce the Rubric

Distribute and discuss the rubric with students before they begin the assignment, focusing attention on the column containing the highest level of performance. Remind students that to receive full credit, they must achieve these objectives.

Make the Assignment

Students can complete this assignment through a wide variety of group projects, ranging from an oral in-class presentation to a writers' collaboration. The emphasis here is on student cooperation with the group. While this rubric presumes students have some experience working in cooperative groups, you may want to review the rules of group work, including respecting others' opinions, waiting for their turn to speak, completing the task the group assigns them, and working as a unit to complete the project. Once they have the assignment, give students a time frame (3 to 5 days) to complete the project.

Assess Student Understanding

Sharing Information
- shares information with all group members

Listening
- makes full eye contact with speaker; asks encouraging, open-ended questions

Nonverbal Communication
- exhibits encouraging, involved gestures and facial expressions

Division of Tasks
- distributes tasks logically based on level of difficulty

Because you will conduct this assessment while observing students in the group setting, keep the rubric at hand during those times. Look for fair division of labor. For example, a student who takes on a particularly complex task should not take on a second task. Make notes about individual behaviors and overall group cooperation. Intervene only when the group's collapse seems inevitable. Otherwise, allow students to work through conflicts independently.

COLLABORATION

Task: Student will participate in a collaborative research project.
Goal/Standard: Participation meets stated criteria

Giving 0 points is an option—no evidence, no credit.

Criteria	1	2	3	4	Total Points
Sharing Information	Shares minimal information	Shares information with a few group members	Shares information with most group members	Shares information with all group members	____ x 3 = ____ points
Listening	Demonstrates adequate listening skills/ behaviors	Makes occasional eye contact with speaker; asks questions	Looks at speaker; asks relevant questions	Makes full eye contact with speaker; asks encouraging, open-ended questions	____ x 4 = ____ points
Nonverbal Communication	Exhibits minimal gestures and facial expressions	Exhibits positive gestures and facial expressions	Exhibits supportive gestures and facial expressions	Exhibits encouraging, involved expressions and gestures	____ x 4 = ____ points
Division of Tasks	Adequate distribution of tasks	Distributes tasks so each group member has same number	Distributes tasks based on time needed to complete them	Distributes tasks logically based on level of difficulty	____ x 4 = ____ points

56–60 = A   47–51 = C
52–55 = B   42–46 = D
           <42 = F

Total score ____/60 = ____

Chapter 7 • Rubrics and the Research Process

How to Use the
COLLABORATION Rubric
at the High School Level

Introduce the Rubric

Distribute and discuss the rubric with students before they begin the assignment, focusing attention on the column containing the highest level of performance. Remind students that to receive full credit, they must achieve these objectives.

Make the Assignment

Students can complete this assignment through a variety of group projects, ranging from an oral in-class presentation to a writers' collaboration. The emphasis is on student cooperation with the group. While this rubric presumes students have some experience working in cooperative groups, you may want to review the rules of group work, including respecting others' opinions, waiting for their turn to speak, completing the task the group assigns them, and working as a unit to complete the project. Give students a time frame (7 to 12 days) to complete the project.

Assess Student Understanding

Sharing Information
- shares information, including source, with all group members

Listening
- models active listening behaviors for other group members

Nonverbal Communication
- exhibits encouraging, involved gestures and facial expressions

Division of Tasks
- distributes tasks logically based on interrelatedness of information

Because you will conduct this assessment while observing students in the group setting, keep the rubric at hand during those times. Look for task distribution based on how tasks relate to one another. Make notes about individual behaviors and overall group cooperation. Intervene only when the group's collapse seems inevitable. Otherwise, allow students to work through conflicts independently.

COLLABORATION

Task: Student will participate in a collaborative research project.
Goal/Standard: Participation meets stated criteria

Giving 0 points is an option—no evidence, no credit.

Criteria	1	2	3	4	Total Points
Sharing Information	Shares information with a few group members	Shares information with most group members	Shares information with all group members	Shares information, including source, with all group members	_____ x 3 = _____ points
Listening	Makes occasional eye contact with speaker; asks questions	Looks at speaker; asks relevant questions	Makes full eye contact with speaker; asks relevant questions	Models active listening behaviors for other group members	_____ x 4 = _____ points .
Nonverbal Communication	Exhibits minimal gestures and facial expressions	Exhibits positive gestures and facial expressions	Exhibits supportive gestures and facial expressions	Exhibits encouraging, involved gestures and facial expressions	_____ x 4 = _____ points
Division of Tasks	Adequate distribution of tasks	Distributes tasks evenly	Distributes tasks logically based on level of difficulty	Distributes tasks logically based on interrelatedness of information	_____ x 4 = _____ points

56–60 = A   47–51 = C
52–55 = B   42–46 = D
        <42 = F

Total score _____/60 = _____

8
Rubrics and Classroom Technology

Michael, a middle school principal, is committed to finding ways of incorporating technology in the classroom. While many of his students demonstrate a high level of proficiency with video games and other tasks, such as programming a VCR, Michael is concerned that they lack more essential skills for desktop publishing or conducting an Internet search. Citing early exposure as a positive factor in developing students' technological expertise, Michael works with Guy, an elementary school principal, to design and implement a technology curriculum, including assessment rubrics to monitor student growth throughout the program.

PREPARING FOR TOMORROW

Michael and Guy join other principals concerned about students' readiness to face the challenges of an increasingly "tech dependent" society. The World Wide Web is a massive clearinghouse of information accessible to those individuals with the ability to harness its resources. E-commerce and e-communication have proved to be more than a passing trend, and tomorrow's leaders must learn to thrive in a world they can access from a desktop.

In addition to the Web, recent advances in the fields of video and audio technology make these areas more student-friendly. No longer limited to printed presentations, students can now share their ideas with others through video and audio productions. These alternate avenues of self-expression can motivate even the most reluctant learner to become actively involved in the learning process. Increasing students' ability to use technology is a must if they are to succeed in a world that grows smaller with distant neighbors only a mouse click away.

The rubrics in this chapter cover the following technological areas: Internet Search, E-Mail Messages, Web Page, Audio Collage, and Video Presentation. The rubrics list full-credit responses to provide teachers with concrete examples of what they may see in student work. A summary of the expectations for the age and grade level follows. In cases when students in more than one grade-level group should have all the skills described, the rubric and assessment guidelines have been combined. In the case of areas not suitable for primary grades, no rubric appears at that level.

Internet Search: E-Search

These rubrics assess students' ability to find information on the World Wide Web with the help of search engines. The goal, or highest degree of accomplishment on the rubric, for each grade level follows:

Primary—student uses appropriate search terms to find correct answer to specific question.

Intermediate—student refines search terms to enhance search and identifies and visits a link to confirm correct answer to specific question.

Middle School and High School—student refines search terms to enhance search and compares search capabilities of single search engine vs. meta-search engine.

E-Mail Message: E-Communication

E-communication is an increasingly common method of communicating both next door and worldwide. Because, in some instances, e-mail replaces telephone or face-to-face interaction, creating the proper tone in these messages is extremely important. The sender may not have the opportunity to clarify intent for the recipient so he or she must pay special attention to phrasing. Students should develop the habit of rereading e-mail messages before sending them to make certain that the tone is positive and nonconfrontational and appropriate considering the sender's relationship (personal, professional) with the recipient. The rubric here applies to all levels and assesses students' ability to compose and send an e-mail message. The goal, or highest degree of accomplishment on the rubric, follows:

Primary, Intermediate, Middle School, and High School—student uses correct address for recipient, uses appropriate greeting and closing in message, and composes message of appropriate, positive tone free of spelling and grammatical errors.

Web Page: Welcome to the Web

An increasing number of schools, classrooms, and students are constructing Web pages to share their ideas and news with a larger audience. An attractive design layout and easy navigation are primary factors in Web page construction. These rubrics assess students' ability to construct a Web page by using graphics and including links. The goal, or highest degree of accomplishment on the rubric, for each grade level follows:

Primary and Intermediate—student composes appropriate title, uses two- or three-color graphics, includes some relevant links on the page, and creates a well-organized, easy-to-read page layout.

Middle School and High School—student composes attention-getting title, uses full-color graphics, includes several relevant, current links, and creates a visually stimulating page layout.

Audio Collage: The Sounds of Life

Audio collages provide students with the unique challenge of expressing themselves nonverbally through sound. Creating an audio collage to represent happiness, autumn, or the color orange requires students to reflect on background sounds and the emotions or images those sounds evoke. These rubrics assess students' ability to produce an audio collage. The goal, or highest degree of accomplishment on the rubric, for each grade level follows:

Intermediate—student uses smooth transition between sounds to clarify theme, uses interrelated sounds relevant to topic, and produces superior sound quality.

Middle School—student employs seamless transition between sounds to unify theme, uses sounds that embody the topic and concept, and produces superior sound quality.

High School—student blends sounds together to conceal transitions and create a seamless collage, uses some subtle yet powerful sounds to convey theme, and produces superior sound quality.

Video Presentation: Lights, Camera, Action

While movies have been part of our culture for decades, student filmmaking is a relatively new venture. New technology provides budding video artists with a number of user-friendly tools for telling stories, expressing opinions, or creating a visual poem to celebrate nature. These rubrics assess students' ability to produce a short (3 to 10 minute) video presentation with visual effects.

Intermediate—student produces video with a well-developed concept, logical sequence, seamless visual effects, and superior overall video quality.

Middle School and High School—student produces video with a well-developed concept ideal for video format, visual effects that unify video, and superior overall quality.

How to Use the
INTERNET SEARCH Rubric
at the Primary Level

Introduce the Rubric

Distribute and discuss the rubric beforehand, focusing attention on the column containing the highest level of performance. Remind students that to receive full credit, they must achieve these objectives. Review terms such as *search engine* and some common operators useful in conducting Internet searches such as AND (+), OR, NOT (-), and quotation marks. Conduct a brainstorming session on how to choose the most useful terms when conducting a search. For help teaching students about conducting Internet searches, visit http://www.askscott.com/. Scott Nicholson's helpful site not only provides an introduction and tutorial for Internet searches (which he may allow you to use in class if you ask permission), it also has a service called Great Scott, which helps searchers choose the most appropriate search engine for their needs. Consider posting a list of common search engines in the room for students to refer to.

Make the Assignment

Conduct this lesson after students have had some basic Internet experiences. Create a list of six or seven questions students must answer by using the Internet, and have them choose one. (To prevent friends from picking the same question, you might number the questions, then have students draw a number from a hat.) Prepare questions that have only one clear answer such as What is the fourth planet from the sun? Who was the 19th president of the United States? What state entered the union in 1818? What year did Alexander Graham Bell invent the telephone? What is the capital of Hawaii? You might consider developing questions related to upcoming curriculum units; current events; or your state's history, current government representatives (governor, senators, congressmen), state flower or bird, and so on.

Before they go to the computer to undertake their search, tell students to write down how they plan to conduct their search, and in particular, what search engine they will use and what terms they will type in to the search field to focus the search. Establish a time frame, about 15 to 20 minutes at this grade level, for students to seek the answer to their question. Tell them that if they revise their search terms, during the search they should write down the new terms, too. Finally, have them write down the answer they found and the name of the site at which they found the answer.

INTERNET SEARCH

Task: Student will conduct an Internet search to obtain the answer to a specific question.

Goal/Standard: Participation meets stated criteria

Criteria	0	1	2	Total Points
Search Terms	Not identified	Too broad	Appropriate terms for search	____ x 5 = ____ points
Search Results	Did not find answer	Gives incomplete or incorrect answer	Gives correct answer	____ x 5 = ____ points

19–20 = A   16–17 = C
18 = B   14–15 = D
<14 = F

Total score ____/20 = ____

Chapter 8 • Rubrics and Classroom Technology

Assess Student Understanding

Search Terms

■ uses appropriate terms for search

Search Results

■ gives correct answer

If the student did not find the answer to the question or the answer is incomplete, look at the search terms the student used. The student may have misspelled a term or, more likely, used a term that has too many meanings or is too broad and produced an unwieldy number of possible sites. If this is the case, work with the student to refine the search terms, perhaps by adding AND (+), NOT (−), or another operator, and allow the student to try the search again.

How to Use the
INTERNET SEARCH Rubric
at the Intermediate Level

Introduce the Rubric

Distribute and discuss the rubric beforehand, focusing attention on the column containing the highest level of performance. Remind students that to receive full credit, they must achieve these objectives. Review terms such as *search engine* and some common operators useful in conducting Internet searches such as AND (+), OR, NOT (-), and quotation marks. Conduct a brainstorming session on how to choose the most useful terms when conducting a search. For help teaching students about conducting Internet searches, visit http://www.askscott.com/. Scott Nicholson's helpful site not only provides an introduction and tutorial for Internet searches (which he may allow you to use in class if you ask permission), it also has a service called Great Scott, which helps searchers choose the most appropriate search engine for their needs. Consider posting a list of common search engines in the room for students to refer to.

Make the Assignment

Create a list of six or seven two-part questions students must answer by using the Internet, and have them choose one. (To prevent friends from picking the same question, you might number the questions, then have students draw a number from a hat.) Some sample questions are What year did Disneyland open and in what city is it located? What date did Paul Revere's ride take place and from what town did he start his ride? What date and where was the Battle of Bull Run fought? What year was Abraham Lincoln assassinated and where did the murder take place? Who was the first woman elected governor and what state did she govern? You might also consider developing questions related to upcoming curriculum units; current events; or your state's history, current government representatives (governor, congressmen), state bird, and so on.

Before they go to the computer to undertake their search, tell students to write down how they plan to conduct their search, in particular, what search engine they will use and what terms they will type in to the search field to focus the search. Establish a time frame, about 15 to 20 minutes at this grade level, for students, first, to seek the answer to their questions, and, second, to follow a link to a second site that confirms the answer. Tell them to write down the answers they found and the names of the two sites they visited to find and confirm the answers.

Next, ask them to reflect on the first search terms they used, then write a different set of terms. Have them test the new terms. Did the new terms take them to the same sites? Did they find the answer more or less quickly?

How to Use the INTERNET SEARCH Rubric at the Intermediate Level

INTERNET SEARCH

Task: Student will conduct an Internet search to obtain the answer to a specific question.

Goal/Standard: Participation meets stated criteria

Giving 0 points is an option—no evidence, no credit.

Criteria	1	2	3	4	Total Points
Search Terms	Too broad	Appropriate terms for search	Appropriate alternate set of terms	Can refine terms to enhance search	_____ x 5 = _____ points
Search Results	1 or 2 answers correct	2 correct answers	2 correct answers and name of site where answers appear	Identifies and visits a link to confirm correct answer	_____ x 5 = _____ points

37–40 = A   31–34 = C
35–36 = B   28–30 = D
         <28 = F

Total score _____/40 = _____

Assess Student Understanding

Search Terms

■ can refine terms to enhance search

Search Results

■ identifies and visits a link to confirm correct answer

Make sure the student has the following: (1) an initial set of search terms; (2) the correct answer to both parts of the question; (3) the names of two sites at which the student found the answer; and (4) an alternate set of search terms with a brief explanation of which set of terms helped the student find the answer most directly. If the student did not find the answers to the question or the answer is incomplete, look at the search terms the student used. The student may have misspelled a term or, more likely, used a term that has too many meanings or is too broad and produced an unwieldy number of possible sites. If this is the case, work with the student to refine the search terms, perhaps by adding AND (+), NOT (-), or another operator, and allow the student to try the search again.

How to Use the
INTERNET SEARCH Rubric
at the Middle School and High School Level

Introduce the Rubric

Distribute and discuss the rubric beforehand, focusing attention on the column containing the highest level of performance. Remind students that to receive full credit, they must achieve these objectives. Review terms such as *search engine* and *meta-search engine* and some common operators useful in conducting Internet searches such as AND (+), OR, NOT (-), and quotation marks. Conduct a brainstorming session on how to choose the most useful terms when conducting a search. For help teaching students about conducting Internet searches, visit http://www.askscott.com/. Scott Nicholson's helpful site not only provides an introduction and tutorial for Internet searches (which he may allow you to use in class if you ask permission), it also has a service called Great Scott, which helps searchers choose the most appropriate search engine for their needs. Consider posting a list of common search engines in the room for students to refer to.

Make the Assignment

For this assignment, students will compare a search conducted by using a single search engine with a search conducted by using a meta-search engine such as Dogpile (http://www.dogpile.com/), SurfWax (http://www.surfwax.com/), or ProFusion (http://www.profusion.com/). Create a list of six or seven questions students must answer by using the Internet, and have them choose one. (To prevent friends from picking the same question, you might number the questions, then have students draw a number from a hat.) Some sample questions are What movie won the Academy Award in the year you were born? Who was the prime minister of England the year you were born? What baseball team won the World Series the year you were born? Who was the governor of the state you were born in the year you were born? For high school students, add a level of challenge; for example, What is the highest mountain in the world, where is it, and how much higher is it than the second highest mountain? Who is the richest American and how much more money did that person make last year than the second richest American? What Steven Spielberg film has grossed the most money worldwide, and how much more did it make than the second highest grossing Spielberg film? You might also consider developing questions related to upcoming curriculum units; current events; or your state's history, current government representatives (governor, senators, congressmen), state flower or bird, and so on.

INTERNET SEARCH

Task: Student will conduct an Internet search to obtain the answer to a specific question.

Goal/Standard: Participation meets stated criteria

Giving 0 points is an option—no evidence, no credit.

Criteria	1	2	3	4	Total Points
Search Terms	Too broad	Appropriate terms for search	Appropriate alternate set of terms	Can refine terms to enhance search	____ x 5 = ____ points
Search Results	Gives incomplete answer	Gives correct answer	Gives correct answer and lists 2 sites where answer appears	Compares search capabilities of single search engine vs. meta-search engine	____ x 5 = ____ points

37–40 = A   31–34 = C
35–36 = B   28–30 = D
            <28 = F

Total score ____/40 = ____

Chapter 8 • Rubrics and Classroom Technology

Before they go to the computer to undertake their search, tell students to write down how they plan to conduct their search, in particular, which two search engines they will use and what terms they will type in to the search field to focus the search. When they finish the searches, tell them to write down the answer to the question, the name of the site(s) that gave them the answer (because they are using two search engines, they may name two different sites), and a brief description of the usefulness of each search engine. Tell them to include such information as which search engine gave them the fewest unrelated sites and which search engine got them to the answer the fastest or the most directly.

Next, ask them to reflect on the first search terms they used, then write a different set of terms. Have them test the new terms with both search engines. Did the new terms take them to the same sites? Did they find the answer more or less quickly?

Assess Student Understanding

Search Terms

■ can refine terms to enhance search

Search Results

■ compares search capabilities of single search engine vs. meta-search engine

Make sure the student has the following: (1) an initial set of search terms; (2) the correct answer to the question; (3) the names of two sites at which the student found the answer; and (4) an alternate set of search terms with a brief explanation of which set of terms helped the student find the answer most directly. If the student did not find the answers to the question or the answer is incomplete, look at the search terms the student used. The student may have misspelled a term or, more likely, used a term that has too many meanings or is too broad and produced an unwieldy number of possible sites. If this is the case, work with the student to refine the search terms, perhaps by adding AND (+), NOT (-), or another operator, and allow the student to try the search again.

How to Use the
E-MAIL MESSAGE Rubric
at All Levels

Introduce the Rubric

Distribute and discuss the rubric. Focus attention on the column containing the highest level of performance, reminding students that to receive full credit, they must achieve these objectives.

Make the Assignment

Instruct students to compose and send an e-mail message to another individual. The person can be a friend, a relative, or a pen pal at another school. The message should be free of spelling and grammatical errors and the topic appropriate for the intended recipient. For example, if a student writes to a grandparent, the topic will differ from that of a message to a good friend. Because the recipient of an e-mail message cannot know the sender's mood from the printed word, users of e-mail communication must reread their messages before sending them and consider whether the recipient could perceive the tone as confrontational or argumentative.

Assess Student Understanding

Recipient Address
- uses correct recipient address

Greeting and Closing
- uses appropriate message greeting and closing

Spelling and Grammar
- has no spelling or grammatical errors

Tone of Message
- keeps tone appropriate for recipient

Examine e-mail messages before students send them to check for spelling and grammatical errors as well as appropriateness of greeting, closing, and message topic. If any of these areas requires revising, instruct students to make changes before they send the message.

TECHNOLOGY   **E-MAIL MESSAGE**   ALL LEVELS

Task: Student will compose and send an e-mail message.
Goal/Standard: Message meets stated criteria

Criteria	0	1	2	Total Points
Recipient Address	Not present	Present but incorrect	Present and correct	____ x 3 = ____ points
Greeting and Closing	Not present	Present but inappropriate	Present and appropriate	____ x 4 = ____ points
Spelling and Grammar	Several errors	Few errors	Error-free	____ x 3 = ____ points
Tone of Message	Unclear	Inappropriate for recipient	Appropriate for recipient	____ x 5 = ____ points

28–30 = A   24–25 = C
26–27 = B   21–23 = D
            <21 = F

Total score ____/30 = ____

How to Use the
WEB PAGE Rubric
at the Primary and Intermediate Level

Introduce the Rubric

Distribute and discuss the rubric beforehand, focusing attention on the column containing the highest level of performance. Remind students that to receive full credit, they must achieve these objectives.

Make the Assignment

Student, class, and school Web pages are becoming increasingly popular due to increased access to the Internet. These pages provide individuals and groups a method of communicating ideas and making announcements far beyond classroom walls. For this reason, students need to reflect on the type and amount of information they will include before they construct a Web page. Several software programs and Internet sites are available to guide students through Web page construction, but exciting graphics and page layout will not compensate for a page with little or no entertaining or informative content. Entertainment or informative value lies, of course, in the site's appeal to Web readers. But even the most avid fan of the Web page topic will want current, accurate information. If Web readers enjoy reading about a particular actor, they will find a Web page that contains new or little-known and frequently updated information about that actor entertaining. A Web reader interested in the solar system will find a Web page with accurate data about the solar system informative. Links at the site direct Web readers to visit other parts of the page or other related pages, giving Web readers a chance to learn more about the subject that interests them.

Instruct students to determine the type of page they wish to produce and where their page will fit in cyberspace. For example, if a student wants to share her interest in helping animals, she might include links to organizations that help animals to make the information accessible to site visitors who share that interest. Bearing an appropriate title with graphics and links that enhance the site, a well-organized student Web page can be a project with far-reaching, worldwide effects.

How to Use the WEB PAGE Rubric at the Primary and Intermediate Level

WEB PAGE

Task: Student will construct a Web page that includes graphics and relevant links.

Goal/Standard: Completed Web page meets stated criteria

Criteria	0	1	2	Total Points
Title	None	Present but inappropriate	Present and appropriate	____ x 3 = ____ points
Graphics	None	Few; 1 color	Several; 2–3 colors	____ x 4 = ____ points
Ease of Navigation	Difficult to navigate; no links	Somewhat difficult to navigate; links are not relevant	Easy to navigate; contains 1–2 relevant, largely accessible links	____ x 4 = ____ points
Page Layout	Drab; mostly text	Text with 1–2 pictures	Well organized and easy to read	____ x 4 = ____ points

28–30 = A 24–25 = C
26–27 = B 21–23 = D
         <21 = F

Total score ____ /30 = ____

Assess Student Understanding

Title
- composes appropriate title

Graphics
- uses graphics with at least two or three colors

Ease of Navigation
- produces page that is easy to navigate and includes one to two relevant, largely accessible links

Page Layout
- creates well-organized and easy-to-understand overall page layout

Review student Web pages for accuracy as well as for overall page layout and information organization. A confusing layout detracts from the page's content and reduces interest of site visitors. The title should be informative and inviting so Web surfers will want to visit the page to learn more. Students should include links relevant to the Web page topic to enhance the site's position in cyberspace, making it a more interesting place to explore. Students should include current, reliable, and lasting links to established organizations such as the Smithsonian Institution or an official author's page. These pages are likely to be around for a long time as opposed to sites such as Joe's Peek at the Universe, which may quickly become outdated or unavailable.

How to Use the

WEB PAGE Rubric

at the Middle and High School Level

Introduce the Rubric

Distribute and discuss the rubric beforehand, focusing attention on the column containing the highest level of performance. Remind students that to receive full credit, they must achieve these objectives.

Make the Assignment

Student, class, and school Web pages are becoming increasingly popular due to increased access to the Internet. These pages provide individuals and groups a method of communicating ideas and making announcements far beyond classroom walls. For this reason, students need to reflect on the type and amount of information they will include before they construct a Web page. Several software programs and Internet sites are available to guide students through Web page construction, but exciting graphics and page layout will not compensate for a page with little or no entertaining or informative content. Instruct students to determine the type of page they wish to produce first and where their page will fit in cyberspace. For example, if a student wants to share her interest in helping animals, she might include links to similar organizations to make the information accessible to site visitors who share that interest.

Bearing an appropriately specific title with graphics and links that enhance the site, a well-organized student Web page can be a project with far-reaching, worldwide effects.

WEB PAGE

Task: Student will construct a Web page that includes graphics and relevant links.

Goal/Standard: Completed Web page meets stated criteria

Giving 0 points is an option—no evidence, no credit.

Criteria	1	2	3	4	Total Points
Title	Present but unspecific	Present and specific to content	Appealing to potential site visitors	Attention grabber!	____ x 3 = ____ points
Graphics	Few; 1 color	Few; 2 colors	Several in full color	Full color with photos and/or clip art	____ x 4 = ____ points
Ease of Navigation	Somewhat difficult to navigate; some links don't work	Easy to navigate; includes links but not all accessible	Easy to navigate; includes 3–5 relevant accessible links	Easy to navigate; includes 3–5 links with regular updates	____ x 4 = ____ points
Page Layout	Text; 1–2 pictures only	Well-organized balance of text and pictures	Uncluttered and inviting	Visually stimulating	____ x 4 = ____ points

56–60 = A   47–51 = C
52–55 = B   42–46 = D
          <42 = F

Total score ____/60 = ____

Chapter 8 • Rubrics and Classroom Technology

Assess Student Understanding

Title

■ composes attention-grabbing page title

Graphics

■ uses full-color graphics, photos, and clip art

Ease of Navigation

■ produces page that is easy to navigate and includes three to five accessible links with regular updates

Page Layout

■ creates visually stimulating overall page layout

Review student Web pages for accuracy as well as for overall page layout and information organization. A confusing layout detracts from the page's content and reduce interest of site visitors. The title should be informative and inviting so Web surfers will want to visit the page to learn more. Students should include relevant links to enhance the site's position in cyberspace, making it a more interesting place to explore. Students should check to make sure that links are current before including them on the page since broken or outdated links are a source of frustration to site visitors.

How to Use the
AUDIO COLLAGE Rubric
at the Intermediate Level

Introduce the Rubric

Distribute and discuss the rubric beforehand. Focus attention on the column containing the highest level of performance, reminding students that to receive full credit, they must achieve these objectives. Burning CDs and making audiotapes are both acceptable for this assignment, depending on students' access to and the availability of audiocassette recorders and computers with read/write capabilities.

Make the Assignment

Audio collages stimulate students' creativity by requiring them to reach beyond the sense of sight to develop a collage of sound that tells a story or conveys an emotion. Instruct students to select a topic, such as happiness or holidays, or a color, such as green, and challenge them to create a sound collage that captures the essence of the topic. For example, an audio happiness collage might contain the sound of children laughing. The collage should create an auditory picture for listeners. Establish a time limit for the recording, 5 to 8 minutes, and encourage students to think about what sounds they associate with the topic.

Assess Student Understanding

Cohesion of Collage
- uses smooth transitions between sounds, clarifying theme

Relevance to Topic
- uses sounds relevant to topic and related to each other

Sound Quality
- produces superior sound quality

Review the collage for cohesiveness of sounds, transitions between them, and their relevance to the topic. For example, if sounds go from loud to soft with nothing to connect them or from discordant to harmonious with nothing as a bridge, the theme is less clear to the listener. In the case of vague or seemingly inappropriate responses, such as use of a siren as a happy sound, ask the student for clarification. The sound quality of the collage should be excellent without fading or slurring due to operator error.

How to Use the AUDIO COLLAGE Rubric at the Intermediate Level

AUDIO COLLAGE

Task: Student will produce an audio collage.

Goal/Standard: Collage meets stated criteria

Giving 0 points is an option—no evidence, no credit.

Criteria	1	2	3	4	Total Points
Cohesion of Collage	Some weak sound transitions	Adequate transition between sounds	Logical, solid transitions; coherent theme	Smooth transition; clarifies theme	____ x 5 = ____ points
Relevance to Topic	Some relevant sounds	Majority of sounds are relevant	All sounds are relevant	All sounds are relevant and interrelated	____ x 5 = ____ points
Sound Quality	Fair	Good	Excellent	Superior	____ x 5 = ____ points

56–60 = A   47–51 = C
52–55 = B   42–46 = D
            <42 = F

Total score ____/60 = ____

How to Use the
AUDIO COLLAGE Rubric
at the Middle School Level

Introduce the Rubric

Distribute and discuss the rubric beforehand. Focus attention on the column containing the highest level of performance, reminding students that to receive full credit, they must achieve these objectives. Burning CDs and making audiotapes are both acceptable for this assignment, depending on students' access to and the availability of audiocassette recorders and computers with read/write capabilities.

Make the Assignment

Audio collages stimulate students' creativity by requiring them to reach beyond the sense of sight to develop a collage of sound that tells a story or conveys an emotion. Instruct students to select a topic, such as happiness or holidays, or a color, such as green, challenging them to create a sound collage that captures the essence of the topic. For example, an audio happiness collage might contain the sound of children laughing. Encourage students to stretch their sound inventory by including sounds of places that promote happiness, such as a baseball game, or sounds that promote peacefulness, such as church bells on a Sunday morning. The collage should create an auditory picture for listeners. Establish a time limit for the recording, 8 to 12 minutes, and encourage students to think about what sounds they associate with the topic.

Assess Student Understanding

Cohesion of Collage
■ employs seamless transition between sounds to unify theme

Relevance to Topic
■ uses relevant sounds that embody topic and concept

Sound Quality
■ produces superior sound quality

Review the collage for cohesiveness and blending of sounds, transitions between them, and their relevance to the topic. In the case of vague or seemingly inappropriate responses, ask the student for clarification. The sound quality of the collage should be superior without fading or slurring due to operator error.

How to Use the AUDIO COLLAGE Rubric at the Middle School Level

AUDIO COLLAGE

Task: Student will produce an audio collage.

Goal/Standard: Collage meets stated criteria

Giving 0 points is an option—no evidence, no credit.

Criteria	1	2	3	4	Total Points
Cohesion of Collage	Adequate transition between sounds	Logical, solid transition; coherent theme	Smooth transition; clarifies theme	Seamless transition; unifies theme	_____ x 5 = _____ points
Relevance to Topic	Majority of sounds are relevant	All sounds are relevant	All sounds are relevant and interrelated	All sounds are relevant and embody theme	_____ x 5 = _____ points
Sound Quality	Fair	Good	Excellent	Superior	_____ x 5 = _____ points

56–60 = A   47–51 = C
52–55 = B   42–46 = D
           <42 = F

Total score _____/60 = _____

How to Use the
AUDIO COLLAGE Rubric
at the High School Level

Introduce the Rubric

Distribute and discuss the rubric beforehand. Focus attention on the column containing the highest level of performance, reminding students that to receive full credit, they must achieve these objectives. Burning CDs and making audiotapes are both acceptable for this assignment, depending on students' access to and the availability of audiocassette recorders and computers with read/write capabilities.

Make the Assignment

Audio collages stimulate students' creativity by requiring them to reach beyond the sense of sight to develop a collage of sound that tells a story or conveys an emotion. Instruct students to select a topic, such as happiness or holidays, or a color, such as green, challenging them to create a sound collage that captures the essence of the topic. For example, an audio happiness collage might contain the sound of children laughing. Encourage students to experiment with less obvious but still powerful sound images. For example, they might record conversation at a Thanksgiving dinner table to convey the theme of a holiday. Students should assemble the sounds in a way that creates an auditory picture for listeners. Establish a time limit for the recording, 12 to 15 minutes, and encourage students to think about what sounds they associate with the topic.

Assess Student Understanding

Cohesion of Collage
■ blends sounds to conceal transitions and create a unique collage

Relevance to Topic
■ uses some subtle yet powerful sounds to convey theme

Sound Quality
■ produces superior sound quality

Review the collage for cohesiveness of sounds, their relevance to the topic, and use of some creative sound associations. In the case of vague or inappropriate responses, ask the student for clarification. The sound quality of the collage should be superior.

How to Use the AUDIO COLLAGE Rubric at the High School Level

TECHNOLOGY **AUDIO COLLAGE** HIGH SCHOOL

Task: Student will produce an audio collage.

Goal/Standard: Collage meets stated criteria

Giving 0 points is an option—no evidence, no credit.

Criteria	1	2	3	4	Total Points
Cohesion of Collage	Logical, solid transition; coherent theme	Smooth transition; clarifies theme	Seamless transition; unifies theme	Blended sounds conceal transition and create a unique sound	_____ x 5 = _____ points
Relevance to Topic	All sounds are relevant	All sounds are relevant and interrelated	All sounds are relevant and embody theme	Some subtle yet powerful sounds help convey theme	_____ x 5 = _____ points
Sound Quality	Fair	Good	Excellent	Superior	_____ x 5 = _____ points

56–60 = A   47–51 = C
52–55 = B   42–46 = D
         <42 = F

Total score _____/60 = _____

How to Use the
VIDEO PRESENTATION Rubric
at the Intermediate Level

Introduce the Rubric

Distribute and discuss the rubric beforehand, focusing attention on the column containing the highest level of performance. Remind students that to receive full credit, they must achieve these objectives.

Make the Assignment

The increased availability of camcorders, digital cameras, and DVD hardware and software has made video a viable option for student response and self-expression. Students strong in visual-spatial intelligence often find this avenue more effective for conveying emotions or information to others. Instruct students to choose a topic. While students become acquainted with this medium, it is best to provide a list of possible topics, such as My Hero(ine). You might also give students a topic from a content area and encourage them to use video to share information they have gathered about it, such as "How recycling helps our planet" for a science video. Establish a time limit for the video production, 10 to 15 minutes for this grade level, and encourage students to look for images that will leave a lasting impression in the minds of viewers.

Assess Student Understanding

Concept Development
- ■ creates well-developed concept with scenes building on each other

Visual Effects
- ■ uses seamless visual effects

Overall Video Quality
- ■ produces superior overall video quality

Reflect on the topics while reviewing the video. Think about how the student has conveyed information to viewers. Images should be effective and relevant to the main topic. Students should use visual effects, such as fade-in and fade-out, to enhance the production quality of the video. The sound and picture quality should be superior.

How to Use the VIDEO PRESENTATION Rubric at the Intermediate Level

VIDEO PRESENTATION

Task: Student will produce a short (3–10 minutes) video presentation.

Goal/Standard: Video meets stated criteria

Giving 0 points is an option—no evidence, no credit.

Criteria	1	2	3	4	Total Points
Concept Development	Underdeveloped or gaps in sequence	Adequate development; logical sequence	Well developed; good sequence	Well developed with scenes building on each other	____ x 5 = ____ points
Visual Effects	Present, but distracting	Present and adequate	Present and effective	Present and seamless	____ x 5 = ____ points
Overall Video Quality	Fair	Good	Excellent	Superior	____ x 5 = ____ points

56–60 = A   47–51 = C
52–55 = B   42–46 = D
          <42 = F

Total score ____/60 = ____

How to Use the
VIDEO PRESENTATION Rubric
at the Middle and High School Level

Introduce the Rubric

Distribute and discuss the rubric beforehand, focusing attention on the column containing the highest level of performance. Remind students that to receive full credit, they must achieve these objectives.

Make the Assignment

The increased availability of camcorders, digital cameras, and DVD hardware and software has made video a viable option for student response and self-expression. Students strong in visual-spatial intelligence often find this avenue more effective for conveying emotions or information to others. Instruct students to choose a topic, and encourage them to use video to share information they have gathered about it, such as "How recycling helps our planet" for a science video. Establish a time limit for the video production, 15 to 25 minutes for this grade level, and encourage students to look for images that will leave a lasting impression in the minds of viewers. Instruct students to experiment with special effects such as split-screen video.

Assess Student Understanding

Concept Development
- creates a well-developed concept ideal for a video format

Visual Effects
- creates visual effects that unify video

Overall Video Quality
- produces superior overall video quality

Reflect on the topics while reviewing the video. Think about how the student has conveyed information about the topic to viewers. Images should be effective and relevant to the main topic. Students should use visual effects that capture and hold viewer's attention and enhance the production quality of the video. The sound and picture quality should be superior.

TECHNOLOGY **VIDEO PRESENTATION** MIDDLE AND HIGH SCHOOL

Task: Student will produce a short (3–10 minutes) video presentation.

Goal/Standard: Video meets stated criteria

Giving 0 points is an option—no evidence, no credit.

Criteria	1	2	3	4	Total Points
Concept Development	Adequate development and sequence	Well developed; logical sequence	Well developed with scenes building on each other	Well developed; ideal for video format	_____ x 5 = _____ points
Visual Effects	Present but not always effective	Present and effective	Present and seamless	Unifies video	_____ x 5 = _____ points
Overall Video Quality	Fair	Good	Excellent	Superior	_____ x 5 = _____ points

56–60 = A   47–51 = C
52–55 = B   42–46 = D
          <42 = F

Total score _____/60 = _____

9

Constructing Rubrics

Intermediate unit teachers Nick and Judy are delighted with a districtwide decision to use rubrics in the student assessment process. Receiving a packet containing several sample rubrics, Nick expresses concern that none of the samples fits a special environmental awareness unit he conducts each year with his fifth-grade class. Judy suggests a miniworkshop for teachers interested in constructing their own rubrics. She adds that she and her colleagues could use many of the strategies developed for such a program to help students create rubrics as a way of comprehending the process and purpose of the rubric. The principal agrees and contacts the university to schedule a workshop with one of the College of Education professors.

TEACHER-CREATED RUBRICS

While this book contains rubrics for every area of the language arts, educators may cover a particular activity in their curriculum more effectively with their own teacher-created rubric. For this reason, teachers should understand how to create their own rubrics. Even if educators find it unnecessary to use a language arts rubric beyond those in this book, they should know how to construct a rubric.

Creating their own rubrics allows teachers to tailor the assessment to the individual needs of their students and the school's curriculum. As the chapter-opening scenario suggests, helping students understand why and how teachers use rubrics is an essential step not only in assessment but in the entire learning process. The discussion of rubric construction in this chapter begins with a detailed description of all that rubric construction involves and includes examples of rubrics under construction. The discussion ends with a step-by-step summary. This chapter also discusses ways to involve students more fully in rubrics assessment.

CONSTRUCTING A RUBRIC

The first step in constructing a rubric is to identify a particular skill, behavior, or attitude to evaluate. This topic should not be too specific (recognizes sound of /ch/ digraph) or too broad (reading) in nature. A good example might be Oral Presentation–Debate. Every objective listed on the rubric must relate to the assessment of student performance during an oral debate.

As this book illustrates, the most common arrangement for a rubric is a grid. On the vertical axis, list the skills, behaviors, and attitudes of a master debater. Reflect on general areas, such as quality of content, vocal projection and clarity, knowledge of subject matter, and professional attitude (Figure 9.1).

The next step involves focusing on each of the areas to evaluate, delineating (in the example of the Oral Presentation–Debate rubric) exactly which skills a master debater possesses. For example, the following elements are essential to the objective Professional Attitude: adheres to specified time limits, does not interrupt opponent, and listens attentively to opponent. Because no one is perfect and even seasoned debaters experience occasional lapses, the rubric identifies several levels of proficiency.

Before evaluating student performance on a task, educators must examine the task, dissecting its components to determine which parts are more essential to an understanding of the task. For example, ability to proofread a written assignment for punctuation and capitalization errors is an essential step in the writing process, but the ability to compose a cohesive and coherent sentence is more crucial to the success of the writing task. Weighted rubrics permit the evaluator to assign more importance or weight to various aspects of a single task.

The arrangement of these elements in a weighted rubric is the evaluator's choice. One method lists the criteria in the first column (Figure 9.2), then delineates in subsequent columns how many criteria students must meet to attain the specific number of points identified in the column heading (students must meet all three criteria to earn 4 points, they must meet two criteria to earn 3 points, etc.).

ORAL PRESENTATION—DEBATE

Criteria					
Quality of Content					
Vocal Projection and Clarity					
Knowledge of Subject Matter					
Professional Attitude					

Figure 9.1

ORAL PRESENTATION—DEBATE

Criteria	1 point	2 points	3 points	4 points	Total Points
Quality of Content					
Vocal Projection and Clarity					
Knowledge of Subject Matter					
Professional Attitude • adheres to time limits • does not interrupt opponent • listens attentively	Evidence of 2+ incomplete elements	1 complete element present	2 complete elements present	3 complete elements present	____ x 3 = ____ points

Figure 9.2

ORAL PRESENTATION—DEBATE

Criteria	1 point	2 points	3 points	4 points	Total Points
Quality of Content					
Vocal Projection and Clarity					
Knowledge of Subject Matter					
Professional Attitude	Some unacceptable behavior	Adheres to time limits	Treats opponent respectfully	Adheres to all debate rules	_____ x 3 = _____ points

Figure 9.3

Another approach lists the objective in the first column (Figure 9.3), and the remaining columns of the rubric illustrate higher standards of performance. Either format is suitable for most tasks. The first method notes whether a certain behavior is present or absent while the second method illustrates specifically what deserves 1, 2, 3, or 4 points.

There is some discussion about the order of degrees of proficiency on the rubric. Some educators believe that putting the easiest standards first encourages students to set their goals too low and settle for a mediocre performance. Other opinions favor this design, claiming that putting the most difficult standards first discourages less proficient students. Again, the choice is the assessor's.

Finally, most assessment rubrics have a conversion chart or key, explaining how the assessor will convert the rubric points to number or letter grades. To create this key, divide the total number of points assessed by the total number of points possible. For example, if the total number of points for an assignment is 30 and the student's score is 27, divide 27 by 30 for a result of .90, which you then convert to 90 percent. Convert this percentage to the grade scale of the school or district (93–100 = A; 86–92 = B; etc.). This final step enables educators to quantify the information contained on an assessment rubric as a concrete evaluation of student performance on a wide variety of tasks. A sample key appears in Figure 9.4. Additional discussion and examples of grade conversion appear in chapter 1.

Sample Grade Conversion Key

28–30 = A
26–27 = B
24–25 = C
21–23 = D
<21 = F

Total score _____/30 = _____

Figure 9.4

Step-by-Step Overview of Rubrics Construction

1. Identify the task (building a Web page) or behavior (listening to a guest speaker) you wish to assess. Rubrics are most effective when ranking extended performance tasks (Gronlund 1998) or those containing a number of objectives.

2. Reflect on the task. Identify its components. If the task requires students to create a class newsletter, they must demonstrate proficiency in areas such as the use of desktop publishing software and page layout in addition to grammar and spelling.

3. Consider how to list the objectives for assessment. You might list objectives with several criteria under a single heading, resulting in a number grade based on the number of elements present in a student's work. Alternatively, you might list the objectives with graduated levels of mastery paired with each number on the scale.

4. Decide on the importance and value of each task component in determining the final score. In the example of a class newsletter, should spelling and grammar have the same weight as page layout? Individual teachers can make these decisions or the decisions can be a consensus among unit team members. Once you have established the criteria and scale, it is important to inform students that you will pay greater attention to certain areas during the assessment process.

5. Assign point values (1, 2, 3, 4) for each objective. Present these numbers alone or in conjunction with an appropriate statement (1–Title present but inappropriate; 4–Creative, relevant title).

6. Indicate how you will convert these scores to a letter or number grade. You might use traditional grading standards (93–100% = A; 87–92% = B; 78–86% = C; etc.) and express them by listing the actual totals on the rubric (15–18 = A; 12–14 = B; etc.).

STUDENT-CREATED RUBRICS

One of the most effective ways to help students understand the rubric assessment process is to allow them to create a rubric. Select a fun activity, such as a birthday party, field trip, or school dance, and brainstorm with students for a list of related components. For example, elements related to a field trip might be conveyance getting there, destination, food, and chaperones. Have students complete the rubric with the range of most and least desired choices in these areas. An example of a student-created rubric appears below.

Participating in this exercise prepares students to take part in constructing genuine assessment rubrics. Begin by identifying a cooperative group task (oral report, puppet show, Web page construction), and brainstorm as a class for the profile of an ideal outcome for the assignment, focusing on various objectives of the project. These ideas will make up the highest score on the rubric. You can add less ideal versions of each objective to fill in the rubric.

When the cooperative group activity is complete, have students complete a rubric for each of their group members.

RUBRIC FOR ASSESSING A FIELD TRIP

Criteria	1 Let's stay in class	2 Sure beats study hall	3 Can we stay all day?	4 Can we stay all year?	Total Points
Getting There	Big, yellow school bus	Soccer mom vans	4 x 4s offroad scrambling	Stretch limo with chauffeur	_____ x 3 = _____ points
Destination	School play-ground	Planetarium	Movie theater	Amusement park	_____ x 4 = _____ points
Food	Brown bag PB & J with chips	Favorite fast food restaurant	Deluxe catered meal	Favorite pizza place	_____ x 4 = _____ points
Chaperones	Neighborhood bullies	Room parents	Favorite teachers	Favorite boy and girl bands	_____ x 4 = _____ points

56–60 = A 47–51 = C
52–55 = B 42–46 = D
            <42 = F

Total score _____/60 = _____

Having students complete the rubric helps them understand the requirements the rubric describes, ensures their active involvement in both the activity and the assessment, and puts responsibility on scoring well on them since they helped create the rubric.

Many educators are familiar with the following Chinese proverb:

> Tell me, I forget
> Show me, I remember
> Involve me, I understand.

By completing the rubric themselves, students have a clearer understanding of what is involved when the teacher evaluates them. While it is likely that some students will still complain about their final grade, many more students will be able to see the connection between this exercise and how the teacher sets up a rubric to assess their performances. This activity also shows students that there is not always a pass/fail element to grades, and certain elements are more important than others and are weighted accordingly. Time spent engaging in this activity saves time down the road trying to make students and their parents understand why students received a certain grade on an assignment.

Student Checklists

Another way to help students understand the rubric and gauge their progress toward achievement of the required rubric elements is to provide them with a checklist to accompany the rubric. The checklist helps students see at a glance the areas they need to work on to complete a task successfully.

NONFICTION CHECKLIST

Task	Yes	Not Yet
Purpose • Can I name the topic of the text? • Can I explain the author's purpose for writing? • Do I know why this topic is important to me/others?		
Format • Do I recognize the way the author organized the text? • Do I know why the text uses charts and graphs for some information? • Can I understand the information in the charts and graphs and explain it in a paragraph?		
Content • Can I use what I know to figure out the meaning of unfamiliar words? • Can I make a connection between the words and pictures in the text? • Have I compared the information in this passage with what I already know about this topic?		

Figure 9.5

Figure 9.5 is a checklist that might accompany the nonfiction reading rubric at the intermediate level (chapter 2), and Figure 9.6 is a checklist that might accompany the autobiography writing rubric at the middle school level (chapter 4).

AUTOBIOGRAPHY CHECKLIST

Task	Yes	Not Yet
Cover Design • Does my cover contain words and pictures or photos? • Does my cover relate to the contents of my autobiography? • Does my cover show some of my favorite things?		
Sequence • Do I tell my life story in order from when I was born to now? • Do I include big events that happened in my life? • Do I get readers excited about reading the big events by using words that will make them curious about what comes next?		
Content • Do I use too many/too few pictures or photos? • Do I include captions to explain the pictures or photos? • Do the pictures or photos explain who I am?		

Figure 9.6

THE FUTURE OF RUBRICS

Are rubrics a passing trend or a genuine form of performance assessment? Will schools still use rubrics in some form five to ten years from now? The durable quality of rubric assessment remains its ability to address individual assignments, evolving with those activities over time. The weighted rubric with its graduated criteria scale will always be welcome in a classroom or school district where teachers explore less traditional methods of recording individual student growth and depth of understanding.

APPENDIX

INTERNET SITES

ONLINE STATE CONTENT STANDARDS

Alabama
http://www.alsde.edu/html/home.asp
Alaska
http://www.educ.state.ak.us/ContentStandards/home.html
Arizona
http://www.ade.state.az.us/standards/
Arkansas
http://arkedu.state.ar.us/standards/index.html
California
http://www.cde.ca.gov/challenge/
Colorado
http://www.cde.state.co.us/index_stnd.htm
Connecticut
http://www.state.ct.us/sde/
Delaware
http://www.doe.state.de.us/DPIServices/DOE_Standards.htm
District of Columbia
http://www.k12.dc.us/DCPS/curriculum/standards.html
Florida
http://www.firn.edu/doe/menu/sss.htm
Georgia
http://www.doe.k12.ga.us/index.asp
Hawaii
http://doe.k12.hi.us/standards/index.htm
Idaho
http://www.sde.state.id.us/Dept/
Illinois
http://www.isbe.state.il.us/
Indiana
http://ideanet.doe.state.in.us/standards/welcome.html
Iowa
http://www.state.ia.us/educate/standards/index.html
Kansas
http://www.ksbe.state.ks.us/assessment/
Kentucky
http://www.kde.state.ky.us/oapd/curric/CoreContent/core_content_index_version_
30.asp
Louisiana
http://www.doe.state.la.us/DOE/assessment/standards/index.asp
Maine
http://www.state.me.us/education/lres/lres.htm

Maryland
http://www.msde.state.md.us/

Massachusetts
http://www.doe.mass.edu/

Michigan
http://michigan.gov/mde/

Minnesota
http://cflapp.state.mn.us/CLASS/stds/index.jsp

Mississippi
http://www.mde.k12.ms.us/accred/MPSAS.doc

Missouri
http://www.dese.state.mo.us/standards/

Montana
http://www.metnet.state.mt.us/

Nebraska
http://www.nde.state.ne.us/AcadStand.html

Nevada
http://www.nde.state.nv.us/sca/standards/index.html

New Hampshire
http://www.ed.state.nh.us/CurriculumFrameworks/curricul.htm

New Jersey
http://www.state.nj.us/njded/stass/index.html

New Mexico
http://www.sde.state.nm.us/

New York
http://www.emsc.nysed.gov/guides/

North Carolina
http://www.dpi.state.nc.us/student_promotion/

North Dakota
http://www.dpi.state.nd.us/standard/index.shtm

Ohio
http://www.ode.state.oh.us/

Oklahoma
http://www.sde.state.ok.us/publ/pass.html

Oregon
http://www.ode.state.or.us/TchgLrngStds/

Pennsylvania
http://www.pde.state.pa.us/stateboard_ed/cwp/view.asp?a=3&Q=76716&state
board_edNav=|5467|&tpde_internetNav=|

Rhode Island
http://www.ridoe.net/standards/

South Carolina
http://www.sde.state.sc.us/offices/csol

South Dakota
http://www.state.sd.us/deca/TA/ContentStandards/index.htm

Tennessee
http://www.state.tn.us/education/ci/cistandards.htm
Texas
http://www.tea.state.tx.us/teks/
Utah
http://www.usoe.k12.ut.us/
Vermont
http://www.state.vt.us/educ/new/html/pubs/framework.htm
Virginia
http://www.pen.k12.va.us/go/Sols/home.shtml
Washington
http://www.k12.wa.us/
West Virginia
http://wvde.state.wv.us/igos/
Wisconsin http://www.dpi.state.wi.us/dpi/standards/index.html
Wyoming http://www.k12.wy.us/publications/standards.html

RUBRIC-RELATED WEB SITES

All About Assessment and Rubrics: a collection of links to Web sites offering an introduction to rubrics, advice on creating them, and many sample rubrics to assess student writing.
http://www.suelebeau.com/assessment.htm

Assessment Rubric Links: a list of links to Web sites that give examples of rubrics for assessing various multimedia projects.
http://www.forsyth.k12.ga.us/jhobson/multimed.htm

Chicago Public Schools, Performance Assessment, Ideas and Rubrics: an introduction to assessment rubrics and tips on rubrics construction.
http://intranet.cps.k12.il.us/Assessments/Ideas_and_Rubrics/
ideas_and_rubrics.html

Evaluation Rubrics for Websites: rubrics for students in primary, intermediate, and secondary grades to evaluate Web sites when conducting research on the Internet.
http://www.siec.k12.in.us/~west/online/eval.htm

Exploring the Environment—Teacher Pages: an introduction to rubrics that includes a rationale for using assessment rubrics and advice on rubric construction.
http://www.cotf.edu/ete/teacher/rubrics.html

Kathy Schrock's Guide for Educators—Assessment Rubrics: a categorized, annotated list of more than 1,600 sites to help educators, teachers, and parents enhance instruction and support the curriculum.
http://school.discovery.com/schrockguide/assess.html

"Kid Language" Writing Rubrics: rubrics geared toward middle school students in the areas of writing to inform or persuade and for personal expression.
http://www.intercom.net/local/school/sdms/mspap/kidwrit.html

Rubrics: a list of links prepared by the College of Education at the University of Missouri-Columbia
http://www.coe.missouri.edu/~prism/html/rubrics.html?

Rubric Sampler—Relearning by Design
http://www.relearning.org/resources/PDF/rubric_sampler.pdf

Rubrics for Web Lessons: a case for using rubrics in authentic assessment, links to articles about rubrics and authentic assessment, holistic rubrics for various topics, a rubric template, and other rubric resources.
http://webquest.sdsu.edu/rubrics/weblessons.htm

The Staff Room for Ontario's Teachers—Rubrics: informative resource offering links to Web sites featuring sample rubrics in the areas of research skills, group work, music, reading, writing, science, dance, social studies, visual arts, math, learning skills, test-taking skills, guidance and career, foreign language skills, thinking skills, speaking skills, physical education, and many more.
http://www.odyssey.on.ca/~elaine.coxon/rubrics.htm

Teach-nology: Handy site with rubric generators—you plug in the type of rubric you want, and it generates a rubric for you, personalized with the school and teacher name. It has rubric generators in all major content areas and some unique areas as well.
http://www.bestteachersites.com/web_tools/rubrics/

"Understanding Rubrics": an article (originally published in *Educational Leadership*) on rubrics, their use, and their design. The article features tips for creating rubrics and examples of analytic rubrics for such areas as book reports, oral presentations, persuasive essays, and more.
http://www.middleweb.com/rubricsHG.html

GENERAL, USEFUL WEB SITES FOR TEACHERS

AskScott
http://www.askscott.com/

Education World—The Educator's Best Friend
http://www.education-world.com/

Inki & Taz's Poetry Corner
http://library.thinkquest.org/11883/

Kathy Schrock's Guide for Educators
http://school.discovery.com/schrockguide/

Teachers Helping Teachers
http://www.pacificnet.net/~mandel/

Teachers.Net
http://www.teachers.net/

Teachnet.com
http://www.teachnet.com/

BIBLIOGRAPHY

Airasian, P. W. 2000. *Classroom assessment: Concepts and applications*, 4th ed. New York: McGraw-Hill.

Alvermann, D. E., and S. F. Phelps. 1998. *Content reading and literacy: Succeeding in today's diverse classroom,* 2nd ed. Needham Heights, MA: Allyn and Bacon.

Andrade, H. G. 2000. Using rubrics to promote thinking and learning. *Educational Leadership,* 57(5).

Arter, J., and J. McTighe. 2001. *Scoring rubrics in the classroom: Using performance criteria for assessing and improving student performance.* Thousand Oaks, CA: Corwin Press.

Barr, M. A. 2000. Looking at the learning record. *Educational Leadership,* 57(5).

Barr, R., and B. Johnson. 1996. *Teaching reading and writing in elementary classrooms,* 2nd ed. Boston: Addison Wesley.

Beamon, G. 2001. *Teaching with adolescent learning in mind.* Arlington Heights, IL: SkyLight Training and Publishing Inc.

Benjamin, A. 2000a. *English teacher's guide to performance tasks and rubrics: High school.* Larchmont, NY: Eye on Education.

———. 2000b. *English teacher's guide to performance tasks and rubrics: Middle school.* Larchmont, NY: Eye on Education.

Berman, S. 1997. *Project learning for the multiple intelligences classroom.* Arlington Heights, IL: SkyLight Training and Publishing Inc.

Black, P., and D. Wiliam. Inside the black box: Raising standards through classroom assessment. *Phi delta kappan,* October, 139.

Bridges, L. 1996. *Assessment: Continuous learning.* Portland, ME: Stenhouse Publishers.

Brualdi, A. 2000, February. Implementing performance assessment in the classroom. *Classroom Leadership Online,* 3(5). Association for Supervision and Curriculum Development.

Burke, K. 1999. *How to assess authentic learning,* 3rd ed. Arlington Heights, IL: Skylight Training and Publishing Inc.

Burke, K., R. Fogarty, and S. Belgrad. 2002. *The portfolio connection: Student work linked to standards,* 2nd ed. Arlington Heights, IL: SkyLight Professional Development.

Claggett, M. F. 1997. *Measure of success: From assignment to assessment in language arts.* Portsmouth, NH: Boynton/Cook Publishers.

Danielson, C. 1996. *Enhancing professional practice: A framework for teaching.* Alexandria, VA: Association for Supervision and Curriculum Development.

Darling-Hammond, L. 1994. Setting standard for students: The case for authentic assessment. *Education Forum,* 59, 14–21.

Depka, E. 2001. *Designing rubrics for mathematics.* Arlington Heights, IL: SkyLight Professional Development.

Falk, B. 2000. *The heart of the matter: Using standards and assessment to learn.* Porstmouth, NH: Heinemann.

Fogarty, R. 1998. *Balanced assessment.* Arlington Heights, IL: SkyLight Training and Publishing Inc.

Foriska, T. 1998. *Restructuring around standards: A practitioner's guide to design and implementation.* Thousand Oaks, CA: Corwin Press.

Gambrell, L. B., and L. M. Morrow, S. B. Neuman, and M. Pressley, eds. 1999. *Best practices in literacy instruction.* New York: Guilford Press.

Glasgow, J., ed. 2002. *Standards-based activities with scoring rubrics: Middle and high school English volume 1: Portfolios.* Larchmont, NY: Eye on Education.

Glatthorn, A. 1999. *Performance standards and authentic learning.* Larchmont, NY: Eye on Education.

Goodrich, H. 1997. Understanding rubrics. *Educational Leadership,* 54(4): 14–17.

Grady, J. B. 1994. Authentic assessment and tasks: Helping students demonstrate their abilities. *NASSP Bulletin,* 78(566): 92–98.

Graves, D. 1994. *A fresh look at writing.* Portsmouth, NH: Heinemann.

Groeber, J. F. 1999. *More than 100 tools for literacy in today's classroom.* Arlington Heights, IL: SkyLight Training and Publishing Inc.

Gronlund, N. E. 1998. *Assessment of student achievement,* 6th ed. Boston, MA: Allyn and Bacon.

Gunning, T. G. 1999. *Creating literacy instruction for all children,* 3rd ed. Boston: Allyn and Bacon.

Harp, B. 2000. *Handbook of literacy assessment and evaluation,* 2nd ed. Norwood, MA: Christopher-Gordon Publishers.

Henning-Stout, M. 1994. *Responsive assessment: A new way of thinking about learning.* San Francisco: Jossey-Bass.

Herman, J. L., P. R. Aschbacher, and L. Winters. 1992. *A practical guide to alternative assessment.* Alexandria, VA: Association for Supervision and Curriculum Development.

Hibbard, K. M., et al. 1996. *A teacher's guide to performance-based learning and assessment.* Alexandria, VA: Association for Supervision and Curriculum Development.

Hill, B. C., and C. Ruptic. 1994. *Practical aspects of authentic assessment: Putting the pieces together.* Norwood, MA: Christopher-Gordon Publishers.

Hill, B. C., C. Ruptic, and L. Norwick. 1998. *Classroom based assessment.* Norwood, MA: Christopher-Gordon Publishers.

Huck, C., S. Hepler, J. Hickman, and B. Keifer. 2001. *Children's literature,* 7th ed. New York: McGraw-Hill.

Jensen, E. 1998. How Julie's brain learns. *Educational leadership,* (56)2. http://www.ascd.org/xchange/threads/nodes/brain/extjensen.html.

Johnston, P. H. 1997. *Knowing literacy: Constructive literacy assessment.* Portland, ME: Stenhouse Publishers.

Lazear, D. 1998. *The rubrics way: Using MI to assess understanding.* Tucson, AZ: Zephyr Press.

Lewin, L., and B. J. Shoemaker. 1999. *Great performances: Creating classroom-based assessment tasks.* Alexandria, VA: Association for Supervision and Curriculum Development.

Marzano, R. J., D. Pickering, and J. McTighe. 1993. *Assessing student outcomes: Performance assessment using the dimensions of learning model.* Alexandria, VA: Association for Supervision and Curriculum Development.

Marzano, R. J., and J. S. Kendall. 1996. *A comprehensive guide to designing standards-based districts, schools, and classrooms.* Alexandria, VA: Association for Supervision and Curriculum Development.

McMillan, J. H. 2001. *Classroom assessment: Principles and practice for effective instruction*. Needham Heights, MA: Allyn and Bacon.

McTighe, J., and S. Ferrara. 1998. *Assessing learning in the classroom*. Washington, DC: National Education Association.

Mehrens, W. A., W. J. Popham, and J. M. Ryan. 1998. How to prepare students for performance assessments. *Educational measurement: Issues and practice,* 17(1).

Mertler, C. 2001. Designing scoring rubrics for your classroom. *Practical assessment, research, and evaluation,* 7(25). http://ericae.net/pare/getvn.asp?v=7&tn=25.

Miller, W. H. 2001. *Alternative assessment techniques for reading and writing*. San Francisco: Jossey-Bass.

Moskal, B. M. 2000. Scoring rubrics: What, when, and how? *Practical assessment, research, and evaluation,* 7(3). http://ericae.net/pare/getvn.asp?v=7&tn=3.

Moskal, B. M., and J. Leydens. 2000. Scoring rubric development: Validity and reliability. *Practical assessment, research, and evaluation,* 7(10). http://ericae.net/pare/getvn.asp?v=7&tn=10.

Nitko, A. J. 2000. *Educational assessment of students,* 3rd ed. Upper Saddle River, NJ: Prentice Hall.

Olson, C. B. 2002. *The reading/writing connection: Strategies for teaching and learning in the secondary classroom*. Needham Heights, MA: Allyn and Bacon.

Olson, L. 2002. Up close and personal. *Education week,* 21(37): 28–33.

Opitz, M. F., and M. P. Ford. 2001. *Reaching readers: Flexible and innovative strategies for guided reading*. Portsmouth, NH: Heinemann.

Popham, W. J. 2001. *Classroom assessment: What teachers need to know,* 3rd ed. Needham Heights, MA: Allyn and Bacon.

———. 1997. What's wrong—and what's right—with rubrics. *Educational leadership,* 55(2). http://www.ascd.org/readingroom/edlead/9710/popham.html.

Pressley, M. 2002. *Reading instruction that works,* 2nd ed. New York: Guilford Press.

Readence, J. E., T. W. Bean, and R. S. Baldwin. 2001. *Content area literacy: An integrated approach*. Dubuque, IA: Kendall/Hunt Publishing Company.

Reutzel, D. R., and R. B. Cooter, Jr. 1999. *Balanced reading strategies and practices: Assessing and assisting readers with special needs*. Upper Saddle River, NJ: Prentice Hall.

Richardson, J. S., and R. F. Morgan. 2000. *Reading to learn in the content areas*. Belmont, CA: Wadsworth Publishing Company.

Rickards, D., and E. Cheek, Jr. 1999. *Designing rubrics for k–6 classroom assessment*. Norwood, MA: Christopher-Gordon Publishers.

Rolheiser, C., B. Bower, and L. Stevahn. 2000. *The portfolio organizer: Succeeding with portfolios in your classroom*. Alexandria, VA: Association for Supervision and Curriculum Development.

Ruddell, M. R. 2000. *Teaching content reading and writing,* 3rd ed. Hoboken, NJ: John Wiley and Sons, Inc.

Schommer, M. 1995. Voices in education on authentic assessment. *Mid-western educational researcher,* 8(2): 13–14.

Sejnost, R., and S. Thiese. 2001. *Reading and writing across content areas.* Arlington Heights, IL: SkyLight Training and Publishing Inc.

Sheffield-Gibbons, K. 2001. *The teacher's right hand: A resource guide of reading and writing strategies, lesson plans, and rubrics.* Bloomington, IN: 1st Books Library.

Simpkins, M. 1999. Designing great rubrics. *Technology and learning,* 20(1): 23–30.

Smith, N. B. 1964. Patterns of writing in different subject areas—part 2. *Journal of reading,* 8, 97–102.

Solomon, P. G. 1998. *The curriculum bridge: From standards to actual classroom practice.* Thousand Oaks, CA: Corwin Press.

———. 2002. *The assessment bridge: Positive ways to link tests to learning, standards, and curriculum development.*

Starr, L. *Creating rubrics: Tools you can use.* Education World. Available online: http://www.middleweb.com/rubricsHG.html.

Stauffer, R. G. 1969. *Directed reading maturity as a cognitive process.* New York: Harper and Row.

Stiggins, R. J. 1994. *Student-centered classroom assessment.* New York: MacMillan.

———. 2002. Assessment crisis: The absence of assessment for learning. *Phi delta kappan.* (83)10: 758–765.

Stix, A. 1997. *Creating rubrics through negotiable contracting and assessment.* ERIC document. http://ericae.net/ericdb/ED411273.htm.

Taggart, G. L., S. J. Phifer, J. A. Nixon, and M. Wood, eds. 1998. *Rubrics: A handbook for construction and use.* Lanham, MD: Scarecrow Education.

Tierney, R. J. 1999. *Reading strategies and practices: A compendium,* 5th ed. Needham Heights, MA: Allyn and Bacon.

Tombari, M., and G. Borich. 1999. *Authentic assessment in the classroom: Applications and practice.* Upper Saddle River, NJ: Merrill.

Treadwell, M. 2000. *1001 of the best internet sites for educators,* 2nd ed. Arlington Heights, IL: SkyLight Training and Publishing Inc.

Vacca, R. T., and J. L. Vacca. 2001. *Content area reading: Literacy and learning across the curriculum,* 7th ed. Needham Heights, MA: Allyn and Bacon.

Valencia, S. W., E. H. Hiebert, and P. Afflerbach, eds. 1993. *Authentic reading assessment: Practices and possibilities.* Newark, DE: International Reading Association.

Wiggins, G. 1989. A true test: Toward more authentic and equitable assessment. *Phi delta kappan,* May, 703–713.

———. 1998. *Educative assessment: Designing assessments to inform and improve student performance.* San Francisco, CA: Jossey-Bass.

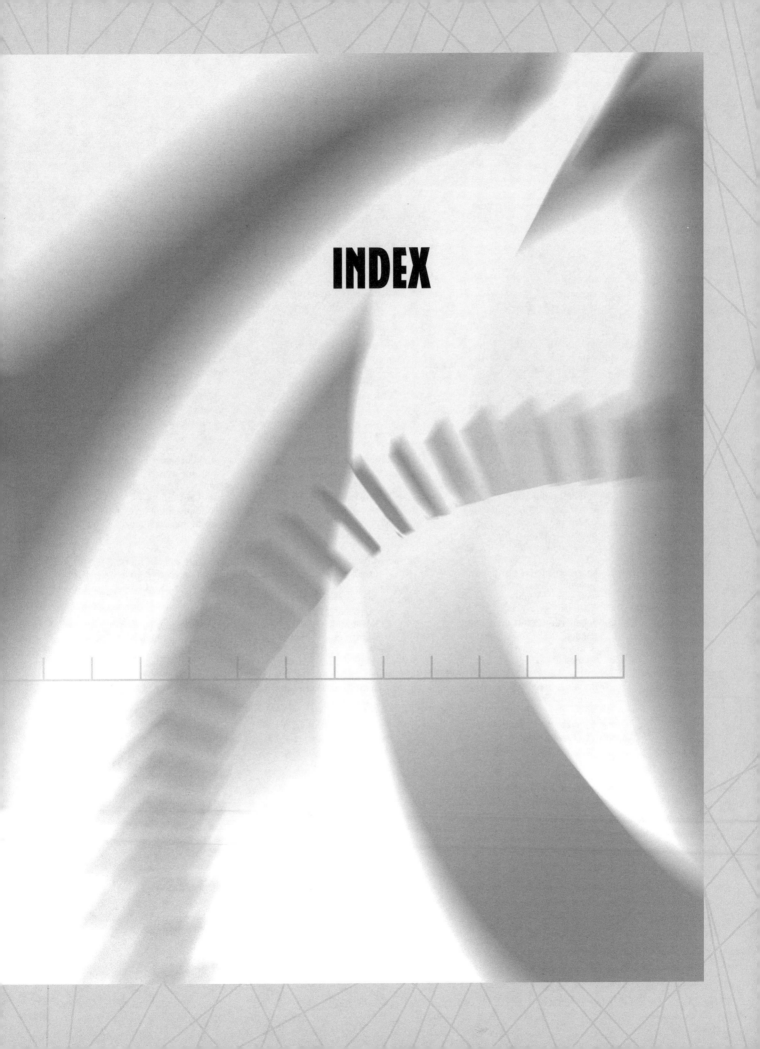

INDEX

INDEX

Accuracy, written report rubric (for research skills) and, 347, 349, 351–353

Activities
    for character, 98
    for instructions, 69
    for plot, 85
    for poetry, 15
    for setting, 113
    for theme, 130
    for writing, 144

Application
    informational speech rubric (for listening skills) and, 253, 256, 259, 262
    theme rubric (for literary elements) and, 133, 136, 139, 142

Assessment tools. See Checklists; Rubric(s)

Assignments
    for audio collage rubrics (for technology skills), 381, 383, 385
    for autobiography rubrics (for five-step writing process), 185, 187, 189, 191
    for biography rubrics (for reading comprehension), 57, 60, 63, 66
    for character rubrics (for literary elements), 99, 102, 106, 110
    for collaboration rubrics (for research skills), 354, 356, 358
    for debate rubrics (for oral language skills), 266, 269, 272
    for discussion rubrics (for oral language skills), 311, 313, 315, 317
    for dramatic presentation rubrics (for oral language skills), 299, 302, 305, 308
    for e-mail message rubrics (for technology skills), 373
    for fiction rubrics (for five-step writing process), 165, 168, 171, 174
    for fiction rubrics (for reading comprehension), 29, 32, 36, 39
    for first-hand experience rubrics (for research skills), 335, 338, 341, 344
    for five-step writing process rubric, 145
    for greeting card rubrics (for five-step writing process), 177, 179, 181, 183
    for guest speaker rubrics (for listening skills), 239, 242, 245, 248

for informational brochure rubrics (for five-step writing process), 194, 197, 200, 202
for informational speech rubrics (for listening skills), 251, 254, 257, 260
for instructions rubrics (for listening skills), 218, 221, 224
for instructions rubrics (for reading comprehension), 70, 73, 76, 79
for Internet search rubrics (for technology skills), 364, 367, 370–372
for letter rubrics (for five-step writing process), 204, 207, 210, 213
for nonfiction rubrics (for reading comprehension), 44, 47, 50, 53
for oral report rubrics (for oral language skills), 275, 278, 281, 284
for plot rubrics (for literary elements), 86, 89, 92, 95
for poetry rubrics (for five-step writing process), 153, 156, 159, 162
for poetry rubrics (for reading comprehension), 16, 19, 22, 25
for reference materials rubrics (for research skills), 323, 326, 329–331, 332
for setting rubrics (for literary elements), 114, 118, 122, 126
for stories rubrics (for listening skills), 227, 230, 233, 236
for storytelling rubrics (for oral language skills), 287, 290, 293, 296
for theme rubrics (for literary elements), 131, 134, 137, 140
for video presentation rubrics (for technology skills), 387, 389
for Web page rubrics (for technology skills), 375, 378
for written report rubrics (for research skills), 347, 349, 351

Atlas, reference materials rubric (for research skills) and, 325, 328, 331, 334

Audio collage rubric (for technology skills)
    goals of, 363
    high school level, 385–386
    intermediate level, 381–382
    middle school level, 383–384

Authentic learning, assessing with rubrics, ix–x, 2

Autobiography checklist (sample), 398

Autobiography rubric (for five-step writing process)
    grade level goals of, 151–152
    at high school level, 191–193
    at intermediate level, 187–188
    middle school level, 189–190
    at primary level, 185–186

Behavior, discussion rubric (for oral language skills) and, 311, 313, 315, 317

Benchmarks, x

Bibliography, written report rubric (for research skills) and, 347, 349, 351–353

Biography
    benefits of, 56
    content and, 59, 62, 65, 68
    format and, 59, 62, 65, 68
    popular varieties of, 56
    purpose and, 57, 60, 63, 66–68

Biography rubric (for reading comprehension)
    at high school level, 66–68
    at intermediate level, 60–62
    at middle school level, 63–65
    at primary level, 57–59

Body of letter, letter rubric (for five-step writing process) and, 206, 209, 212, 213

Character
    activities for, 98
    comparison and, 101, 104, 108, 112
    description and, 99–101, 102–104, 106–108, 110
    evaluation and, 101, 105, 109, 112
    fiction rubric (for five-step writing process) and, 165–167, 168–170, 173, 176
    inference and, 101, 104, 108, 112
    stories rubric (for listening skills) and, 227, 232, 235, 238

Character rubric (for literary elements)
    at high school level, 110–112
    at intermediate level, 102–105
    at middle school level, 106–109
    at primary level, 99–101

Checklists
    rubrics vs., 7
    student, 397–398

Classification, fiction rubric (for reading comprehension) and, 29, 32–34, 36, 39–41

Closing. See also Greeting and closing letter rubric (for five-step writing process) and, 206, 209, 212, 213

Cohesion of collage, audio collage rubric (for technology skills) and, 381, 383, 385

Collaboration rubric (for research skills)
goals of, 321–322
high school level, 358–359
intermediate and middle school level, 356–357
primary level, 354–355

Comparison
character rubric (for literary elements) and, 101, 104, 108, 112
setting rubric (for literary elements) and, 116, 120, 124, 128
theme rubric (for literary elements) and, 133, 134–136, 139, 140–142

Concept development, video presentation rubric (for technology skills) and, 387, 389

Conferences, benefits of rubric use for student/teacher, 6

Conflict
fiction rubric (for reading comprehension) and, 31, 34, 38, 41
plot rubric (for literary elements) and, 88, 91, 94, 97

Contact information, informational brochure rubric (for five-step writing process) and, 196, 199, 200, 202

Content
autobiography rubric (for five-step writing process) and, 185, 187, 189, 193
biography rubric (for reading comprehension) and, 59, 62, 65, 68
debate rubric (for oral language skills) and, 266–267, 269–271, 274
discussion rubric (for oral language skills) and, 311, 313, 315, 317
greeting card rubric (for five-step writing process) and, 177, 179, 181, 183
nonfiction rubric (for reading comprehension) and, 46, 49, 52, 55
oral report rubric (for oral language skills) and, 275–277, 278–280, 281–283, 284–286

Conversion chart/key, grade (sample), 10, 394–395

Cooperative group activity, student-created rubrics and, 396–397

Costumes
dramatic presentation rubric (for oral language skills) and, 301, 304, 307, 310
storytelling rubric (for oral language skills) and, 287–289, 290–292, 295, 298

Cover design
autobiography rubric (for five-step writing process) and, 185, 187, 189, 193
greeting card rubric (for five-step writing process) and, 177, 179, 181, 183
informational brochure rubric (for five-step writing process) and, 196, 199, 200, 202

Debate rubric (for oral language skills)
goals of, 264
high school level, 272–274
intermediate level, 266–268
middle school level, 269–271

Depth of understanding, written report rubric (for research skills) and, 347, 349, 351-353

Description
character rubric (for literary elements) and, 99–101, 102–104, 106–108, 110
setting rubric (for literary elements) and, 114–116, 118–120, 122–124, 126

Description of services, informational brochure rubric (for five-step writing process) and, 196, 199, 200, 202

Dictionary, reference materials rubric (for research skills) and, 325, 328, 331, 334

Discussion rubric (for oral language skills)
goals of, 265
high school level, 317–318
intermediate level, 313–314
middle school level, 315–316
primary level, 311–312

Division of tasks, collaboration rubric (for research skills) and, 354, 356, 358

Drafting, five-step writing process rubric and, 147

Dramatic presentation rubric (for oral language skills)
goals of, 265
high school level, 308–310
intermediate level, 302–304
middle school level, 305–307
primary level, 299–301

Ease of navigation, Web page rubric (for technology skills) and, 377, 380

Editing, five-step writing process rubric and, 148

E-mail message rubric (for technology skills)
all levels, 373–374
goals of, 362–363

Encyclopedia, reference materials rubric (for research skills) and, 325, 328, 331, 334

Envelope, letter rubric (for five-step writing process) and, 206, 209, 212, 213

Evaluation
character rubric (for literary elements) and, 101, 105, 109, 112
setting rubric (for literary elements) and, 117, 121, 125, 129
theme rubric (for literary elements) and, 133, 136, 139, 142

Extension of ideas, guest speaker rubric (for listening skills) and, 241, 244, 247, 250

Eye contact
debate rubric (for oral language skills) and, 266–267, 269–271, 274
oral report rubric (for oral language skills) and, 275–277, 278–280, 281–283, 284–286

Fiction
categories of, 28
classification of, 29, 32–34, 36, 39–41
conflict, 31, 34, 38, 41
plot, 31, 34, 38, 41
reader comprehension of, 14
theme, 31, 34, 38, 42

Fiction rubric (for five-step writing process)
grade level goals of, 150–151
at high school level, 174–176
at intermediate level, 168–170
at middle school level, 171–173
at primary level, 165–167

Fiction rubric (for reading comprehension)
at high school level, 39–42
at intermediate level, 32–35
at middle school level, 36–38
at primary level, 29–31

Field trip assessment rubric (sample), 396

Figurative language, poetry rubric (for five-step writing process) and, 153–155, 156–158, 159–161, 162–164

First-hand experience rubric (for research skills)
goals of 321
high school level, 344–346
intermediate level, 338–340
middle school level, 341–343
primary level, 335–337

Five-step writing process rubric, 145–152
drafting and, 147
editing and, 148
prewriting and, 145–147
publishing and, 149
revising and, 148

Format
biography rubric (for reading comprehension) and, 59, 62, 65, 68

nonfiction rubric (for reading comprehension) and, 46, 49, 52, 55

Gestures and movements, dramatic presentation rubric (for oral language skills) and, 301, 304, 307, 310
Grade and Percentage Scoring for Rubric Based on a 30-Point Scale, 10
Grade conversion
    converting rubric scores to letter/number, 9, 10
    sample key, 394–395
Grammar. See Spelling and grammar
Graphics, Web page rubric (for technology skills) and, 377, 380
Greeting and closing, e-mail message rubric (for technology skills) and, 373
Greeting card rubric (for five-step writing process)
    grade level goals of, 151
    at high school level, 183–184
    at intermediate level, 179–180
    at middle school level, 181–182
    at primary level, 177–180
Grid, for rubrics, 3
Guest speaker rubric (for listening skills)
    goals of, 217
    high school level, 248–250
    intermediate level, 242–244
    middle school level, 245–247
    primary level, 239–241

High school level
    audio collage rubric (for technology skills), 385–386
    autobiography rubric (for five-step writing process), 191–193
    biography rubric (for reading comprehension), 66–68
    character activities for, 98
    character rubric (for literary elements) at, 110–112
    collaboration rubric (for research skills), 358–359
    debate rubric (for oral language skills), 272–274
    discussion rubric (for oral language skills), 317–318
    dramatic presentation rubric (for oral language skills), 308–310
    e-mail message rubric (for technology skills), 373–374
    fiction rubric (for five-step writing process), 174–176
    fiction rubric (for reading comprehension), 39–42
    first-hand experience rubric (for research skills), 344–346
    five-step writing process rubric for, 145–152

greeting card rubric (for five-step writing process), 183–184
guest speaker rubric (for listening skills), 248–250
informational brochure rubric (for five-step writing process), 202–203
informational speech rubric (for listening skills), 260–262
instructions rubric (for listening skills), 224–226
instructions rubric (for reading comprehension), 79–81
Internet search rubric (for technology skills), 370–372
letter rubric (for five-step writing process), 213–214
nonfiction rubric (for reading comprehension), 53–55
plot activities for, 85
plot rubric (for literary elements) at, 95–97
poetry rubric (for five-step writing process), 162–164
poetry rubric (for reading comprehension), 25–27
reference materials rubric (for research skills), 332–334
setting activities for, 113
setting rubric (for literary elements) at, 126–129
stories rubric (for listening skills), 236–238
storytelling rubric (for oral language skills), 296–298
theme activities for, 130
theme rubric (for literary elements) at, 140–141
video presentation rubric (for technology skills), 389–390
Web page rubric (for technology skills), 378–380
written report rubric (for research skills), 351–353

Identification, theme rubric (for literary elements) and, 131, 134, 137, 140
Illinois Board of Education Learning Standards for English and Language Arts, x
Imagery
    poetry rubric (for five-step writing process) and, 153–155, 156–158, 159–161, 162–164
    poetry rubric (for reading comprehension) and, 18, 21, 24, 27
Implementation, instructions rubric and, 72, 75, 78, 79
Inference
    character rubric (for literary elements) and, 101, 104, 108, 112
    setting rubric (for literary elements) and, 116, 120, 124–125, 128

Informational brochure rubric (for five-step writing process)
    grade level goals of, 152
    at high school level, 202–203
    at intermediate level, 197–199
    at middle school level, 200–201
    at primary level, 194–196
Informational speech rubric (for listening skills)
    goals of, 217
    high school level, 260–262
    intermediate level, 254–256
    middle school level, 257–259
    primary level, 251–253
Instructions
    activities/projects for, 69
    implementation and, 72, 75, 78, 79
    preparation and, 70, 73, 76–78, 79
    sequence and, 72, 75, 78, 79
    strategy for reading, 69
Instructions rubric (for listening skills)
    goals of, 216
    high school level, 224–226
    intermediate and middle school level, 221–223
    primary level, 218–220
Instructions rubric (for reading comprehension)
    at high school level, 79–81
    at intermediate level, 73–75
    at middle school level, 76–78
    at primary level, 70–72
Intermediate level
    audio collage rubric (for technology skills), 381–382
    autobiography rubric (for five-step writing process), 187–188
    biography rubric (for reading comprehension), 60–62
    character activities for, 98
    character rubric (for literary elements) at, 102–105
    collaboration rubric (for research skills), 356–357
    debate rubric (for oral language skills), 266–268
    discussion rubric (for oral language skills), 313–314
    dramatic presentation rubric (for oral language skills), 302–304
    e-mail message rubric (for technology skills), 373–374
    fiction rubric (for five-step writing process), 168–170
    fiction rubric (for reading comprehension), 32–35
    first-hand experience rubric (for research skills), 338–340
    five-step writing process rubric for, 145–152
    greeting card rubric (for five-step writing process), 179–180
    guest speaker rubric (for listening skills), 242–244

informational brochure rubric (for five-step writing process), 197–199
informational speech rubric (for listening skills), 254–256
instructions rubric (for listening skills), 221–223
instructions rubric (for reading comprehension), 73–75
Internet search rubric (for technology skills), 367–369
letter rubric (for five-step writing process), 207–209
nonfiction rubric (for reading comprehension), 47–49
plot activities for, 85
plot rubric (for literary elements) at, 89–91
poetry rubric (for five-step writing process), 156–158
poetry rubric (for reading comprehension), 19–21
reference materials rubric (for research skills), 326–328
setting activities for, 113
setting rubric (for literary elements) at, 118–121
stories rubric (for listening skills), 230–232
storytelling rubric (for oral language skills), 290–292
theme activities for, 130
theme rubric (for literary elements) at, 134–136
video presentation rubric (for technology skills), 387–388
Web page rubric (for technology skills), 375–377
written report rubric (for research skills), 347–348
Internet searches, Web site on, 364
Internet search rubric (for technology skills)
goals of, 362
intermediate level, 367–369
at middle school and high school level, 370–372
primary level, 364–366
Internet sites. See Web sites
Interview, first-hand experience rubric (for research skills) and, 337, 340, 343, 346

Language, poetry rubric (for reading comprehension) and, 16, 19–21, 22–24, 25–27
Learning, process vs. product approach to, 2
Lesson, distribution of rubric at start of, 8
Letter grading, converting rubric scores to, 9, 10, 394–395
Letter rubric (for five-step writing process)
grade level goals of, 152
at high school level, 213–214
at intermediate level, 207–209
at middle school level, 210–212
at primary level, 204–206

Listening
art and science of, 216–217
collaboration rubric (for research skills) and, 354, 356, 358
Listening behaviors, guest speaker rubric (for listening skills) and, 239, 242, 245, 248
Listening skills rubrics, 215–262
goals of, 216–217
guest speaker rubric, 217, 239–250
informational speech rubric, 217, 251–262
instructions rubric, 216, 218–226
stories rubric, 216–217, 227–238
Literary elements, 84. See also specific elements
character, 98–112
plot, 85–97
setting, 113–129
theme, 130–142

Middle school level
audio collage rubric (for technology skills), 383–384
autobiography rubric (for five-step writing process), 189–190
biography rubric (for reading comprehension), 63–65
character activities for, 98
character rubric (for literary elements) at, 106–109
collaboration rubric (for research skills), 356–357
debate rubric (for oral language skills), 269–271
discussion rubric (for oral language skills), 315–316
dramatic presentation rubric (for oral language skills), 305–307
e-mail message rubric (for technology skills), 373–374
fiction rubric (for five-step writing process), 171–173
fiction rubric (for reading comprehension), 36–38
first-hand experience rubric (for research skills), 341–343
five-step writing process rubric for, 145–152
greeting card rubric (for five-step writing process), 181–182
guest speaker rubric (for listening skills), 245–247
informational brochure rubric (for five-step writing process), 200–201
informational speech rubric (for listening skills), 257–259
instructions rubric (for listening skills), 221–223
instructions rubric (for reading comprehension), 76–78
Internet search rubric (for technology skills), 362
letter rubric (for five-step writing process), 210–212

nonfiction rubric (for reading comprehension), 50–52
plot activities for, 85
plot rubric (for literary elements) at, 92–94
poetry rubric (for five-step writing process), 159–161
poetry rubric (for reading comprehension), 22–24
reference materials rubric (for research skills), 329–331
setting activities for, 113
setting rubric (for literary elements) at, 122–125
stories rubric (for listening skills), 233–235
storytelling rubric (for oral language skills), 293–295
theme activities for, 130
theme rubric (for literary elements) at, 137–139
video presentation rubric (for technology skills), 389–390
Web page rubric (for technology skills), 378–380
written report rubric (for research skills), 349–350
Movements. See Gestures and movements

Nonfiction
content, 46, 49, 52, 55
format, 46, 49, 52, 55
purpose, 46, 47–49, 50, 53
reader comprehension of, 14
text structures, vocabulary context clues, and, 43
Nonfiction checklist (sample), 397
Nonfiction rubric (for reading comprehension)
at high school level, 53–55
at intermediate level, 47–49
at middle school level, 50–52
at primary level, 44–46
Nonverbal communication, collaboration rubric (for research skills) and, 354, 356, 358
Number grading, converting rubric scores to, 9, 10, 394–395

Observation, first-hand experience rubric (for research skills) and, 337, 340, 343, 346
Omissions, instructions rubric (for listening skills) and, 220, 223, 226
Oral language skills rubrics
debate rubrics, 264, 266–274
discussion rubrics, 265, 311–318
dramatic presentation rubrics, 299–310
oral report rubrics, 264–265, 275–286
storytelling rubrics, 287–298
Oral Presentation-Debate rubric (example), 392–395
Oral Presentation Rubric, 3, 5, 11

Oral report rubric (for oral language skills)
    goals of, 264
    high school level, 284–286
    intermediate level, 278–280
    middle school level, 281–283
    primary level, 275–277
Overall appearance, greeting card rubric (for five-step writing process) and, 177, 179, 181, 183
Overall video quality, video presentation rubric (for technology skills) and, 387, 389

Page layout, Web page rubric (for technology skills) and, 377, 380
Parents/guardians, benefits of rubric use for, 6
Participation, first-hand experience rubric (for research skills) and, 337, 340, 343, 346
Performance standards. See Standards
Plot
    activities for, 85
    conflict and, 88, 91, 94, 97
    fiction rubric (for five-step writing process) and, 165–167, 168–170, 173, 176
    fiction rubric (for reading comprehension) and, 31, 34, 38, 41
    prediction and, 86, 89, 92, 95
    sequence and, 86–88, 91, 94, 97
    stories rubric (for listening skills) and, 227, 230, 233, 236
    summary and, 88, 91, 94, 97
Plot rubric (for literary elements)
    at high school level, 95–97
    at intermediate level, 89–91
    at middle school level, 92–94
    at primary level, 86–88
Poetry
    forms of, 15
    imagery in, 18, 21, 24, 27
    language and, 16, 19–21, 22–24, 25–27
    theme in, 18, 21, 24, 27
    workshop activities for, 15
Poetry rubric (for five-step writing process)
    grade level goals of, 150
    at high school level, 162–164
    at intermediate level, 156–158
    at middle school level, 159–161
    at primary level, 153–155
Poetry rubric (for reading comprehension)
    at high school level, 25–27
    at intermediate level, 19–21
    at middle school level, 22–24
    at primary level, 16–18
Prediction
    instructions rubric (for listening skills) and, 220, 223, 226
    plot rubric (for literary elements) and, 86, 89, 92, 95

Preparation, instructions rubric (for reading comprehension) and, 70, 73, 76–78, 79
Prewriting, 144
    five-step writing process rubric and, 145–147
Primary level
    autobiography rubric (for five-step writing process), 185–186
    biography rubric (for reading comprehension), 57–59
    character activities for, 98
    character rubric (for literary elements) at, 99–101
    collaboration rubric (for research skills), 354–355
    discussion rubric (for oral language skills), 311–312
    dramatic presentation rubric (for oral language skills), 299–301
    e-mail message rubric (for technology skills), 373–374
    fiction rubric (for five-step writing process), 165–167
    fiction rubric (for reading comprehension, 29–31
    first-hand experience rubric (for research skills), 335–337
    five-step writing process rubric for, 145–152
    greeting card rubric (for five-step writing process), 177–178
    guest speaker rubric (for listening skills), 239–241
    informational brochure rubric (for five-step writing process), 194–196
    informational speech rubric (for listening skills), 251–253
    instructions rubric (for listening skills), 218–220
    instructions rubric (for reading comprehension), 70–72
    Internet search rubric (for technology skills), 364–366
    letter rubric (for five-step writing process), 204–206
    nonfiction rubric (for reading comprehension), 44–46
    plot activities for, 85
    plot rubric (for literary elements) at, 86–88
    poetry rubric (for five-step writing process), 153–155
    poetry rubric (for reading comprehension), 16–18
    range on rubrics for, 3
    reference materials rubric (for research skills), 323–325
    setting activities for, 113
    setting rubric (for literary elements) at, 114–117
    stories rubric (for listening skills), 227–229
    storytelling rubric (for oral language skills), 287–289
    theme activities for, 130

    theme rubric (for literary elements) at, 131–133
    Web page rubric (for technology skills), 375–377

Procedure, debate rubric (for oral language skills) and, 266–267, 269–271, 274
Process vs. product approach, to learning, 2
Props
    dramatic presentation rubric (for oral language skills) and, 301, 304, 307, 310
    storytelling rubric (for oral language skills) and, 287–289, 290–292, 295, 298
Publishing, five-step writing process rubric and, 149
Punctuation Checklist for Written Report, 7
Purpose
    biography rubric (for reading comprehension) and, 57, 60, 63, 66–68
    nonfiction rubric (for reading comprehension) and, 46, 47–49, 50, 53

Questions and comments, guest speaker rubric (for listening skills) and, 239, 242, 245, 250

Range of achievement, on rubric, 3, 4
Reading comprehension, 12
Reading comprehension rubrics
    biography rubric and, 56–68
    components of, 14
    fiction rubric and, 28–42
    instructions rubric and, 69–81
    nonfiction rubric and, 43–55
    poetry rubric and, 15–27
Reading process, 12
Recall, informational speech rubric (for listening skills) and, 253, 256, 259, 262
Recipient address, e-mail message rubric (for technology skills) and, 373
Reference materials rubric (for research skills)
    goals of, 320–321
    high school level, 332–334
    intermediate level, 326–328
    middle school level, 329–331
    primary level, 323–325
Relevance to topic, audio collage rubric (for technology skills) and, 381, 383, 385
Research rubrics
    collaboration rubrics, 321–322, 354–359
    first-hand experience rubric, 321, 335–346
    reference materials rubric, 320–321, 323–334
    written report rubrics, 321, 347–353

Reversals, instructions rubric (for listening skills) and, 218, 221, 224

Revising, five-step writing process rubric and, 148

Rhythm, poetry rubric (for five-step writing process) and, 153–155, 156–158, 159–161, 162–164

Rubric(s), ix–xi. See also specific rubrics
  as assessment tool and more, 9–12
  for authentic learning, 2
  vs. checklists, 7
  constructing, 392–394
  defined, ix, 2–4
  features of, 3–4, 5
  future of, 398
  grade conversion key (sample), 10, 394–395
  grid arrangement for, 3
  Oral Presentation-Debate rubric (example), 392–395
  primary-level, 3
  reasons for using, 4–6
  standards relationship with rubric range, 4
  step-by-step overview of construction, 395
  student checklists and, 397–398
  student-created, 9, 396–398
  teacher-created, 392
  use of, ix–x, 8
  weighted, 4, 5, 392–393, 398

Rubric Conversion Key, 10, 395

Rubric scores, converting to school districts' grading system, 9, 10, 394–395

Salutation, letter rubric (for five-step writing process) and, 206, 209, 212, 213

Search results, Internet search rubric (for technology skills) and, 366, 369, 372

Search terms, Internet search rubric (for technology skills) and, 366, 369, 372

Selection, storytelling rubric (for oral language skills) and, 287–289, 290–292, 295, 298

Sequence
  autobiography rubric (for five-step writing process) and, 185, 187, 189, 193
  instructions rubric (for reading comprehension) and, 72, 75, 78, 79
  plot rubric (for literary elements) and, 86–88, 91, 94, 97
  storytelling rubric (for oral language skills) and, 287–289, 290–292, 295, 298

Setting
  activities for, 113
  comparison and, 116, 120, 124, 128
  description and, 114–116, 118–120, 122–124, 126

evaluation and, 117, 121, 125, 129
  fiction rubric (for five-step writing process) and, 165–167, 168–170, 173, 176
  inference and, 116, 120, 124–125, 128
  stories rubric (for listening skills) and, 229, 232, 235, 238

Setting rubric (for literary elements)
  at high school level, 126–129
  at intermediate level, 118–121
  at middle school level, 122–125
  at primary level, 114–117

Sharing information, collaboration rubric (for research skills) and, 354, 356, 358

Sound quality, audio collage rubric (for technology skills) and, 381, 383, 385

Spelling and grammar, e-mail message rubric (for technology skills) and, 373

Standards
  benefits of rubric use and, 6
  related to rubric range, 4
  Stories rubric (for listening skills)
    goals of, 216–217
    high school level, 236–238
    intermediate level, 230–232
    middle school level, 233–235
    primary level, 227–229

Story structure, 12

Storytelling rubric (for oral language skills)
  goals of, 265
  at high school level, 296–298
  at intermediate level, 290–292
  at middle school level, 293–295
  at primary level, 287–289

Structure, informational speech rubric (for listening skills) and, 251–253, 254, 257–259, 260–262

Student(s)
  benefits of rubric use for, 6
  use of rubric at start of lesson/unit, 8

Student checklists, 397–398

Student-created rubrics, 9, 396–398

Student performance, quantifying with rubrics, 4–6

Substitutions, instructions rubric (for listening skills) and, 220, 223, 226

Summary, plot rubric (for literary elements) and, 88, 91, 94, 97

Teacher-created rubrics, 392

Teachers, benefits of rubric use for, 6

Technology skills rubrics
  audio collage rubrics, 363, 381–386
  e-mail message rubrics, 362–363, 373–374
  Internet search rubrics, 362, 364–372

video presentation rubrics, 387–390
  Web page rubrics, 363, 375–380

Theme
  activities for, 130
  application and, 133, 136, 139, 142
  comparison and, 133, 134–136, 139, 140–142
  evaluation and, 133, 136, 139, 142
  fiction rubric (for five-step writing process) and, 165–167, 168–170, 173, 176
  fiction rubric (for reading comprehension) and, 31, 34, 38, 42
  identification and, 131, 134, 137, 140
  poetry rubric (for reading comprehension) and, 18, 21, 24, 27
  stories rubric (for listening skills) and, 229, 232, 235, 238

Theme rubric (for literary elements)
  at high school level, 140–141
  at intermediate level, 134–136
  at middle school level, 137–139
  at primary level, 131–133

Title
  poetry rubric (for five-step writing process) and, 153–155, 156–158, 159–161, 162–164
  Web page rubric (for technology skills) and, 377, 380

Tone of message, e-mail message rubric (for technology skills) and, 373

Topic, written report rubric (for research skills) and, 347, 349, 351–353

Topic sentence, letter rubric (for five-step writing process) and, 206, 209, 212, 213

Unit, distribution of rubric at start of, 8

Video presentation rubric (for technology skills)
  goals of, 363
  intermediate level, 387–388
  middle and high school level, 389–390

Visual aids, oral report rubric (for oral language skills) and, 275–277, 278–280, 281–283, 284–286

Visual effects, video presentation rubric (for technology skills) and, 387, 389

Vocal delivery
  debate rubric (for oral language skills) and, 266–267, 269–271, 274
  dramatic presentation rubric (for oral language skills) and, 301, 304, 307, 310
  oral report rubric (for oral language skills) and, 275–277, 278–280, 281–283, 284–286

storytelling rubric (for oral language skills) and, 287–289, 290–292, 295, 298

Web page rubric (for technology skills)
  goals of, 363
  middle and high school level, 378–380
  primary and intermediate level, 375–377
Web sites
  for formula poems, 15
  general, useful sites for teachers, 403
  on Internet searches, 364
  on-line state content standards, 400–401

rubric-related, 401–402
  for text structures, 43
Weighted rubrics, 4, 5, 392–393, 398
Writing
  activities for, 144
  five-step process, 144
Writing rubrics
  autobiography rubric, 151–152, 185–193
  fiction rubric, 150–151, 165–176
  five-step writing process rubric, 145–152
  greeting card rubric, 151, 177–184
  informational brochure rubric, 152, 194–203
  letter rubric, 152, 204–214
  poetry rubric, 150, 153–164

Written report rubric (for research skills)
  goals of, 321
  high school level, 351–353
  intermediate level, 347–348
  middle school level, 349–350